## International Political Economy Series

General Editor: **Timothy M. Shaw**, Professor of Political Science and International Development Studies, and Director of the Centre for Foreign Policy Studies, Dalhousie University, Halifax, Nova Scotia

*Titles include*:

Glenn Adler and Johnny Steinberg (*editors*)
FROM COMRADES TO CITIZENS
The South African Civics Movement and the Transition to Democracy

Glenn Adler and Eddie Webster (*editors*)
TRADE UNIONS AND DEMOCRATIZATION IN SOUTH AFRICA, 1985–1997

Einar Braathen, Morten Bøås and Gutermund Sæther (*editors*)
ETHNICITY KILLS
The Politics of War, Peace and Ethnicity in SubSaharan Africa

Deborah Bräutigam
CHINESE AID AND AFRICAN DEVELOPMENT
Exporting Green Revolution

Gavin Cawthra
SECURING SOUTH AFRICA'S DEMOCRACY
Defence, Development and Security in Transition

Jennifer Clapp
ADJUSTMENT AND AGRICULTURE IN AFRICA
Farmers, the State and the World Bank in Guinea

Neta C. Crawford and Audie Klotz (*editors*)
HOW SANCTIONS WORK
Lessons from South Africa

Susan Dicklitch
THE ELUSIVE PROMISE OF NGOs IN AFRICA
Lessons from Uganda

Kees Kingma (*editor*)
DEMOBILIZATION IN SUB-SAHARAN AFRICA
The Development and Security Impacts

International Political Economy Series
Series Standing Order ISBN 0–333–71708–2 hardcover
Series Standing Order ISBN 0–333–71110–6 paperback
(*outside North America only*)

You can receive future titles in this series as they are published by placing a standing order. Please contact your bookseller or, in case of difficulty, write to us at the address below with your name and address, the title of the series and one of the ISBNs quoted above.

Customer Services Department, Macmillan Distribution Ltd, Houndmills, Basingstoke, Hampshire RG21 6XS, England

The Bonn International Center for Conversion (BICC) is an independent non-profit-making organization dedicated to promoting and facilitating the processes whereby people, skills, technology, equipment, and financial and economic resources can be shifted away from the defence sector and applied to alternative civilian uses.

Further information can be found on BICC's internet website at:
http://www.bicc.de

# Demobilization in Sub-Saharan Africa

## The Development and Security Impacts

Edited by

Kees Kingma
*Project Leader*
*Demobilization and Peace-building*
*Bonn International Center for Conversion*
*Germany*

BONN INTERNATIONAL CENTER FOR CONVERSION
B I C C

in association with
BONN INTERNATIONAL
CENTER FOR CONVERSION

First published in Great Britain 2000 by
**MACMILLAN PRESS LTD**
Houndmills, Basingstoke, Hampshire RG21 6XS and London
Companies and representatives throughout the world

A catalogue record for this book is available from the British Library.

ISBN 0–333–78986–5 hardcover
ISBN 0–333–92129–1 paperback

First published in the United States of America 2000 by
**ST. MARTIN'S PRESS, INC.,**
Scholarly and Reference Division,
175 Fifth Avenue, New York, N.Y. 10010

ISBN 0–312–22955–0

Library of Congress Cataloging-in-Publication Data
Demobilization in Sub-Saharan Africa : the development and security impacts /
edited by Kees Kingma.
p.   cm. — (International political economy series)
Includes bibliographical references and index.
ISBN 0–312–22955–0 (cloth)
1. Africa, Sub-Saharan—Armed Forces—Demobilization—Economic aspects. 2.
Eritrea—Armed Forces—Demobilization—Economic aspects. 3. Ethiopia—
Armed Forces—Demobilization—Economic aspects. 4. Mozambique–Armed
Forces—Demobilization—Economic aspects. 5. Disarmament—Economic
aspects—Africa, Sub-Saharan. 6. Disarmament—Economic aspects—Eritrea. 7.
Disarmament—Economic aspects—Ethiopia. 8. Disarmament—Economic
aspects—Mozambique. I. Kingma, Kees. II. Bonn International Center for
Conversion. III. Series.
HC800.Z9 D4528   2000
338.963'009'049—dc21                                     99–053447

This book is printed on paper suitable for recycling and made from fully managed and sustained
forest sources.

10   9   8   7   6   5   4   3   2   1
09   08   07   06   05   04   03   02   01   00

Printed and bound in Great Britain by
Antony Rowe Ltd, Chippenham, Wiltshire

# Contents

# Part III  Conclusions

# List of Tables

## Conclusions

## Appendices

# List of Boxes

# List of Figures

# Preface

This volume reflects the results of a cooperative research endeavour of the Bonn International Center for Conversion (BICC) with several researchers in Africa and elsewhere. The study assesses the development and security impact of recent demobilizations of armed forces in Africa – particularly those in Eritrea, Ethiopia and Mozambique. It provides several key lessons as well as inspiration for future demobilization exercises and peace-building. As this study finds, demobilization is not a 'magic bullet' to address development and security challenges in a simple way. However, if it is well planned and implemented in conjunction with broader postwar rehabilitation, it can make a considerable contribution to sustainable human security and human development. The book thereby provides substance for efforts to develop and work with 'new' concepts of security – putting people in the centre.

In 1998 a violent conflict broke out between Eritrea and Ethiopia, causing a dramatic reversion of some of the disarmament studied in this volume. It shows how unpredictable the responses to perceived security threats can be in the region, despite the potential positive effects of demobilization on development and security. Improvements in broader development and security terms have to be matched at least with the willingness of leaders to explore all non-violent means of resolving conflicts. But the war also implies that some of the very countries that were studied are likely to face the challenge of demobilization again, once the armed conflicts have been ended.

As project leader for this research, I thank all the authors of this book for their diligent research and fruitful and stimulating discussions. In addition, I express my sincere thanks to my colleagues at BICC, in particular Michael Brzoska, Kiflemariam Gebrewold, Garry Gehyigon and Herbert Wulf, who have all assisted and encouraged me in putting this volume together. I am also grateful to the people who provided suggestions for the conceptual basis of the research: in addition to the contributors to this volume, these were Nicole Ball, Kathrin Eikenberg, Ivor Fung, Moses Kiggundu, Stefan Klingebiel and Dirk Kohnert. I also acknowledge the support and encouragement of Timothy Shaw to bring the research together in this book.

There are many other people working on demobilization issues – on implementation or research – with whom I have cooperated and shared ideas and views during the research and writing process. They are too many to mention; but their information, views and feedback have certainly been a great support. Lastly, BICC is very grateful to the Volkswagen Foundation for its financial support to the research for this volume.

K.K.

# List of Abbreviations

| | |
|---|---|
| ACDA | United States Arms Control and Disarmament Agency |
| ACORD | Agency for Cooperation and Research in Development |
| ACRI | African Crisis Response Initiative |
| ADENIMO | Association of Disabled Demobilized Soldiers (Mozambique) |
| AMODEG | Mozambican Association for the Demobilized Soldiers |
| APLA | Azanian People's Liberation Army (armed wing of the Pan-Africanist Congress – PAC) (South Africa) |
| BICC | Bonn International Center for Conversion |
| BMI | body mass index |
| BPD | People's Development Bank (Mozambique) |
| CAII | Creative Associates International Inc. |
| CB | Commercial Bank (Eritrea) |
| CBM | confidence-building measure |
| CEEI | Centre for Strategic and International Studies, of the Higher Institute for International Relations (ISRI) (Mozambique) |
| CERA | Commission of Eritrean Refugee Affairs |
| CORE | Commission for Reintegration (Mozambique) |
| CRS | Catholic Relief Services |
| DoD | Department of Defence |
| DRC | Democratic Republic of Congo |
| ECOMOG | ECOWAS Monitoring Group (West Africa) |
| ECOWAS | Economic Community of West African States |
| ELF | Eritrean Liberation Front |
| ENDF | Ethiopian National Defence Force |
| EPLF | Eritrean People's Liberation Front |
| EPRDF | Ethiopian People's Revolutionary Democratic Front |
| ERCS | Ethiopian Red Cross Society |
| ERHS | Ethiopian Rural Household Survey |
| ERRA | Eritrean Relief and Rehabilitation Agency (formerly Eritrean Relief Association) |
| ERREC | Eritrean Relief and Refugee Commission |
| ERRP | Economic Rehabilitation and Reconstruction Programme (Ethiopia) |
| ESRF | Ethiopian Social Rehabilitation Fund |
| EU | European Union |
| EWDFA | Eritrean War Disabled Fighters Association |

| | |
|---|---|
| FADM | Mozambican Defence Force |
| FAM | Mozambican Armed Forces |
| FPLM | People's Liberation Army of Mozambique |
| Frelimo | Mozambican Liberation Front |
| GDP | Gross Domestic Product |
| GNP | Gross National Product |
| GPA | General Peace Agreement (for Mozambique in Rome, 4 October 1992) |
| GTZ | German Agency for Technical Cooperation |
| GTZ-RP | GTZ-Reintegration Programme (Ethiopia) |
| ICRC | International Committee of the Red Cross |
| IISS | International Institute for Strategic Studies |
| ILO | International Labour Organization |
| IMF | International Monetary Fund |
| IOM | International Organization for Migration |
| IRS | Information and Referral Service (Mozambique) |
| ISRI | Higher Institute for International Relations (Mozambique) |
| LRA | Lord's Resistance Army (Uganda) |
| MK | *Umkhonto We Sizwe* (armed wing of the African National Congress – ANC) (South Africa) |
| MONAMO | Mozambican National Movement |
| MOZMO | Mozambican Mine-clearance Organization |
| NATO | North Atlantic Treaty Organization |
| NGO | Non-governmental Organization |
| NRA | National Resistance Army (Uganda) |
| NRM | National Resistance Movement (Uganda) |
| NUEWn | National Union of Eritrean Women |
| NUEYS | National Union of Eritrean Youths and Students |
| OAU | Organization of African Unity |
| OBS | Otto-Benecke-Stiftung |
| ODA | Official Development Assistance |
| OLF | Oromo Liberation Front (Ethiopia) |
| ORF | Open Reintegration Fund (Mozambique) |
| OSD | Occupational Skills Development project (Mozambique) |
| PF | Provincial Fund (Mozambique) |
| PFDJ | People's Front for Democracy and Justice (successor of the EPLF) |
| Renamo | Mozambican National Resistance |
| RLF | Revolving Loan Fund (Eritrea) |
| RRPE | Recovery and Rehabilitation Programme for Eritrea |
| RSS | Reintegration Support Scheme (Mozambique) |

| RUF | Revolutionary United Front (Sierra Leone) |
| SADC | Southern African Development Community |
| SADF | South African Defence Force (before 1994) |
| SANDF | South African National Defence Force |
| SAP | Structural Adjustment Programme |
| SIPRI | Stockholm International Peace Research Institute |
| SPLA | Sudan People's Liberation Army |
| TGE | Transitional Government of Ethiopia |
| TPLF | Tigrayan People's Liberation Front (Ethiopia) |
| UN | United Nations |
| UNDP | United Nations Development Programme |
| UNHCR | United Nations High Commissioner for Refugees |
| UNITA | National Union for the Total Independence of Angola |
| UNOMOZ | United Nations Operation in Mozambique |
| UNRISD | United Nations Research Institute for Social Development |
| UPDF | Uganda People's Defence Force |
| USAID | United States Agency for International Development |
| UVAB | Uganda Veterans Assistance Board |
| UXO | unexploded ordnance |
| WFP | World Food Programme |
| WTS | War-torn Societies Project (UNRISD) |
| ZANLA | Zimbabwean African National Liberation Army |

# Notes on the Contributors

**Daniel Ayalew** is Lecturer at the Department of Economics, Addis Ababa University, Ethiopia. He is currently on a study leave at the Katholieke Universiteit Leuven, Belgium. His research interest is rural household economics, particularly household consumption and savings decisions, and responses to different types of shocks.

**Iraê Baptista Lundin** is a social anthropologist and Head of the Department of Socio-Political and Cultural Studies at the Centre for Strategic and International Studies (CEEI) of the Higher Institute for International Relations (ISRI), Maputo, Mozambique. She is also a lecturer at ISRI.

**Eva-Maria Bruchhaus** is an independent development consultant, based in Cologne, Germany. She has extensive experience in design, implementation and evaluation of development projects and programmes in Africa, particularly for self-help and women in rural areas. Previously she was Africa reporter for the German World Service (*Deutsche Welle*), for which she first reported on Eritrea in 1968. From 1994 to 1996 she was adviser to the Eritrean Department for Demobilization and Reintegration of Ex-combatants (*Mitias*).

**Martinho Chachiua** has a masters degree in international relations (Birmingham, UK) and is assistant lecturer at ISRI (Mozambique) in the theory of international relations. He is also a research fellow at the Department of Peace Studies and Security of CEEI.

**Stefan Dercon** is a Professor of Economics at the Katholieke Universiteit Leuven (Belgium) and a Research Officer at the Centre for the Study of African Economies at Oxford University (UK). His research focuses on the microeconomic analysis of poverty and income growth in Africa, and the consequences of risk and shocks on households. He has worked extensively on Tanzania, Burkina Faso and Ethiopia. Besides his work on demobilization in Ethiopia he has also studied the consequences of war and peace on the functioning of grain markets.

**António Gaspar** has a degree in international relations. He is Deputy Director and Head of the Department of Peace Studies and Security at the CEEI (Mozambique). He is also Assistant Lecturer in Peace and Conflict Studies at ISRI. Previously he was an officer in the Mozambican Armed Forces.

**Garry Gehyigon** is a Liberian political economist. In 1996–97 he worked at BICC, specializing in demobilization in Africa. He was educated at the University of Liberia (BSc, Economics), Institute of Social Studies in the Hague, the Netherlands (MA, Development Studies) and the University of Amsterdam (MA, International Relations). He was Director for Training and Human Resources Development in the Ministry of Posts and Telecommunications in Liberia. Currently he is the coordinator of the United Nations Volunteers programme in Kenya.

**Habiba Guebuza** has a masters degree in international relations. She is Assistant Lecturer at ISRI (Mozambique) in the Practice of Diplomacy and research fellow in the Department of Economy and Development of the CEEI.

**Kees Kingma** is a Dutch economist, and since 1994 has been BICC's Project Leader for Demobilization and Peace-building, directing and implementing several research and advisory projects. He previously worked with the Free University Amsterdam, the United Nations Development Programme (UNDP) in Uganda and New York, and with the Evert Vermeer Foundation in Amsterdam. He has published and lectured widely on several development issues and conducted advisory and other consultancy work for several multilateral, governmental and non-governmental organizations. He was a member of the UNDP team preparing the *Human Development Report* (1991, 1992 and 1993), and contributed the sections on global demobilization and reintegration to BICC's *Conversion Survey* (1996, 1997, 1998 and 1999).

**Guilherme Mbilana** has a degree in history, and is a researcher with the UNRISD War-torn Societies Project in Mozambique.

**Amanuel Mehreteab** is currently a PhD student in development studies at the University of Leeds, UK. He fought with the EPLF from 1975 till the liberation of Eritrea in 1991. From 1993 until

1996 he was the Director of the Eritrean Department for Demobilization and Reintegration of Ex-combatants (*Mitias*). In 1997 he completed his MA at the University of Leeds, with a thesis on 'Assessment of Demobilisation and Reintegration of Ex-fighters in Eritrea'.

**Irmgard Nübler** is Assistant Professor at the Institute for World Economics at the Free University of Berlin, Germany. Her current research interest is on knowledge and economic development and she teaches development economics and international trade. Previously she worked with the International Labour Organization (ILO) on training policy and training systems, and at the Institute for Development Studies at the University of Nairobi (Kenya) on industrial training. Her PhD thesis on training for women entrepreneurs in the informal sector was published in 1995.

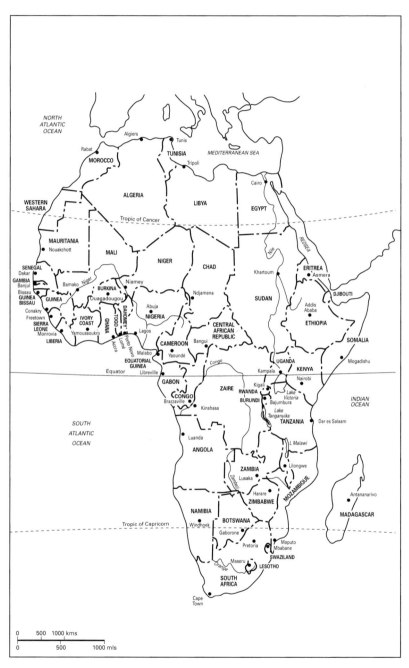

Map of Africa

# Part I
# Overview

# 1
# Introduction

*Kees Kingma*

## 1 Conversion in Africa?

International attention on the interplay between conflicts, (dis)armament and development in Africa has in recent years increased. Political changes in Africa and their relation to changes in the rest of the world raise questions about whether Africa is taking part in – and benefiting from – the global post-Cold War disarmament trend since the late 1980s (BICC, 1998). Or is the disappearance of the East–West conflict actually affecting Africa negatively? Clear geopolitical divisions and ideological disputes in Africa, such as in the struggle against apartheid and alliances with either the Soviet or western camp, have disappeared. Over the past decade several wars in Africa have indeed ended. But new ones have also ignited, mostly as a result of struggles for state power by individuals or groups, frustration with ruling elites, or strife for the control of natural resources. Most of these violent conflicts have at least some active involvement of other countries. So despite the termination of several wars, a number of African countries and communities are still subjected to large-scale violent conflicts. Millions of people suffer directly from violence and the destruction of their livelihoods, or indirectly through the limitation of their development opportunities. Women and children especially bear the brunt of these wars.

This book looks at the experiences of those African countries that demobilized part of their armed forces in the early and mid-1990s. Despite the destruction caused by long-standing wars and the danger of recurrence of some of these conflicts, development opportunities exist after armed conflicts have ended. Given Africa's enormous development challenges and the millions of people living in poverty, an important question is to what extent have the recent demobilizations actually contributed to peace and human development? To what extent have they also improved security? Can we learn from the different approaches that have been taken? Is demobilization possibly a means to address the development and security needs simultaneously? Can the lessons of demobilization even be an incentive for fighting parties to enter into peace agreements? These questions are again part of larger questions regarding the link between development and conflict, and concerning processes of demilitarization, security and peace-building in postwar societies.

The study of demobilization and its impact is seen as a relatively new topic relevant in academic fields such as peace research, international relations, and in development and regional studies. As will be shown, this study also provides substance for efforts to develop 'new' concepts of security and to link academic and policy debates on development with those on security. Questions regarding demobilization and reintegration should also be seen in their context, which often includes issues such as foreign policy, development cooperation, peace-keeping and broader peace-building support.

This introductory chapter will provide the context in which the above questions are posed. It will give background on how these questions concerning the link between the security sector and development have come to the forefront in recent years. It will also briefly outline the recent development trends in Africa and the peace and security environment and challenges. Subsequently it will place the demobilization issue in the context of other issues of postwar reconstruction. Finally, the last section of the chapter will provide a brief guide to the next chapters of the book.

## 2  Disarmament and development

The overall use of scarce resources by the military in Sub-Saharan Africa has declined considerably over the past decade – although at a lower rate than the world average[1] (BICC, 1998). The picture regarding the trends in military resource use in different African countries is however mixed. The Southern African region showed a reduction of military resource use almost as high as the world average, while in Central Africa especially such use was barely reduced. As will be elaborated and analysed in Chapter 4, military expenditures in Sub-Saharan Africa were in 1996 down to less than three-quarters of their peak in 1990. The military sector in Sub-

Saharan Africa currently absorbs about 3 per cent of the region's total GDP (compared to 2.3 per cent as the global average). In the same period the total number of armed forces in Sub-Saharan Africa declined by about 350 000 (24 per cent). Since 1990 more countries in Sub-Saharan Africa have reduced the size of their forces than have increased them. In particular those countries that have come out of a war have made large cuts in their armed forces.

Debates on the relationship between disarmament and development have been long and extensive from the 1960s on to the 1980s (see for example Graham *et al.*, 1986; Brzoska *et al.*, 1995). During this Cold War era, however, they have been largely theoretical and driven by 'wishful thinking'. They centred around the question to what extent a disarmament process could potentially benefit development. Declines in military expenditure and demobilization are generally perceived to allow for more productive use of the financial resources, contribute to limiting the political power of the military establishment and to free manpower and skills for more productive activities. Along with a reduction in the number and size of violent conflicts it could support and facilitate human development. Advancing human development – again – increases social justice and might reduce tensions between people. On the other hand, more recently – but increasingly – it is also recognized that, in order to use these resources and this possible 'momentum' for development and security, considerable demilitarization investments will have to be made; for example in the closure of military facilities, resettlement of ex-combatants,[2] demining of land, and the disposal of other 'surplus weapons' (BICC, 1996).

For a considerable period of time this discussion remained theoretical in respect to large parts of Africa and other regions. The actual relationship between disarmament and development has rarely been assessed on the basis of broad empirical research in Africa. Recent disarmament experiences in parts of Africa seem to allow for an assessment of the actual impact of the downsizing of the military on development. The working hypothesis of the broad research reported in this book was that, despite Africa's large development problems and the enormous devastation and human suffering caused by wars and civil conflict, demobilization related to recent changes in the international political environment might have had a favourable impact on development and security. It was also hoped that if disarmament lessons become available and known, these could inform development and security policies in Africa.

With actual disarmament experiences in Africa a parallel shift has taken place in the international development debate and support efforts, since the early 1990s. For people involved in national and international development strategies and cooperation programmes, military and security issues have till – say – the late 1980s remained largely outside their scope.[3] These issues were not part of the mainstream of development policy making. Increasingly, however, the analytical and practical connection is being made between development on the one hand and conflicts and resources used by the military on the other. The share of military expenditure in national budgets has drawn much attention in the early 1990s, in the development literature (for example Kaldor, 1991; UNDP, 1994), at the national policy level in various countries, and in the policy dialogue between African governments and donor agencies (Ball, 1993; OECD/DAC, 1998a, b). The security sector is increasingly included in the emphasis on 'governance' in the aid dialogues, which generally involves issues such as public sector efficiency, accountability, transparency, human rights, open policy debates in civil society, and maintenance of law and order. There is also an increasing concern with the role humanitarian and development assistance might play in unintentionally fuelling and/or prolonging violent conflict (de Waal, 1997; United Nations, 1998; Kingma and Gebrewold, 1998).

The UN recognizes demobilization and reintegration as critical parts of postwar peace-building. This has been highlighted in several major UN policy documents (Boutros-Ghali, 1994, p. 7; and 1995, para. 50) and the *Copenhagen Declaration* adopted by the World Summit for Social Development in 1995. The 1998 report of UN Secretary-General Kofi Annan on 'The Causes of Conflict and the Promotion of Peace and Sustainable Development in Africa' lists 'the reintegration of ex-combatants and others into productive society' as one of the priorities of post-conflict peace-building (United Nations, 1998, p. 14).

The above debates have actually shifted the operational development assistance programmes of several international development cooperation agencies over the past few years. These organizations have largely overcome their initial reluctance (or legal constraints) to get involved in development activities closely related to the military and other parts of the security sector. Particularly the opportunities, problems and policy issues concerning demobilization and reintegration of ex-combatants have received increasing attention. Multilateral, bilateral and non-governmental donor agencies have provided support for example to the financing of UN peace operations, demobilization packages, special services during demobilization, technical assistance, and programmes to facilitate reintegration. As an alternative or complement to hard conditionalities, support to demobilization exercises is seen as a positive measure (Brzoska, 1993) to shift resources from the military to development purposes. Some donor agencies have also increased support to judicial systems and reform of civil police forces, particularly in countries that have come out of war.

We should also note that military establishments have generally become more open to think about and discuss broader development concerns. Cooperation of the military in humanitarian relief operations has played an important role in this 'opening up'. The interdependence and need to cooperate are increasingly recognized. This clearly relates to changing concepts of security, discussed in Chapter 2.

## 3 Africa's development challenge

The extent of the general development problems and challenges in Africa is known; but some figures will help to highlight the width and depth of these problems. The GDP per capita in Sub-Saharan Africa is only US$507 (1993, in 1987 US$), while in 1980 it was still US$634 (data based on UNDP, 1997a). Economic growth over the past decade has clearly been slower than population growth. Per-capita GDP in Sub-Saharan Africa is only 15 per cent of the world average. Disparities between African countries and within countries are also large. More than half of the population in Sub-Saharan Africa lives in absolute poverty. Life expectancy at birth is only 50 years, compared to 63 years in the world as a whole; only 42 per cent of the population has access to safe drinking water; and 54 per cent of the adult population in Sub-Saharan Africa is illiterate. Sub-Saharan Africa is still highly dependent on external aid. Official Development Assistance (ODA) amounted in 1995 to about 12 per cent of Sub-Saharan Africa's total GNP. ODA per capita stood at US$32.

The causes of Africa's economic decline can be found in a cluster of interrelated factors – internal as well as external. National policies have in most countries not been able to provide a framework beneficial to economic diversification and growth. Meanwhile, declining international commodity prices, droughts and increasing debt burden all had a negative impact on income growth and development opportunities. Africa's growth and development have also been seriously affected by wars and civil strife. Violent conflicts not only took millions of human lives over the past few decades. They caused tremendous suffering, health problems, educational gaps, and destruction of infrastructure and other types of physical capital (Green, 1993; Stewart, 1993). Social services, such as health facilities and school systems, deteriorated or were totally destroyed. More indirectly, all the resources spent on the military were not spent on direct human needs and development. As a result of economic hardship and conflicts, many educated and skilled people left the continent. Most people in countries that have suffered from major wars and civil strife live at very low levels of development. Twelve African countries with major wars (in the recent past) – Angola, Burundi, Chad, Djibouti, Ethiopia, Eritrea, Mali, Mozambique, Rwanda, Sierra Leone, Sudan, Uganda – rank among the lowest 20 countries in terms of the Human Development Index (UNDP, 1997a, p. 148).

As a response to the economic problems most African governments have since the early 1980s started to implement structural adjustment programmes (SAPs). Pressure by the IMF and World Bank played an important role in the way these policies were designed. These policies aim at restoring and strengthening development processes by correcting the macroeconomic balances and improving the incentive structure of the economy. They usually imply liberalization of exchange rates and trade, and cutbacks in government budgets: reductions in social subsidies, retrenching public servants (Kiggundu, 1997), privatization of public enterprises, etc. These SAPs have been the subject of heated debates in academic and policy circles in Africa, in countries providing development assistance and in international development and financial institutions. There has been a considerable consensus that some kind of adjustment was (or still is) necessary in most countries to attain sustainable growth and poverty alleviation. But controversies exist about the precise content and phasing of the adjustment measures, and their relationship with broader societal questions of democracy and the appropriate institutions for managing development (van der Hoeven and van der Kraaij, 1994). After criticism of their narrow economic focus, SAPs and associated programmes have increasingly addressed the short-term social costs of adjustment and issues related to institutional capacity. Still, however, alarming increases in poverty occurred in some countries implementing SAPs. On the other hand,

it has in some cases been shown to be possible to succeed in pro-
tecting the poor while adjusting (Stewart, 1995). In the first decade
of structural adjustment policies little attention was paid to military expenditure. With the inclusion of issues of good governance,
security and disarmament in the development debate, this has slowly
started to change.

## 4  Africa's peace and security environment and challenge

The general security situation in the region has been varied and
extremely dynamic over the past decade. Africa has experienced
many wars and other violent conflicts – varying in scope, intensity
and nature. At different levels and from different perspectives, violent conflicts, threats and responses have changed over recent years.
Wars have ended, but new ones have ignited. By late 1998 several
African countries still suffered from violent conflicts, for example
Angola, Burundi, the Democratic Republic of Congo (DRC), Rwanda,
Somalia and Sudan. Rwanda experienced a horrific genocide in 1994,
killing an estimated 800 000 people. Relatively short wars were fought
in 1997 and early 1998 in Congo (B), between Eritrea and Ethiopia,
and in Guinea Bissau. All these wars cause various types of suffering
and damage: death, trauma, injuries, refugees, internal displacement,
destruction of livelihoods, 'brain drain', physical destruction,
repressed investment, and diversion of public funding and development policy.

It can also be observed that several wars have ended in their
violent form, namely in the Central African Republic, Chad, Djibouti,
Eritrea, Ethiopia, Liberia, Mali, Mozambique, Namibia, Uganda and
South Africa. However, in most of these cases we could place a
question mark. Large battles were fought in a border dispute
between Eritrea and Ethiopia in 1998. In most of the other countries
there is also still some sort of violent conflict happening. In
Uganda, for example, a large civil war ended in January 1986.
However, especially since around 1994, different groups in the north,
east and – more recently – west of the country have made attacks
on government troops in these regions and threatened, abducted
and killed large numbers of civilians. Also in Sierra Leone by late
1998 rebel activities continued in some parts of the country. This
clearly shows that we have to consider peace processes, rather than
declarations.

Not only violent conflict affects security in Africa. Especially in the light of a broadening concept of security (see Chapter 2) the development issues indicated in the previous section could actually be perceived as the predominant security concerns for people in Sub-Saharan Africa. Environmental degradation, infectious diseases, drug trafficking and violent crime are perceived as 'new' major security threats in Africa. In addition, especially in postwar countries, millions of people are confronted with the threat or effects of land mines, unexploded ordnance (UXO) and small-arms proliferation. The exact location of mines is usually unknown; and they thus continue to threaten to kill or maim indiscriminately, long after the end of the fighting. The problem is particularly bad in Angola and Mozambique. Estimates of the number of mines in Angola alone range between 10 and 20 million.

The current peace and security trends in Africa are too complex and diverse to generalize. A few examples of significant trends could however provide useful background for the analysis of the impact of demobilization.

- As a relatively recent phenomenon, several regimes in Africa have been overthrown by rebel forces operating largely from within the country (Clapham, 1998). This happened in Uganda in 1986, when the (then) rebel National Resistance Army (NRA), led by Yoweri Museveni, overthrew the military government. Similar take-overs took place in Ethiopia (then including Eritrea) in 1991, Rwanda in 1994 and Zaire in 1997.

- In the news media – and some academic literature – the observation is often made that since the end of the Cold War conflicts in Africa have become internal, rather than external. This is however questionable – and at least misleading. Hardly any of the so-called *internal* conflicts in Africa has no significant external (regional) component. The conventional distinction between interstate and intrastate conflicts has actually lost much of its meaning in Africa (Anglin, 1997, p. 4). Over the past few years there have been several cases where neighbouring countries have been involved in what could be perceived as basically national conflicts. The overthrow of the Mobutu regime in (then) Zaire in May 1997 was made possible by the support of countries such as Angola, Burundi, Rwanda, and Uganda to the opposition forces led by Laurent Kabila. Similarly, Angola supported the take-over by the former military ruler Denis Sassou Nguesso in Congo (B). The conflicts in Rwanda and Burundi are intertwined, and the governments of Uganda and Sudan are supporting rebel groups in each other's country. In West Africa there were close links between the forces of Charles Taylor in Liberia, before he was elected President in 1997, and the Revolutionary United Front (RUF) in Sierra Leone, providing mutual support and refuge. The uprising in Guinea Bissau in mid-1998 was closely related to the ongoing guerrilla war in the Casamance region in Senegal. Arms often flow from one country into another once a peace settlement is reached or an ally in the neighbouring country is in short supply. And, of course, the enormous flows of refugees have drawn neighbouring countries into conflicts.

- As a result of wars, weak states and thousands of refugees looking for security, very complex 'emergency' situations have developed, particularly in the area of the Great Lakes. Large refugee camps, sheltering (ex-)combatants produce considerable policy dilemmas. If assistance is not provided through emergency operations, enormous human suffering is taking place, especially involving women and children. But there is also increasing evidence of misuse of emergency aid during conflict. Ex-soldiers have often shown to be hiding out (and rearming) in refugee camps, while food and refugees are often manipulated by the fighting parties.

- Over the past decade or so one can observe changes in status of military forces and the nature of warfare in Africa. Many African militaries can these days not be perceived as formal coherent structures. Observers have noted a 'fragmentation of government military mobilisation' (de Waal, 1996, p. 10). In Mobutu's Zaire for example the security services and armed forces were fragmented in order to reduce their threat to the regime (de Waal, 1996, p. 7). The national army consisted only of about 20 000 poorly equipped and underpaid soldiers – if paid at all. The main task of the *actual* security forces was to protect the President and the group around him. These forces consisted of several different elite units. Other strategies of direct or indirect support by informal armed forces are also used. Several African governments have made use of mercenaries, mostly in times of armed conflict. Special arrangements are made for the protection of private (foreign) interests, such as oil exploitation and mining. This is often partially due to the weakness of the police forces.

- Wars affect societies as a whole. The weakening of states has had an impact on the military (poorly paid, badly equipped) and the security of people. Civilians are often not only victims, but actually targets of the violence. There seems to be an increasing ruthlessness of warfare, including systematic brutalization, sexual violence and the use of child soldiers. In current armed conflicts in Africa most casualties are civilian. It is, however, at times difficult to distinguish between civilians and combatants, since guerrillas might rely heavily on support from rural communities – voluntary or through force. In many cases, due to weakening states and availability of light weapons, there is a nebulous distinction between civil war and banditry. Rebel forces generally have a rather narrow political agenda, with little ideological content. Economic interests are increasingly the driving force. The forces of Laurent Kabila came to power largely on the ticket 'to get rid of Mobutu'. Many of the fighting groups during the civil war in Liberia were mainly after direct economic benefits. In Sierra Leone the word 'sobel' was introduced to describe soldiers fighting in the regular army during the day, but joining rebel groups in robbing and looting at night.

- Over the past decades the involvement of children in hostilities in Africa has increased. The reduction of the weight of weapons has made it easier for children to fight. Even small boys and girls can handle common weapons such as M-16 or AK-47 assault rifles (Brett and McCallin, 1996). It is believed that commanders often prefer child soldiers, because they can be well disciplined, are not afraid and able to use very severe violence. Children enter armies in multiple ways, voluntarily or by force. In some countries, such as Ethiopia under the Derg, young men were frequently rounded up at market places or in churches. Renamo in Mozambique also systematically used forced recruitment of children, through abduction (see Chapter 7). Reports from Liberia and on the Lord's Resistance Army (LRA) in Northern Uganda (in 1998) show similar patterns. Often the young children – sometimes as young as seven – have to commit horrific acts on each other or their family. It has been reported that both sides of the war in Angola were forcing children into their ranks in 1998. The line between voluntary and forced recruitment, however, is sometimes fuzzy. In Uganda before 1986 the rebel NRA became a 'family substitute' by absorbing a large number of children that had become orphans due to the genocidal tactics of the government army.

- Extreme, but real, cases of weak states are the so-called *collapsed (or failed) states*. Several African countries have in recent years –

at least for a period of time – done without an actual state and functioning government (Herbst, 1996). For different reasons, but always involving civil strife, some states collapsed, such as in Liberia, Somalia and Zaire (now the DRC). Particularly in Somalia and Zaire it followed a long period where the state had been used entirely for the benefit of its head and his close circle. After the fall of Siad Bare and Mobutu Sese Seko, respectively, there was little to hold it together and *things fell apart*. Even if there formally is a government, it lacks internal control and does not fulfil the other key functions of the state. Control over the security forces is often lost. If civil society is not able to respond to the crisis and rallies around a successor, the process of weakening of the state ends in collapse (Zartman, 1995). This of course provides an entirely different perspective on *security*. Overcoming these problems requires nation-building and state formation, more than defence efforts. Often, in these cases, some parts of the country are controlled by certain armed groups or in some cases even commercial companies.

• In countries that did have sufficient state capacity the above trends have pressurized governments to act and consider military reforms. Most African governments have had to reconsider their security institutions as a result of shifting security concerns and alliances. Debates are ongoing at various levels about the role of the armed forces, including the role as peace-keepers in other (African) countries. There is an increasing recognition about the fact that new security threats are related to new concepts of security (see Chapter 2). Some people argue that there are new roles for armed forces in supporting environmental protection, infrastructural development, in addition to the more traditional non-military role of emergency preparedness. General democratization processes also require improved civilian control over the armed forces and civil military relations in general. African armed forces remain to be characterized by a lack of transparency and weak civilian oversight capability. Civilians, and even parliamentarians and other politicians, usually know very little about their country's armies. Actual military reforms going on are, however, limited. The clearest example of reform is in South Africa, where there is a process of reassessment, military reform and improvement of civil–military relations (Cawthra, 1997; Cock and McKenzie, 1998).

• The changing environment and efforts to reform the military have also led to rethinking of joint arrangements for regional security. There are efforts in Africa to reduce the dependence on non-African forces to resolve crises and maintain regional stability (Shaw *et al.*, 1998). The Conflict Management Centre at the OAU, the SADC Organ on Politics, Defence and Security in Southern Africa and the ECOMOG (ECOWAS Monitoring Group) troops in West Africa are examples of international African security co-operation. *Ad-hoc* groups of Heads of States convene to mediate in certain crises. There is an increasingly important role for regional powers. With the democratic government in South Africa in power since 1994, the influence of South Africa in the region, particularly in the Southern cone, has gradually increased. Also Nigeria has increased its regional influence, particularly as a result of its dominant role in the ECOMOG operations in Liberia and Sierra Leone. There are also non-African initiatives to develop new security arrangements in Africa. The African Crisis Response Initiative (ACRI) is, for example, a US initiative announced in 1996 to form an African force trained and supported by the US and some European countries.

- During the East–West conflict the superpowers competed for clients in Africa through support for governments or opposition groups. This type of military support has reduced dramatically, since the late 1980s. The justifications for involvement of non-African countries in African security issues are changing. But security issues in Africa are still influenced by larger international relations. In many ways the major military and economic powers in Europe and North America are still searching for new roles towards Africa. France has traditionally provided military assistance to its former colonies and some other countries. It is now revising its policy towards Africa, including its security role. The total number of French troops permanently based in Africa will be reduced from 8500 to 5000 in the year 2000 (*Jane's Defence Weekly*, 15 April 1998, p. 23). The US has become increasingly reluctant to become directly involved in peace-keeping or peace-enforcement operations in Africa after 15 US soldiers were killed in Somalia in 1993. The UK's security policy in Africa is also being revised.

## 5  Postwar reconstruction

As mentioned above, most demobilizations in Sub-Saharan Africa took – or are taking – place after the termination of a violent conflict. When the peace settles in, these countries undergo several processes simultaneously, ranging from constitutional reform and economic adjustment to reconciliation and healing of trauma (see for example Matthies, 1995; Kumar, 1997). Traces of war can be very deep and take a long time to vanish. The war has usually affected the economy as a whole, but also community cohesion and people's self-confidence. Many groups of people – including returning refugees, ex-child soldiers and war widows – have to find themselves a new livelihood.

---

**Box 1.1  Possible aspects of postwar rehabilitation and development**

**Military related**
- demobilization of government and non-government troops
- reform of armed forces or creation of a new force
- absorption of former rebels into the regular forces
- withdrawal of foreign troops
- micro-disarmament, including clearing of land mines and UXO

**Political**
- establishment of a transitional government
- constitutional reform
- transformation of guerrilla movements into political parties
- electoral process
- political reform, possibly including power-sharing between previously fighting parties
- dealing with past human rights violations (e.g. prosecution and/or 'Truth Commission')
- re-establishment or strengthening of government institutions,[4] including those for policy design and implementation, and the legal system

**Socioeconomic**
- relief services (food, water, health, shelter, etc.)
- relocation of people who were unable to move during the war

---

- return of economic and political refugees
- reintegration of war-affected groups (ex-combatants, refugees, internally displaced)
- privatization or other types of redistribution of assets
- economic stabilization and adjustment programmes (SAPs)
- liquid assets are gradually switched into investment
- reduction of security expenditures
- increasing external finance
- increasing tax revenues
- rehabilitation of physical infrastructure: roads, bridges, water supply, etc.
- rehabilitation of social infrastructure: health centres, schools, etc.
- agricultural rehabilitation
- rebuilding community structures
- reconciliation
- addressing psychosocial problems, including post-traumatic stress disorder

At the economic level we usually observe a shift from a wartime mixture of centrally controlled and survival economy to a market-led economy. Governments with often little institutional capacity are faced with difficult structural and management issues. Economic reforms have to be initiated, new institutions have to be created and meanwhile the government has to mobilize external resources, increase revenues, control inflation, etc. Remnants of the war economy, such as mismanagement, corruption and profiteering, also have to be dealt with. In addition, there is usually some pressure to show quick impact. In a broader process of peace-building it is important for people to see that the peace is 'paying off'.

Box 1.1 shows many of the different aspects that these postwar[5] rehabilitation and development processes can have. Most are closely related to each other and can be seen as fitting in a, so called, *relief to development continuum.*[6] It should be noted that some of the aspects listed in the box are interventions, or the direct result of interventions. For example, clearance of land mines, organizing elections and the provision of food aid are part of policies and programmes. Other aspects, however, are processes, largely the result of people responding to the changing security situation and new opportunities associated with the new situation. Deeper processes, such as rebuilding communities and reconciliation, depend almost entirely on the confidence and effort of individual people and groups. Clearly, the processes are often the result of both. For example, agricultural rehabilitation would usually be based on re-habilitation of roads, credit and subsidies, demining, etc.; but the farmers have to return to the land, make the extra effort and take the risks.

In the complex social and economic dynamics of postwar processes and interventions the demobilization and reintegration process is often quite central (Ball and Halevy, 1996; Colletta *et al.*, 1996a). Converting the people who were most directly involved in the vio-lence is significant in economic, political as well as social terms. It also has a symbolic impact. In Eritrea and Uganda, for example, the demobilization was also presented as a 'confidence-building measure' (CBM) for neighbouring countries. It should be noted, however, that in postwar situations ex-combatants are usually not the largest group that has to reintegrate. Returning refugees and internally displaced people usually outnumber the ex-combatants.

There is a clear tension between the political uncertainty that usually exists in a country emerging from a war and the need for advance planning. Nevertheless, important preparatory work for demobilization includes needs assessment, sensitization of stakehold-ers, mobilization of resources, and linking demobilization with reintegration efforts. Programmes for resettlement and reintegration should start soon after the end of the war, since armies might be-gin to disintegrate before formal demobilization. If the encampment takes too long and the demobilized have to do without informa-tion and opportunities to see their relatives, violent activities and rebellion could undermine the demobilization – and the entire peace process. Clarity about resettlement and reintegration programmes will provide confidence to the ex-combatants and their leaders in the peace agreement and their future in society.

As will be clearly shown by the case studies in this book, the actual process of demobilization and the institutions involved are different in each case. Generally, once the decision to demobilize is taken, practical plans have to be worked out and financing ensured. The combatants that are to be demobilized are in some cases brought to assembly areas, where they are registered, disarmed and given an identification card. In other cases soldiers are demobilized directly out of the barracks. In the assembly areas or barracks they may receive health care and be assisted with reorientation and counselling. In Uganda, for example, the ex-soldiers and their dependants went through pre-discharge briefings, providing them details on how to open a bank account, how to start income-generating activities, environmental and legal issues, family planning, and HIV/AIDS prevention. At time of demobilization a 'package' in cash and/or kind is usually provided to assist the ex-combatants in the initial stages of resettlement. These packages may include food-stuffs, civilian clothing, household utensils, building material, seeds or agricultural implements. The package could also include the payment of school fees for a veteran's children. Generally, the demobilized receive a cash payment at the time of demobilization and then at subsequent intervals. Considerable support is often required to transport the ex-combatants to where they will resettle.

Once the ex-combatants have reached the location of their choice the real reintegration begins. This process takes time, since it is by nature a comprehensive social, economic and psychological process. They all have to find their way to build up a livelihood for themselves and their families – often after a long period in the military. The economic environment in which they face this task is usually not easy, with high levels of un(der)employment. The skills that they obtained in the military are often not appropriate for the existing economic opportunities. If they intend to (re)turn to farming, land is not always available. It appears also to be hard to adjust attitudes and expectations.

## 6  Assessing the impact of demobilization

As indicated above, recent incidences of military downsizing in Sub-Saharan Africa mostly centred around a demobilization exercise.[7] Much of the strength of current African armies depends on their number of soldiers, and the payroll takes the bulk of the military expenditure. When a war is over, pressure is felt to reduce the number of soldiers; especially after conflicts that were close-linked to the Cold War, since in those cases arms and other equipment were often provided for free or with soft loans.

Demobilization is more than a process of linking demand and supply in the labour market, or a conversion of the human resources. It is a complex process in which basically each of the ex-combatants has to find a new civilian life, and re-establish some *roots* in society. As for the larger process of postwar rehabilitation and development, the demobilization and reintegration process forms a *continuum*. Different components are sequenced or overlapping, according to the specific circumstances. The actual phasing of the demobilization depends particularly on the time available – or taken – to prepare for demobilization, resettlement and reintegration support. The experience shows that risks exist that these processes may fail, or produce negative side-effects. Therefore, the argument to provide support to demobilization and reintegration is often that, while it might be costly, long-term costs for society – or even the region – could be larger if the ex-combatants were unable to find new livelihoods. It could lead to increasing unemployment and social deprivation, which could again lead to rising crime rates and political instability. Frustrated ex-combatants may also jeopardize the broader peace and development process. In such cases they might pick up their guns again. Indeed, a complex relationship appears to exist between demobilization, development and security. On the positive side, the skills of ex-soldiers might be very useful in the development of communities and the country as a whole.

Little research had been done on the impact of the actual demobilizations on development and security, due to the complexity of the issues and the lack of reliable data. For economists and other development policy makers these issues are relatively new, since – as we saw above – most development organizations and analysts have traditionally shied away from issues that were related to the military or national security in general. A pioneering effort was made by an *ad-hoc* team in the World Bank (World Bank, 1993), which looked at the design and management of demobilization and reintegration programmes. It was the first comprehensive study and provided useful insights into demobilization programmes. A major step forward was made by the World Bank's follow-up study, published in 1996. The team led by Nat Colletta produced thorough country studies on Ethiopia, Namibia and Uganda, and an overall best-practices assessment (Colletta *et al.*, 1996a, b). Meanwhile, other more focused work has been conducted, some on particular countries or issues (see for example Ball, 1997; Berdal, 1996; Coelho and Vines, 1994; Dolan and Schafer, 1997; Klingebiel *et al.*, 1995; Preston, 1994). Several assessments and evaluations have also been conducted by or for international development agencies, mainly focusing on the impact of the external assistance to the processes.

## 7   This study

From several perspectives it seems relevant or important to actually assess the impact that recent demobilizations have had on development and security in the respective countries or regions. Demobilizations have brought an extra level of complexity to the decisions around development policy and as a result development cooperation. Given the huge development challenges and the complex and dynamic security situation in Sub-Saharan Africa, what has been demobilization's role, and its impact in terms of human development and security? Has the momentum of a demobilization been used for peace and development? What is the likelihood of replication?

Indeed, if we raise the question so broad, the actual demobilization and reintegration processes should be assessed; not just the short-term relief and containment effects, but the demobilization as a part of the broader peace-building process. One needs to look beyond the typical donor perspective and time-frame, both at the peace and security side as well as the impact on development. The questions addressed in this study are thus broader than in the studies referred to above. These studies, particularly the detailed work by the World Bank (Colletta *et al.*, 1996b) have, however, provided important empirical information, also for this study.

The purpose of this study by the Bonn International Center for Conversion (BICC), in close cooperation with several researchers in Africa and elsewhere, is thus to analyse the development and security impact of demobilizations in Sub-Saharan Africa. It also explores and utilizes the contributions that economic analysis is able to make to such an effort. It applies some of the general approaches and perspectives of development economics to issues of demilitarization and peace-building. The study is meant as a contribution to bridging the gap between the fields of military, peace and security studies on the one hand and development and area studies on the other, assisting those people with policy and operational responsibilities in development activities in postwar situations. This study fits into current debates on 'new' concepts of security in the study of international relations theory and policy. The work is thus ultimately meant to contribute to more effective and efficient conversion – reintegration of ex-combatants into productive civilian life and utilization of the resources freed from the military for processes of peace-building and development.

Chapters 2 and 3 of this book provide the core of the conceptual framework[8] for a comprehensive analysis of the impact of demobilization on development and security. They deal with the political economy and social impact, and with human resources development. They outline the different economic aspects and their relevance for the issues concerned.

Chapter 4 presents an overview of the resources engaged in the military sector of all Sub-Saharan African countries, based on the standard sources available and complemented by press reports and other information. It includes an overview of recent demobilizations in Africa and of military expenditure trends in the region. The evidence on the demobilization in Uganda which is elaborated in this chapter has been largely based on literature and other available data, verified and complemented during a visit to the country in April 1997.

Chapters 5–7 are the case studies to describe, quantify and analyse the development and security impact of demobilization. The case studies in Eritrea, Ethiopia and Mozambique are based on research in the countries themselves. The demobilization processes in these countries were relatively recent, but enough time has passed to assess the impact of the processes. The four countries (including Uganda in Chapter 4) show considerable differences in context of the demobilization. In Eritrea and Ethiopia the former army had been defeated. In Mozambique the demobilization had been agreed upon in a peace agreement between the fighting parties. In Uganda, armed conflict virtually disappeared several years before the demobilization was initiated.

The field work for the case studies was mostly conducted in 1997. This implies that the development trends and particularly political events in 1998 are not reflected upon in Chapters 4–7. In the concluding Chapter 8, however, they are also looked at in the light of the tensions between Eritrea and Ethiopia and the continuing insecurity in Uganda and its military activities in the DRC.

Chapter 8 addresses the main questions posed in this research on the basis of the country studies and in the light of the other demobilization experiences in Africa. In the last section of Chapter 8 some condensed perspectives are given on the findings and what they imply for future demobilization and peace-building in Africa.

## Notes

1 This trend is based on the Conversion, Disarmament, Demilitarization and Demobilization (BIC3D) Index, reflecting changes over the past decade in military expenditure, weapon holdings, armed forces personnel and employment in arms production. For details see BICC, 1998, p. 21.

2 The term *combatants* is used to reflect that the demobilized could be former government soldiers as well as former members of armed opposition groups. It is important to note that, in the context of Mozambique, the term 'ex-combatants' is normally used to refer specifically to veterans of the liberation war. However, for the purpose of consistency throughout this book, the term will also be used for those demobilized in Mozambique after the peace agreement in 1992.

3 The author's personal experience within the UN system in Uganda in the late 1980s confirms this. Although that was at a time that trying to find or maximize a 'peace dividend' would have made sense, security sector reform or the reallocation of funds from the military to development purposes were not on the agenda – and hardly part of the analysis.

4 In the case of Eritrea, a government apparatus was virtually non-existent at the time of independence, shortly before the demobilization was initiated.

5 The study uses the term *postwar* rather than *post-conflict* since in virtually all cases the conflict is actually not yet over when the war has come to an end. Actually, the phrase violent conflict would be the most appropriate, since it would allow for making the difference between, so-called, low- and high-intensity conflicts. Similarly, we will perceive *peace* as more than merely the absence of war or physical violence (Galtung, 1969), and would therefore rather use the concept of *peace process*.

6 This 'continuum' will be discussed in Chapter 2.

7 An exception is South Africa, where the demilitarization also had a major impact on the industrial sector and the use of land.

8 Drafts for the framework were initially discussed in a meeting of a group of experts in September 1996.

# 2
# Assessing Demobilization: Conceptual Issues

*Kees Kingma*

## 1 Clarifying key concepts

For an assessment of the impact of demobilization one needs to ask the right questions, have a clear and consistent set of concepts, and gather the required data and be aware of its limitations. After the central questions of this research have been presented in the previous chapter, this chapter will present the basic concepts used in this analysis and subsequently identify and discuss some relevant economic aspects, and the approaches to address these questions. (Aspects related to human resources development and utilization will be dealt with in Chapter 3.) The systematic presentation in this chapter is not meant as a blueprint for demobilization, since the process will be different according to the circumstances, but rather as outlining a framework for analysis.

### 1.1 Peace dividend

Assessing the impact of demobilization is part of the larger question of measuring the, so-called, *peace dividend*. The peace dividend can be – and has been – defined in many different ways. The United Nations Development Programme (UNDP) estimated world-wide fiscal savings from military expenditures. Given the historic high in global military expenditures of US$1 trillion in 1987 (in 1991 prices and exchange rates), the UNDP team estimated that a peace dividend of US$935 billion was generated between 1987 and 1994 (UNDP, 1994, p. 58). This figure represents the cumulative reduction in military expenditure by comparing each subsequent year to the 1987 peak. BICC's *Conversion Survey 1996* (BICC, 1996) suggests using a broader concept of peace dividend than merely the fiscal perspective.

When military expenditures are reduced, it is not just a matter of reallocating these resources. The process of disarmament also has costs, such as the clean-up of military bases, reinvestment to convert arms industry, social security and retraining for workers and ex-soldiers, and the safe disposal of weapon systems (BICC, 1996; Renner, 1996); and potential positive impact goes far beyond the direct fiscal impact – especially in the longer term. BICC proposed to look at the *resource dividend* (the total reductions in the defence budget minus the additional spending required by the military downsizing) as well as the *product dividend*. The latter is the total of effects that arise due to increased civilian government spending, tax cuts, budget deficit reductions or other alternative uses of the resource dividend. The resulting *welfare dividend* is the positive welfare effect resulting from the resources released from the military (Brömmelhörster, forthcoming). In this study on demobilization in Africa we take the broad peace dividend as the overarching concept. The reduction in military resource use could for example have direct impact on people's development opportunities through increased education and health expenditure, but it could also have more indirect effects. For example, it could reduce inflation and interest rates, and subsequently increase investments and employment opportunities. Eventually what counts is the impact it has on people's lives.

## 1.2   Conversion

A second basic concept to clarify is that of conversion. *Conversion* is basically perceived as the civilian (re)use of resources that were formerly used for military activities. If managed well, it channels resources to productive activities, leading to increased employment, social justice and decreasing social tension. An effective conversion process is also likely to encourage and facilitate further disarmament. In its *Conversion Survey 1996*, BICC presented six aspects of conversion (BICC, 1996):

(1)  reduction of military expenditures,
(2)  reorientation of military research and development,
(3)  conversion of the arms industry,
(4)  demobilization and reintegration,
(5)  base closure and redevelopment, and
(6)  safe disposal or management of 'surplus weapons'.

Demobilization is thus perceived as one aspect of conversion. It relates closely to some of the other aspects, which are all related in a critical way to development. Particularly in poor countries, reductions in armed forces are closely linked to reductions in security expenditures,[1] as personnel-related costs absorb most of the military and other security budgets. In these countries, therefore, demobilization implies that human as well as financial resources become available for development activities. Demobilization is also closely linked to the management of, so-called, 'surplus weapons'. At time of demobilization, ex-combatants need to be disarmed. This often creates 'surplus weapons' and involves the risk of weapons ending up uncontrolled in society. Scrapping or controlling these weapons improves the security situation directly by preventing their eventual disposition into the 'wrong hands'.

### 1.3 Peace-building

*An Agenda for Peace*, published by the UN in 1992, defined post-conflict *peace-building* as 'action to identify and support structures which will tend to strengthen and solidify peace in order to avoid a relapse into conflict' (Boutros-Ghali, 1992, p. 11). Peace-building efforts should advance a sense of confidence and well-being among people, and address the root causes of conflicts. Over the past few years the term peace-building is, however, increasingly used to indicate a process which has political, economic, social and psychological aspects. The broad peace-building process could indeed be supported by activities such as: election monitoring, strengthening and sensitizing a police force, development activities involving people from various sides in the conflict, psychosocial counselling, support to human rights advocacy and monitoring groups, etc. It should be noted that women often play a particularly important role in peace-building processes.

The concept of peace-building provides an important link between the debates on development and security. Increased security and stability, for example, are likely to lead to development progress. To put it simply, peace is required for development, but development is required for peace.

The concept is also closely related to the concept of the *relief to development 'continuum'* which has developed in debates within the academic and development and relief communities (Buchanan-Smith and Maxwell, 1994; Longhurst, 1994). Emergency situations require a direct response to save lives and livelihoods, and to alleviate pain and misery. But in order not to create or augment a situation of dependency, the assistance should be provided in the perspective of a self-sustained development process. Several processes and interventions are therefore to take place in a closely integrated way – often simultaneously. In a postwar situation these are, for example, implementation and monitoring of the cease-fire and peace accords, provision of humanitarian relief, capacity building, micro-disarmament, strengthening of food-security systems, infrastructural rehabilitation etc. (see Box 1.1). The development and awareness of this continuum is to improve both the emergency and development interventions. Relief activities would take the longer-term development requirements into account, while development efforts could help to reduce the frequency, intensity and impact of shocks, which will in turn reduce the need for emergency relief (Buchanan-Smith and Maxwell, 1994).

## 1.4 Demobilization

This study uses the term *demobilization* for the process that significantly reduces the number of personnel in the armed forces. It includes the reduction of the size of regular military and paramilitary forces, as well as the number of civilian personnel employed by the armed forces. In several cases demobilization also incorporates the process of disbanding opposition forces – sometimes after their integration into the (new) regular armed forces. This definition does not include the general 'turnover' of personnel that occurs in each army. In terms of the process itself, this study considers

---

**Box 2.1  Components of demobilization exercise**

A typical postwar demobilization in Africa includes the following activities:
- selection and preparation of assembly areas
- planning of logistics, including transport, basic needs supply, etc.
- resource mobilization (domestic and foreign)
- selection of those who will be demobilized
- cantonment
- registration
- disarmament
- needs assessment
- provision of services, such as health-care and basic training
- pre-discharge orientation and counselling
- discharge and transport to home areas

soldiers to be demobilized as soon as they have been disarmed, received their discharge papers and have – officially and *de facto* – left the military command structure.

It should be noted that demobilization does not always imply *demilitarization*. In some cases the reduction of the number of people in the armed forces might actually be part of a modernization effort, making the forces 'leaner and meaner'. Along the same line, it could be noted that demobilization does not necessarily imply a reduction of security expenditure. It is also possible that the demobilized soldiers would still be available as part-time forces or reserves. Reserves are not counted in the statistics, when not under arms; but they might be very quickly remobilizable. Another conceptual difficulty occurs when ex-combatants are turned into policemen. Very often this is important in postwar countries lacking a functioning law-and-order system. They are usually counted as demobilized; but are they really? And then there is the privatization of security services. In Luanda, Angola, the number of security services increased from two in 1992 to almost 100 in 1996. Indeed, most of their employees had a military background (*Onze Wereld* (Netherlands), July/August 1996, p. 73).

## 1.5 Resettlement

After demobilization usually follows *resettlement* of the ex-combatants in the location where they prefer to live. At time of demobilization a package in cash and/or kind is usually provided to assist the ex-combatants in the initial stages of resettlement. In some cases the demobilized receive a cash payment at the time of demobilization and at subsequent intervals in the reintegration process. Often the government or foreign development agencies assist in transport to the home region. In this study the term resettlement will be used, rather than *reinsertion* that has been used in World Bank publications (Colletta *et al.*, 1996a, b). The latter might leave the impression of taking the perspective of top-down policy and programming, rather than of a socioeconomic process in which people find their way into locations and communities in which they wish to reintegrate. Reluctance of World Bank staff to use the term 'resettlement' is likely to be caused by internal World Bank sensitivities, namely the negative experience it has had with 'resettlement programmes' in connection with the construction of large power and irrigation dams.

## 1.6   Reintegration

After resettlement follows the process of *reintegration*.[2] Although this is basically one complex process, a distinction is made between different aspects of reintegration: social, political and economic (Mondo, 1995; Colletta *et al.*, 1996a). In most cases the reintegration process takes a number of years and involves not only the ex-combatants themselves, but also their family unit. *Social reintegration* is defined as the process through which the ex-combatant and his or her family feel part of and are accepted by the community. One should thus not only consider the ex-combatants and their families, but also the attitude of the communities towards the ex-combatants. This remains relevant throughout the reintegration process, since communities might not, for example, appreciate special reintegration support to the ex-combatants. *Political reintegration* refers to the process through which the ex-combatant and his or her family become a full part of decision-making processes. *Economic reintegration* is the process though which the ex-combatant's household builds up its livelihood, through production and other types of gainful employment. For the economic reintegration one should consider the position of ex-combatants – with often little education, few skills and poor health – in societies where it is already difficult to start a small enterprise or find employment.

## 1.7   Demobilization and reintegration support

It is important to make an analytical distinction between the demobilization and reintegration process, on the one hand, and the support programmes to facilitate the process, on the other. Very often, particularly in circles of donor agencies, these are (implicitly) used as synonyms. The ex-combatants and their families carry the heaviest day-to-day burden of reintegration. They make the bulk of the efforts, set priorities and make decisions. If those managing the support activities are not sufficiently aware of this, their efforts might in fact not support the local reintegration processes, nor lead to local capacity and sustainability of the achievements. It is also useful to distinguish between the various providers of support, for example between national governments, national NGOs, foreign governments, international NGOs, UN agencies, etc. Usually international involvement is, in post-conflict situations, more needed and more prominent in the entire process than in general development cooperation in African countries.

Support programmes could take many different forms, according to the local circumstances, the target groups and the availability of resources. The institutional set-up through which the support effort is conducted can also differ from case to case. Box 2.2 lists some of the possible components of resettlement and reintegration support programmes. It should be noted that some of the reintegration support is not targeted entirely at the ex-combatants. This makes good sense in many cases, as discussed in the section on 'broader political economy', below. It does, however, make the assessment of the impact of demobilization and the costs of the support efforts more difficult.

---

**Box 2.2  Possible components of resettlement/reintegration support programmes**

Resettlement and reintegration support programmes could contain several of the following elements:
- cash payments (in instalments)
- foodstuffs (or coupons)
- health care
- civilian clothing
- household utensils
- building material
- tools
- seeds or agricultural implements
- agricultural extension services
- school fees for children
- counselling
- legal and/or business advice
- job placement
- general referral services
- land distribution
- housing support
- public works and other (temporary) public sector job creation
- wage subsidies
- credit schemes
- managerial and technical training

## 1.8   Development

The concept of *development* has shown continuous changes over the past few decades. In the 1950s and 1960s it was very generally used interchangeably with economic development. It was often even equated with economic growth. In the words of Amartya Sen, 'The close link between economic development and economic growth is simultaneously a matter of importance as well as a source of considerable confusion' (Sen, 1988, p. 12). Too often, in the past – but also implicitly by many today – has development been equated with economic growth. Output per capita is still frequently used as an indicator for development, which could lead to major misperceptions. In countries with similar average income levels the well-being of the average inhabitant can differ dramatically. 'Even if GNP did everything it is expected to do (and there are very strong reasons for doubting this possibility), even then the information provided by GNP must remain fundamentally inadequate for the concept of development' (Sen, 1988, p. 15).

Since the 1960s, changes in development policy perspectives and approaches have affected the (explicit and implicit) concept of development. In the 1970s increasing attention was given to people's (basic) needs and integrated rural development. In the 1980s the neo-liberal counterrevolution dominated at the macroeconomic policy level, while simultaneously the concept of development was influenced by participatory approaches in development interventions and an increasing awareness of the role of women and non-state actors in the development process. Established thinking on people's behaviour and social and economic development is still being challenged by new thinking. Over the past decade the concepts gaining dominance among academics and practitioners are those of human development and sustainable development.

The concept of *human development*, as defined in UNDP's 1990 Human Development Report, puts people at the centre (UNDP, 1990). The Human Development Reports argue that development should be defined in terms of the quality of people's lives, since people are not only the most important means, but also the ultimate end of development. Human development is therefore defined as the creation and utilization of people's choices and capabilities. As such it has two sides. One is the formation of human capabilities, such as improved health or knowledge. The other is the use that people make of their acquired capabilities – for work, leisure or personal growth. What the human development perspective clearly shows is that no automatic link exists between growth of national income and human progress, and that other aspects of development should be included in the measurement of development. The Human Development Reports have therefore also introduced a new way of measuring development: the Human Development Index. This is based on three of the most essential choices in people's lives: a long and healthy life, access to knowledge, and the availability of sufficient resources for decent living standards. Chapter 3 (sections 3.3 and 3.4) discusses the importance of the human development concept in assessing the impact of demobilization.

The concept of *sustainable development* was brought to the centre of development thinking in 1987 by the 'Brundtland Commission' (World Commission on Environment and Development). The Commission defined the concept as 'development that meets the needs of the present without compromising the ability of future generations to meet their own needs' (WCED, 1987, p. 43). This definition of sustainable development begs in practice more questions than it provides answers. What are the needs of the present and the future generations? How to deal with possible trade-offs, if environmental protection would imply serious deprivation in the present? Several publications have made the point that sustainable development is not simply environmental protection, but a comprehensive concept – embracing all facets of human life and activities. 'Sustainable development is a process in which economic, fiscal, trade, energy, agricultural, industrial and all other policies are so designed as to bring about development that is economically, socially and ecologically sustainable' (Pronk and Haq, 1992). A working definition of sustainable development suggested by David Pearce and Kerry Turner is: 'it involves maximising the net benefits of economic development, subject to maintaining the services and quality of natural resources over time' (Pearce and Turner, 1990, p. 24). Based on the economic aspects of the concept, environmental economists have formalized sustainability, using existing theories of capital accumulation and depreciation. In conventional economics the capital stock usually only includes human-made capital assets, such as buildings, roads, machines, factories and vehicles. Environmental economics also considers natural resources as part of the capital stock: 'natural capital'. Just as in the concept of economic development, depreciating capital has to be replaced. This implies the need for continuous reinvestment in physical and natural capital.

A major weakness of the current concepts of sustainable development is that development is usually not defined. Most of the theory and the discussion is on the sustainability; but what needs to be sustained is rarely made very explicit. The concept of sustainable development could thus be built on the concept of human development, since the latter is explicit about what would have to be sustained, namely the process of increasing people's capabilities and choices.

## 1.9  Security

The assessment of the impact of demobilization also requires clarity on the concept of *security*. Space does not allow discussion here of the development of various different security concepts, but this section will illustrate that clear shifts have taken place over the past decade or so in how security is perceived and defined (Brzoska *et al.*, 1995). In broad terms there has been a shift from the security of states ensured by military means to the security of people through prevention of conflicts and other threats. Barry Buzan, Ole Wæver and Jaap de Wilde (1998) see that current security threats appear in five different sectors: military, environmental, economic, social and political. The shift in the thinking on security is largely the result of the end of the East–West conflict, changes in economic and military power balances, increased environmental awareness, and – last but not least – an increasing recognition that people should be the ultimate beneficiaries of security and development policies.

Traditionally, the concept of security has dealt with the protection of sovereign states (*national security*) and their people against external attacks and other threats. This concept has a strong emphasis on military means (*military security*). Subsequently, concepts of common security and collective security have been developed and used. The term *common security* was used in the report of the 'Palme Commission' (Independent Commission on Disarmament and Security Issues, 1982), which emphasized that security cannot be achieved against an adversary, but only together with him. In a *collective security* system governments of all states accept that the security of one state is the concern of all, and they agree to join in a collective response to aggression or coercion to gain advantage. The UN Charter aims to establish a system based on this concept. If peaceful means fail to adequately address a threat to the peace, breach of the peace or act of aggression, the UN Security Council is allowed to authorize other means. The UN 'Agenda for Peace' was an effort to map out ways towards a global collective security system (Boutros-Ghali, 1992). A more recently developed concept is that of *cooperative security*. The major objective of cooperative security is to move from a security system based on deterrence to one based on reassurance. This emphasizes the process that is required to change the present military-based security concept. The concept has several phases in which confidence building and risk reduction proceed along with disarmament and restructuring of defence capabilities (Forsberg, 1992).

Over the past decade an increasing number of arguments have been put forward to include *environmental security* in the concept of security. The 'Brundtland Commission' noted in 1987 that 'The whole notion of security as traditionally understood – in terms of political and military threats to national sovereignty – must be expanded to include the growing impacts of environmental stress – locally, nationally, regionally and globally' (WCED, 1987, p. 19). It has been argued that national security should be redefined in order to include all the threats that come from environmental changes, such as increasing population pressure, depletion of non-renewable resources, genetic erosion, soil degradation and climate change (Mathews, 1989).

The *Human Development Report 1994* made an effort to contribute to the redefinition of security from the perspective of people and their communities (UNDP, 1994); it suggested the notion of *human security* as an all-encompassing concept. This includes economic security, environmental security, food security, health security, personal security, community security and political security (UNDP, 1994, pp. 24–5). 'It means safety from the constant threat of hunger, disease, crime and repression. It also means protection from sudden and hurtful disruptions in the pattern of our daily lives – whether in our homes, in our jobs, in our communities or in our environment' (UNDP, 1994, p. 3). As presented, the concept is close to the concept of human development and does not provide clear links to the more 'traditional' security threats, from a state sovereignty perspective. It seems, however, to allow for a link with the concept of cooperative security.

Also in Africa, the way the concept of security is perceived is widening, and tends to get very close to the concept of human security. The 'Kampala Document', reflecting the views of a wide range of influential African scholars and politicians, states for example that: 'The concept of security goes beyond military considerations. It embraces all aspects of the society including economic, political and social dimensions of individual, family, community, local and national life. The security of a nation must be construed in terms of the security of the individual citizen to live in peace with access to basic necessities of life while fully participating in the affairs of his/her society in freedom and enjoying all fundamental human rights' (Africa Leadership Forum, 1991, p. 9). The government White Paper on Defence in South Africa defines security as 'an all-encompassing condition in which individual citizens live in freedom, peace and safety; participate fully in the process of governance; enjoy the protection of fundamental rights; have access to resources and the basic necessities of life; and inhabit an environment which is not detrimental to their health and well-being' (Government of South Africa, 1996, p. 5).

National security, based on military means, was the guiding principle of the Cold War period. A combination of the concepts of cooperative and human security has gained relevance in the 1990s. These new security concepts also help to show the relationship between demobilization, human development and security.

## 2   Economic aspects of demobilization and reintegration

Basically, what happens in economic terms during and after a demobilization is that the government (and possibly an armed opposition) releases a large number of soldiers from the payroll, cuts security expenditure accordingly,[3] and releases these people and their productive capabilities into the labour market. Meanwhile the government – often supported by outside donors – spends public funds on the management of the demobilization and resettlement and on programmes to facilitate the reintegration of the ex-combatants into civilian life. Several economic concepts and approaches exist that might shed light on questions regarding the impact of demobilization.

### 2.1   Costs of war

Looking at the impact of peace from a different angle than the concept of peace dividend as presented above, it could be noted that peace would first of all bring benefits by ending the *costs of the war*. Africa's growth and development has indeed been seriously affected by wars and other violent conflicts. Over the past four decades more than 30 violent conflicts have taken place in Sub-Saharan Africa, causing the loss of an estimated seven million human lives. These conflicts not only took human lives. They caused tremendous suffering, health problems, educational gaps, loss of livestock, and destroyed infrastructure and other types of physical capital (Bennett *et al.*, 1995; Crana, 1994; Green, 1993; Stewart, 1993). Social services, such as health facilities and school systems, deteriorated or were totally destroyed. Lack of investment and of production below full capacity led to output far below the potential. Wars in Africa also eroded the institutions of civil society, causing a decline in the stock of social capital (Collier, 1994c). More indirect costs of war were caused by the fact that all the resources spent on the military were not spent on development.

Several methods have been used to estimate the costs of violent conflicts. Economic costs can, for example, be estimated by adding up physical damage, loss of exports, erosion of tax revenue, excess transport costs and military spending (ADB, 1995). Studies have also been conducted on the cost of conflict defined as the difference between the estimated GDP growth in the absence of war (counterfactual) and the actual (estimated) GDP growth. All these methods still have large difficulties in estimating the costs, but they could be useful to show the order of magnitude of the costs of war. In a postwar situation they are, however, less useful, since they do not provide much insight into the actual recovery.

## 2.2 Macroeconomic aspects

Questions regarding the *macroeconomic impact* of demobilization might draw on the theory and debate regarding the relation between security expenditure and economic growth. Several models and numerous empirical studies have been developed and applied over the past decades to assess this relation. An early and well-known study in this field was conducted by Emile Benoit in the early 1970s (Benoit, 1973). He found, on the basis of a cross-sectional statistical analysis, a positive correlation between the share of GDP devoted to defence and the rate of growth of non-military output. The method and results of his study have been rather influential, but also seriously criticized. Nicole Ball argues that conceptually and methodologically it is one of the weakest of all statistical examinations of the relationship between security expenditure and growth (Ball, 1988).

A discussion of the method used by Benoit and the critique is beyond the scope of this chapter. Todd Sandler and Keith Hartley argue that: 'Although individual studies on the impact of defense on growth contain *seemingly* contradictory findings, there is a greater consistency in the findings than is usually supposed. Models that include demand-side influences, whereby defense can crowd out investments, found that defense had a negative impact on growth. In contrast, almost every supply-side model either found a small positive defense impact or no impact at all. The findings are amazingly consistent despite differences in the sample of countries, the time periods, and the economic estimating procedures. Since we suspect that these supply-side models exclude some negative influences of defense on growth, we must conclude that the net impact of defense on growth is negative, but small' (Sandler and Hartley, 1995, p. 220).

Most of these models and research efforts look at the level of military expenditure and the changes in national output. For the questions in this study it would be necessary to consider the actual decline in military expenditure and its impact. But we should note that specifically in complex postwar African economies, macroeconomic modelling and statistical techniques have many serious limitations. It is extremely difficult to distinguish the impact of the demobilization – through reduced military spending – from the impact of economic stabilization and adjustment policies, increased aid flows, foreign and domestic investment, rehabilitation of agriculture and industrial capacity, repatriation of refugees, increased tax revenues,[4] increased investor and consumer confidence, etc.

Regarding the various postwar processes and interventions, some of the changes take place as a result of market responses, others directly as a result of policy initiatives. For example, when prices change, new investment decisions are made, trade patterns change, employment opportunities develop, people move within and between countries, etc. These responses could, however, take time, for example because of poor infrastructure (roads) and lack of working capital. As a result of policy interventions, public works, subsidies and services have a direct impact on social and physical infrastructure and employment. The general atmosphere and the level of expectations could also play a role. Expectations for targeted interventions and general improvements of standards of living can be high. Some groups could take a waiting attitude or apply political pressures. Others might take initiatives and respond to new opportunities that develop in the postwar environment.

To assess the direct *employment impact* one should first of all find out where the demobilized went and what type of income-generating activity they found, if any. On the one hand, the number of people in the labour market increases as a result of the demobilization. On the other hand, skills and other capabilities of ex-combatants might lead to new employment opportunities (see Chapter 3). Establishing the general unemployment and underemployment situation and the ratio of the demobilized in the total labour force is important in assessing to what extent the demobilized are 'crowding out' other civilians in the labour market.

In countries with a sophisticated military apparatus and a domestic defence industry, demobilization could also have an impact on the local economy as a result of fewer orders from the military. In Sub-Saharan Africa, with the exception of South Africa, this is unlikely to be the case. It is important, however, to trace the impact of the change in spending by the (demobilized) combatants. Where did the soldiers spend their money, while still serving? When and where did the demobilized soldiers spend the cash component of their demobilization packages? Together with the question of how these packages were financed, this could have an impact both on the inflationary pressures as well as on the purchasing power and distribution of income in the different regions in the country.

There are several ways in which the demobilization exercise and subsequent resettlement and reintegration support could lead to increased *inflation*. External funding to the programmes as a whole increases the money supply, cash payments to the demobilized increase purchasing power in a rather constrained economy, and if the whole programme is supported or coordinated by the United Nations, this would most likely lead to substantial import of foreign exchange (Colletta *et al.*, 1996a). The latter is not directly the result of the demobilization, but as will be shown in Chapter 7, the large expenditures made during the UN operations in Mozambique, for example – and their subsequent withdrawal – led to major distortions and shocks in the fragile economy. On the other hand, there are strong arguments that security expenditures are inherently inflationary since they create effective demand without offsetting increases in consumable output or in productive capacity to meet future consumption requirements (demand-pull). Excess demand creates an upward pressure on prices throughout the economy (BICC, 1996, p. 66). Reduction of the security expenditures as a result of demobilization would therefore also reduce inflationary pressures. The actual weight of these pressures and their net impact on price levels in a specific situation remains an empirical question. Clearly, however, as with most other macroeconomic indicators in postwar countries, the impact of the demobilization as such is very hard to establish.

One has to consider that in postwar economies considerable *time lags* could occur. Basic investments in the infrastructure have to be implemented. Investors' confidence takes time to take root. On the other hand, inflows of foreign aid could considerably boost the growth rate, especially given the low starting level. In those cases, however, the sustainability of the growth should be questioned. As is generally true for conversion processes, long-term gains might require some short-term pains.

### 2.3 Micro-foundation for analysis

Taking the above limitations of a macroeconomic analysis into account, it becomes more important to explore the options of assessing the impact at the *micro-level*. The analysis could then be built on a micro-foundation. For example, the development impact could be assessed on the basis of *household surveys*, providing data on income, income sources, assets, health situation, educational level, access to services, household composition, etc. Such an analysis would deal with questions such as: what type of activities did the ex-combatants end up doing, in which sectors, and what is their income? Depending on the coverage of the survey, it could be estimated how many of them have found or created employment. Monitoring systems of demobilization and reintegration programmes also help to answer some of these questions.

If data are available over a period of time, household surveys could also help to address the specifics in certain regions and of different subgroups of the demobilized and their families. One could, for example, assess the impact of the demobilization on female ex-combatants, or on specific groups, such as the disabled, ex-child soldiers and dependants of ex-combatants. It could be found whether any redistribution of income or assets took place as a result of the demobilization. An *entitlement approach* might also be able to shed light on the micro-level changes as a result of the demobilization.

### 2.4 Financial and economic returns

The questions about the impact of demobilization can also be addressed in a more limited way by looking at the costs and the savings. Direct and indirect financial savings on the military (security) budget as a result of the demobilization might be observed if reasonably reliable defence expenditure data are available. One could also calculate the total costs of the demobilization and reintegration exercise. *Financial and economic returns* could be calculated subsequently. The *financial multiplier* – the ratio of budgetary savings to the costs of demobilization – indicates the savings for each dollar spent on the demobilization and reintegration programme. Along similar lines, the *economic multiplier* is the ratio of the total income of the ex-combatants to the costs of the demobilization and reintegration programme (Colletta *et al.*, 1996a).

It should be kept in mind that savings as a result of the demobilization might be (partially) compensated by increases in other lines of the defence budget, or by increases in salaries. The funding sources of the different components of the demobilization and reintegration activities might complicate this picture. These activities might be funded from government budgets. But the recent experience in Africa shows that substantive proportions of the activities have been funded by external donors, either through loans or grants. Loans obviously increase the debt burden of the country concerned.

World Bank research points out several of the limitations of using a calculation of financial returns (Colletta *et al.*, 1996a). Particularly in postwar countries, data on security expenditure are usually hard to obtain. Much expenditure does not pass through the usual procedures, but comes from special accounts as, so-called, off-budget expenses. During civil wars a major share of the resources used in the conflict came from the opposition side. Their actual expenditures and the size of the non-government forces are obviously even more difficult to trace. In some cases also the direct contributions from outside parties such as arms suppliers and foreign armies should be considered. Considering these limitations it is likely that, using formal calculations, the real net benefits of the demobilization will be underestimated. Only dealing with the defence budgets might also overlook that demobilizations could possibly indirectly increase public expenditure elsewhere, because of additional needs for government services.

On the impact side, limitations of calculating the returns of the demobilization and reintegration programme are that they provide very little indication about the actual reintegration of the ex-combatants. If reliable estimates on the income earned by the ex-combatants were available, the economic returns could give at least some useful indication of the economic impact.

## 2.5   Broader political economy

To assess the impact of the demobilization, one should also consider the broader *political economy* of the entire process. Different
approaches and perceptions exist, ranging from defensive approaches
to demobilization (budgetary savings, preventing insecurity by paying
off soldiers, etc.) to positive proactive approaches (improve security
through development opportunities; try to utilize skills for development, etc.). Already during the decision-making and planning
process certain outcomes can be built in along the lines of the
interests of different groups. Box 2.3 provides an overview of possible actors during the demobilization and reintegration process. These
actors usually have different interests. Were there any groups of
people that actually had an interest in the war continuing? Black-
marketeers could be such a group. What was done to prevent these
groups from disrupting the peace process or taking up arms again?
In Mozambique, for example, special payments were made to officers
of Renamo, in order to keep them happy. Did the soldiers and
military leadership resist the decision to demobilize, which would
possibly reduce their influence in a wider sphere? Demobilization
might imply that the military has to withdraw from some productive sectors in the economy. How voluntary was the demobilization,
and how were the soldiers selected who were to be demobilized?
For some of these questions and settings a *game-theory* approach
might provide insights (Azam, 1994). Other questions might require
different types of political analysis.

After demobilization one could consider how ex-combatants organized themselves and what interests they defended. Did they
establish associations, and what type of activities did these undertake? Other types of mutual support among ex-combatants might
also exist. Some groups might have benefited from the demobilization exercise because of the large logistical effort that was conducted
and the money that was spent during the operation, including the
packages provided to the ex-combatants. Of course money might
also have 'leaked' during such a large-scale operation.

Support programmes have to strike a balance between supporting
different groups. Special treatment of ex-combatants may upset others
in need. From a short-term, conflict-resolution point of view, one
may be inclined to please the ex-combatants to forestall a return
to arms. There appears to be a trade-off between short-term security and long-term development and security. It could even be argued

---

**Box 2.3 Possible actors in demobilization processes**

(1) demobilized combatants
   • male and female ex-combatants
   • ex-child soldiers
   • ex-government soldiers and ex-guerrillas
   • associations of demobilized combatants
(2) families of ex-combatants
(3) communities in which ex-combatants resettle
(4) other groups trying to reintegrate (e.g. returned refugees and internally displaced people)
(5) local business community
(6) government agencies
(7) armed forces, and other security forces
(8) local NGOs
(9) the UN and its agencies
(10) donor agencies
(11) international NGOs

---

that the reintegration support in one country might be an incentive to pick up arms elsewhere. If experiences in other countries are known, why would a government army of guerrilla force demobilize before the international community has committed ample resources?

## 2.6  International involvement

International involvement adds an extra level to the analysis of demobilization and reintegration. Several bilateral, multilateral and non-governmental agencies are sometimes involved in the planning, often committing substantive financial and technical assistance. This might influence the effectiveness and redistributive effect of the entire process. Heavy involvement by external donors and development agencies in the process of demobilization and reintegration could also affect the sustainability of the efforts.

## 2.7  Other economic and non-economic factors

There are clearly numerous *non-economic factors* in postwar situations that influence the impact of demobilization. War often leaves deep scars in society, communities, families and individual life. As indicated above, the conflict is often not yet (fully) resolved and a positive peace – more than a mere absence of violence – not yet attained. Social acceptance in the community might take a long time and employers might have a reluctance to hire ex-combatants, based on their perceptions of them. Tensions might also develop because of the high expectations of the ex-fighters. Especially if they have fought for the liberation of their country and have succeeded, they might have very little patience and understanding for the slowness of certain processes. A factor that must be considered in any comparative analysis is the role of family and community support in difficult circumstances.

Special attention should also be given to affected groups such as female ex-combatants, their children, wives of ex-combatants and former child soldiers. Women have usually acquired new roles during wars, and are often expected by men to return to their traditional roles. Despite the fact that many former child soldiers might have become adults in the meantime, they have additional problems in reintegration. Disabled ex-combatants also require special support and health care for effective reintegration. Psychosocial aspects of leaving the army and re-entering civilian life should not be overlooked. It is often difficult to adjust their attitudes and expectations.

These questions regarding the impact of demobilization could be seen in the perspective of a long-standing debate on the role of the military in development. Since the 1960s there are basically two schools of thought on this issue. The so-called *modernizers* emphasize the positive impact of the military on development. Their arguments centre around the work done by Emile Benoit in the 1970s (Benoit, 1973). They used three basic arguments to explain why the military had a constructive development role (Wulf, 1992): (1) the organizational format of the military and their control over the instruments of power would allow the military to reshape traditional society into a modern society; (2) because of its technological and managerial know-how, the military would be able not only to handle military affairs, but also civilian affairs; and (3) the recruitment of military personnel from different classes in society would allow the military to contribute to nation-building and to the prevention of conflict arising from regionalism or ethnic particularism. These arguments are opposed by representatives of the other school, who have viewed the military as consumers of scarce and valuable resources, which are thus lost for development. Regarding the role of the military in development, Nicole Ball (1988, pp. 30–1) concludes that: 'To obtain a complete picture of the importance of the armed forces in shaping the future of developing countries, it is necessary to include as many different kinds of information as possible. Differences occur not only from country to country, but also over time within the same country. Neither of the two approaches used during the last thirty years for analyzing the role played by the armed forces have succeeded in integrating all the different kinds of information necessary to produce a comprehensive image of the military in development.'

## 3 Conclusions

This chapter suggests and discusses the concepts of peace dividend, conversion, peace-building, demobilization, resettlement, reintegration, support measures, development and security. To assess the impact of demobilization one has to consider the resources involved, the dynamic processes of production and redistribution, and the different actors in policy making and implementation. We found that an assessment needs to take a broad perspective and analyse impact at different levels. Several economic concepts and approaches exist that could contribute to such an assessment – best if applied in combination. Other disciplines and methods can complement the picture of how the demobilization worked out in terms of human development and security.

The analysis could best be based on a broad set of empirical data. There are, however, serious data constraints, particularly in countries coming out of protracted wars. In these countries usually very little even basic data is available. The assessment methods used could therefore take different approaches, based on the availability of data.

## Notes

1  The terms *security expenditure* and *security sector* are as terms preferred over the more commonly used *military expenditure* and *military sector*, since they include paramilitary forces that might be quite considerable in Sub-Saharan African countries (Ball, 1988, p. xvi).

2  We are using the word *reintegration*, but often ex-combatants actually settled in areas where they have never lived before. The word *integration* would in those cases be more correct. It has been reported that in Mozambique about one-third of the demobilized combatants settled in new areas rather than return home (*WSP Research Update* No. 3, p. 2, UNRISD War-torn Societies Project, November 1996).

3  As discussed above, it is possible that a demobilization will not lead to a reduction of security spending.
4  It should be noted that in Ethiopia the tax revenue actually declined directly after the war, since the new government abandoned the coercive measures for revenue raising applied during the war (Chapter 6).

# 3

# Human Resources Development and Utilization in Demobilization and Reintegration Programmes[1]

*Irmgard Nübler*

## 1 Introduction

The ultimate objective of demobilization and reintegration efforts should be to improve the welfare of people. At the same time, people and their capabilities are considered an important means and instrument in achieving the various economic, social and political objectives of demobilization and reintegration. Demobilization of combatants frees human potentials that can contribute to achieving these objectives if available skills and competence are used effectively and if people without any skills, or with only few, are endowed with useful skills and qualifications.

Based on mainly economic theories and approaches, this chapter develops a conceptual framework for analysis and assessment of effective utilization and development of human capabilities and resources during demobilization and reintegration. Section 2 identifies short-, medium- and long-term objectives of demobilization and reintegration. Policies in human resource management have to be analysed and assessed in terms of these objectives. Section 3 presents three different concepts – human capital, human resources and human development – which explain the relevance of human beings in development. The review shows that, in the light of the objectives, the human resource approach represents an appropriate framework for analysing the role of former soldiers and their capabilities.

Sections 4 and 5 discuss the relevance of human resource management in the context of demobilization and reintegration. The scarcity of resources available for demobilization and reintegration programmes requires effective use of these resources. Section 4 deals with effective utilization of ex-combatants' competencies. Interventions must first analyse competencies of ex-combatants which they may have acquired prior to recruitment or during military time. Second, to what extent these competencies are applicable and useful in civilian activities must be analysed. Third, policy measures are required that facilitate the actual deployment and use of skills. Section 5 addresses the development of human resources. Education and training can play an important role in facilitating economic and social integration which in turn contributes to political stability and security. The chapter discusses the design of training programmes for effective economic and social integration. In addition, the complexity and diversity of training systems and their implications for training policies are examined. While the first sections have focused on the analysis of human resource management, Section 6 deals with the evaluation of projects and policy measures aiming at effective human resource management. Several evaluation methodologies are presented which are examined in terms of their suitability and feasibility to evaluate human resource management interventions in demobilization and reintegration strategies.

## 2   The objectives of demobilization and reintegration strategies

In general, the demobilization and reintegration process is related to a variety of objectives at the economic, social, political and human levels. The various objectives imply short-, medium- and long-term goals. In light of the objectives identified here, an appropriate concept is identified for the analysis of people's role during the demobilization process. Furthermore, measures, policies and projects in human resource management have to be evaluated in terms of these objectives.

The long-term objectives of the reintegration process are to enhance economic and human development and to foster and sustain political stability, security and peace (Kingma, 1996). Collier and Pradhan (1994) argue that the removal of legitimate authority and the erosion of institutions of civil society make the consequences of civil war quite different from those of a conventional international war. 'The longer a society stays in a state of civil war the more do conventions of legitimate conduct decay' (Collier and Pradhan, 1994,

p. 120). They conclude that the restoration of peace is tightly linked to the reconstruction of systems of legitimacy. Boyce (1995, p. 2069) concludes that 'in the aftermath of a civil war, the "soundness" of policies can be ascertained only in the light of the political economy of the peace process'.

A critical short- and medium-term objective of demobilization strategies is to integrate ex-combatants into productive civilian life. Economic integration contributes to financial independence and self-reliance which is viewed as essential for achieving objectives of demobilization at the social and political level. Demobilized soldiers have to cope with an environment which is characterized by high rates of unemployment or underemployment. In addition to the general employment situation, wars negatively affect the level and composition of production and expenditures. The decline in productivity and aggregate output usually comes with a change in structure where resources are shifted to less productive activities, and expenditure is shifted out of investment and the public sector. The recovery of production and the reversion of the structures to prewar characteristics seems to be a slow process (Collier and Pradhan, 1994). Consequently, employment opportunities emerge slowly. In the formal sector they are normally extremely limited in the short run. Engagement in the agricultural or informal sectors may be promising but lack of skills, capital, land or licences and entrepreneurial experience may present constraints.

Another short- and medium-term objective is to integrate ex-combatants and their families into society. War-torn countries are characterized by fragmented societies. Special groups within the group of ex-combatants, such as women, child soldiers, disabled combatants, need to be integrated socially.

Effective human resource management, i.e. the development and utilization of people's skills, knowledge and competence, is considered a critical element of the demobilization process. There is evidence that, in general, investment in human resource management is efficient, i.e. the benefits outweigh the costs, and that the rates on investment in human capital are at least as high as in alternative uses (Psacharopoulos, 1988).

# 3   Human capital, human resources and human development

The role and relevance of people in development may be analysed by three different concepts – human capital, human resources and human development. Although these terms are sometimes used as synonyms, they refer to different concepts.

## 3.1   Human capital theory

Human capital theory represents the neoclassical approach to the economics of education and training. It highlights the qualitative aspect of labour: 'human capital refers to the productive capacities of human beings as income producing agents in the economy' (Rosen, 1987, p. 681). According to Schultz (1961), human capital consists of health and of skills and knowledge, which have economic value. The investment aspect is essential in human capital theory. The acquisition of human capital is an investment in the sense that the individual forgoes current income for increased earnings potential in the future.

The theory of human capital analyses the effects of human capital on productivity and income at the micro- and macroeconomic level. At the microeconomic level, human capital theory maintains that good health, knowledge and skills raise labour productivity, which in turn influences economic activity and societal well-being. The acquisition of cognitive abilities, the formation of competence and the transfer of information are considered the major link between schooling/training and productivity (Bowman, 1980). The basic assumption of human capital theory is that the wage rate is determined by the marginal productivity of the worker. At the macroeconomic level, new growth theories have formulated models to explain long-run growth of per-capita income by introducing human capital into the neoclassical growth model. The effect of human capital on growth is the enhancement of labour productivity. The increase in 'effective labour' (or labour in efficiency units) provides permanent incentives to accumulate production factors, thereby stimulating long-term growth of per-capita income (Lucas, 1988).

## 3.2   Human resource approach

Although many authors tend to use the term 'human resource' and 'human capital' synonymously, a closer look reveals substantial differences between these two approaches. First, 'human resources' includes both the quantitative (size of population, age structure) and qualitative aspects of human beings. Schultz (1961, p. 8) maintains that 'Human resources obviously have both quantitative and qualitative dimensions. The number of people, the proportion who enter upon useful work, and hours worked are . . . quantitative characteristics. . . . I shall neglect these and consider only such quality components as skill, knowledge and similar attributes that affect particular human capabilities to do productive work.' This viewpoint is also taken by Smith, Say, Mill, Bentham and List (Kiker, 1966, p. 487). In contrast, Walras, von Thünen and Fisher consider human beings as capital, which reflects the notion of human resources. Following Fisher's definition of capital, the skill of an individual is not capital in addition to the individual himself. 'It is the skilled individual who should be placed in the category of capital' (Fisher, quoted in Kiker, 1966, p. 488).

Second, while human capital theory considers knowledge and cognitive skills the most important link to productivity, the human resource approach takes into account a variety of links between individuals' capabilities and their productivity. People are born with different talents and individual traits that may make them inherently more productive in certain occupations. The socialization and 'correspondence' approaches (Colclough, 1982) stress the role of non-cognitive or affective, as well as motivational and psychological dimensions of human resources in productivity. Education and training may have an important impact on a person's values, attitudes, norms (socialization effect), on motivation and expectations (psychological effects), and on behaviour (McNabb and Whitfield, 1994). These factors influence a person's capacity as well as willingness to work effectively, and are considered an important element of human resources.

Third, the human resource approach is oriented to the development as well as to the utilization of human resources. Human resource utilization is the extent to which available human resources are deployed effectively for the maximum achievement of individual, collective, organizational or national goals and objectives. Effective human resource utilization for development may involve human resource allocation, maintenance and further development (Kiggundu, 1989, p. 151). 'Human resources . . . constitute the ultimate basis for the wealth of nations. . . . The goals of development are the maximum possible utilization of human beings in more productive activity and the fullest possible development of the skills, knowl-edge and capacities of the labor force' (Harbison, 1973, pp. 3, 115). Fourth, while human capital refers only to the productive value of people, the human resource approach refers to economic as well as political and social development objectives. Human resource development and utilization are regarded as the means to meet basic human needs and to contribute to overall development by reducing fertility; by transmitting cultural, religious, political, and technological values; and by preserving national identity, cohesiveness and stability (Cohen, 1994).

### 3.3 Human development concept

The concept of human development is based on the ideas of A.K. Sen, designed by Mahbub ul Haq and promoted by UNDP. Sen defines development in terms of functionings achieved, 'one of the functionings that may be thought to be particularly important in assessing the nature of development is the freedom to choose' (Sen, 1988, p. 16). Human development is defined as enlarging people's choices, where the choices range from political, economic and social freedom to opportunities for being creative and productive, and enjoying personal self-respect and human rights (UNDP, 1990).

The human development concept is based on five essential ideas. First, human development becomes the real end of activities which moves people to centre-stage of development. Second, human de-velopment relates to the formation of human capabilities and the use people make of their acquired capabilities. Third, a distinction is made between ends and means. People are regarded as the ends; however, they are also means of development. Fourth, the human development concept embraces all of society. The political, cultural and social factors are given as much attention as economic factors (Haq, 1995). Haq considers four essential components of human development and to each of them human resources are assigned an important role. The four pillars are equitable access to oppor-tunities, sustainability of human opportunities, productivity and growth, and empowerment of people, meaning that people are placed in a position to exercise their own choices (Haq, 1995). The level achieved on each of these pillars indicates the extent of people's economic, social, political and cultural choices.

The formation and utilization of human resources is regarded as one important policy measure to enhance the levels of the various pillars. Human resource development removes barriers that limit the access of women, minorities or other groups to key economic and political opportunities. Higher productivity and growth require investment in people and in human capital. Empowerment among many other factors requires investing in education and health so that people can take advantage of market opportunities as well as social and political opportunities, and are able to participate in those activities, events and processes that shape their lives (Haq, 1995).

## 3.4  Selecting the appropriate concept

An appropriate concept has to be selected for analysing issues related to demobilization and reintegration of ex-combatants in Africa. The discussion of human capital, human resources and human development reveals that human capital theory takes a rather narrow view by focusing on human competencies for productive purposes. This approach would mainly allow for the analysis of ex-combatants' contribution to income and productivity. The human resource approach takes a much broader view by relating to both the formation and utilization of human capabilities and to economic, social and political objectives. In fact, human capital may be considered as one facet in the human resource approach. Within the human resources framework a wide range of issues related to demobilization and reintegration may be analysed. Human resource management can be linked not only to economic goals but also to social and political objectives. Furthermore, analysis of the relation between human resources and the various objectives of demobilization is not restricted to the role of cognitive abilities, but may consider a broad range of variables, such as different types of skills, motivation, expectations and ambitions.

While the human capital and the human resource concept view human beings as a means, the human development concept highlights the dual role of people both as means and end of development. The human development approach, however, is not considered to be the most appropriate concept to analyse the role of ex-combatants. The approach is considered to be too broad for the nature of the given task, since it includes many more means – of equal importance – to achieve the human development objective. Furthermore, the human development approach still faces several weaknesses at the theoretical and conceptual level.

The human resource approach may in fact be considered as an integral part of the human development concept. Expanding people's choices constitutes the ultimate objective of development where choices relate to economic, political and social variables. Hence, the abstract variable human development is defined by economic, social and political dimensions. It has been pointed out that the human resource approach also relates to economic, social and political development goals. In this sense human development, as the ultimate objective of development, sets the norms, goals and standards to be achieved by human resource management. The human resources concept provides the analytical framework.

One can conclude that the human resources approach represents the most appropriate and useful concept to discuss and analyse issues related to demobilization and reintegration of ex-combatants. The impact of the demobilization and reintegration process and the accompanying human resource policies, however, have to be ultimately assessed in terms of human development.

## 4   Human resource utilization and reintegration

Human resource utilization during demobilization and reintegration refers to the effective deployment of existing skills, qualifications and competencies of ex-combatants for the maximum achievement of individual, social, organizational or national goals and objectives of demobilization.

### 4.1   Identification and taxonomy of skills

An important first step in achieving effectiveness and efficiency in human resource management during demobilization and reintegration is to identify existing skills of former combatants. Qualifications, skills and competencies may be classified according to different criteria depending on the nature of the task to be performed.

#### 4.1.1   *A broad view on human capabilities*

Most studies on demobilization in Africa tend to give a minor role to the aspect of utilization of existing skills. They conclude from surveys that most ex-combatants have very few or no skills and knowledge (ILO, 1995a; Klingebiel *et al.*, 1995; World Bank, 1993). Consequently, little consideration is given to utilization of existing competence and the focus is on human resource development.

Although little information is given on the methodology of data collection, it seems that data on existing skills are mainly collected in interviews, in which former combatants indicate what kind of skills they have acquired. The literature on empirical research methodologies discusses a range of reasons why the data obtained from self-reporting may not be reliable. In addition, it appears that a rather narrow view is taken in terms of skills variety. Reference is made implicitly to (formal) vocational, technical and basic general skills. The world of skills, however, is diverse. Human capabilities and competencies relate to knowledge, abilities, skills, values, attitudes and norms. These are the results of intentional learning, learning-by-doing, and the socialization process in the education and training system, as well as the employment system.

The development of human capabilities takes place at three levels: the cognitive, affective and psychomotor levels. The cognitive area includes knowledge, understanding, problem solving and theory, and distinguishes between formal and idiosyncratic knowledge. Formal knowledge refers to knowledge and skills that can be transmitted in written or verbal instructions. Idiosyncratic knowledge is defined as 'that intuitive knowledge, based upon training and experience, that is incapable of translation into written form' (Williamson, 1975, p. 35). Idiosyncratic experience is characteristic of many skills acquired while performing difficult tasks.

At the affective level human resource formation comprises emotions, attitudes, values and norms. Socialization effects such as punctuality, respect for authority, self-reliance, attitude towards work, and the ability to make decisions may be induced at the level of the family, school or at work. Manual and practical skills including physical agility belong to the psychomotor area (Nölker and Schoenfeldt, 1985). Taking a broad view on skills and human competencies, a more rigorous methodology may reveal some skills and qualifications in ex-combatants that can be of benefit to the individual and society.

### 4.1.2 *Applicability of acquired qualifications in civilian activities*

When people have acquired skills and qualifications during their military service, the central question is whether these skills can be transferred to civilian occupations. Two different concepts are presented which allow the distinction of skills in terms of transferability. One concept, which may be called the inter-occupational approach, distinguishes between functional and extra-functional qualifications. Functional or process-related qualifications relate to the performance, experience, knowledge and skills required for a particular type of job. Extra-functional or process-independent qualifications refer to technical and economic qualifications not tied to one very specific type of work. These include competencies such as the ability to cooperate and communicate, logical thinking, mastery of symbolic languages, technical understanding and creativity. In addition to economic qualifications, there are general and social qualifications such as diligence, attentiveness, thrift, responsibility, ability to adjust, flexibility and openness to life-long learning, change of social role, solidarity and opportunities for freedom of action (Nölker and Schoenfeldt, 1985).

Extra-functional qualifications are transferable between different types of professions and therefore also transferable from the military to the civilian sector. These qualifications may have been acquired during the time in the military at various levels. First, it is argued that training in the use of weapons and equipment may induce changes at the affective level. Soldiers are supposed to acquire modern attitudes and aptitudes by working with modern machinery, following instructions, etc. (Ball, 1988). This attitude is considered to contribute to innovative behaviour, adoption of new technologies and economic development (Inkeles and Smith, 1974). Second, tolerance may be enhanced between people belonging to different ethnic groups or religions. In Eritrea it was observed that there was a greater convergence of different viewpoints in the military than in civilian life. A high level of tolerance contributes to the social and political integration of demobilized soldiers (Klingebiel *et al.*, 1995). Third, during their military time, many combatants may undergo a social transformation (Matthies, 1994). There is evidence that people change from a rural to an urban mentality. Women combatants experienced a relationship to male colleagues as equals, and were very reluctant to return to their traditional roles in society, which were characterized by subordination to men. In many armed forces, female combatants had equal rights and duties during the war and developed a high level of self-confidence. Finally, military service tends to enhance the ability to cooperate in teams. Evidence from Eritrea shows that fighters are used to working in groups for many years, which enhances their ability to cooperate. Group leaders have the opportunity to achieve competence in leadership.

A second concept that is useful in analysing skills in terms of transferability from military to civilian has been introduced by Becker (1975). Skills may be classified as either firm-specific or general skills. General training was defined as raising the worker's productivity in both the training firm and other firms. General skills, therefore, are useful in many firms and are transferable between firms. Specific training increases the productivity of a trainee in the firm providing the training, but not in other firms. Most skills are neither completely general nor specific; the distinction, however, serves as a useful analytical tool.

In the context of military-related skills we define those skills as general which are applicable and useful in both the military and the civilian sectors. In contrast, military-specific or even weapon-specific skills are not useful in the civilian sector. Becker refers to the military sector as the producer of general skills. 'The military offers some forms of training that are extremely useful in the civilian sector, . . . for example, a machinist trained in the army finds his skills of value in steel and aircraft firms . . . and others that are only of minor use to civilians, i.e. astronauts, fighter pilots, and missile men. Such training falls within the scope of specific training because productivity is raised in the military but not (much) elsewhere' (Becker, 1975, pp. 19, 26).

General skills of demobilized soldiers may have been acquired in the military at various levels through training and experience. Capabilities may be provided in basic skills such as reading and writing, in vocational and technical skills such as plumbing, printing, metal-working, learning to drive and repair vehicles, as well as at more advanced levels in electrical, chemical and mechanical engineering (Ball, 1988). Military personnel may acquire skills in improved agricultural techniques since many armed forces in developing countries grow a portion of their own food. Training may also be provided in the health sector imparting medical expertise. Skills acquired during the performance of relatively less skilled non-occupational military tasks such as guard duty or proficiency in using weapons may still be of value in the civilian sector, for example in security services, in the police or as game wardens. Ball concludes that some of the skills taught by the military can benefit the civilian sector; however, studies from industrialized countries suggest that transferability of military skills to the civilian sector is limited (Ball, 1988).

### 4.1.3 Skills for different labour markets and occupations

Policies for effective allocation of demobilized workers in the labour market and job placement measures, as well as policies to promote self-employment, require analysis of available skills according to their relevance in different labour market segments and occupations. Former combatants may be employed in the formal or informal sector as workers or as managers; they may start their own enterprise or work on their own farm. These different tasks and occupations require different patterns of skills and competencies. One can distinguish between vocational/technical, management and entrepreneurial skills.

Vocational and technical qualifications relate to those skills, knowledge and attitudes required for effective and efficient performance within an occupation or group of occupations. Different levels of vocational and technical skills can be identified, such as semi-skilled workers, skilled workers, master craftsmen and technicians (ILO, 1986). Vocational skills can further be distinguished as skills for traditional and non-traditional or 'parallel' occupations (King, 1990). Traditional trades are confined to the informal sector. Parallel trades refer to occupations which exist in both the formal and informal sectors. These skilled trades such as car mechanic, metalworker, carpenter, builder, or tailor may be acquired in traditional apprenticeship as well as in the formal sector. Obviously, skill identification among ex-combatants requires taking into account not only non-traditional, but also traditional, skills such as knowledge on traditional healing methods or food processing.

Business management skills relate to abilities required to operate an enterprise or farm. These skills refer to the ability to use planning, monitoring and evaluation tools effectively, and coordinate and control production for successful business performance. They also refer to abilities such as managing human relations within the firm, dealing with public bureaucracy and managing customer and supplier relations. Management skills may be acquired through formal training, training on the job or learning by doing (Metcalf, 1984). Experience from small enterprise development programmes shows that both vocational and management skills may be required for successful performance. Some studies assign a dominant role to management. Kilby (1988) considers the low capacity among small-scale entrepreneurs in African countries in performing day-to-day management functions to be a major constraint. Proponents of management training maintain that technically and vocationally skilled individuals who lack business management skills are more likely to experience difficulties in operating their business than someone with lower vocational skills but management ability (McLaughlin, 1989).

Entrepreneurial skills relate to the 'ability to deal with disequilibria', i.e. the 'efficiency of human beings to perceive, to interpret correctly, and to take action that will appropriately reallocate their resources' (Schultz, 1975, p. 827). These skills refer to abilities such as making investment decisions, innovating, imitating, and filling gaps in fragmented markets. Programmes to assist ex-combatants in starting a micro-enterprise may in particular select those who possess entrepreneurial skills and provide management and vocational skills training.

Finally, occupational-oriented distinction can be made between strategic and core skills (Benson, 1989). Strategic skills are skills that are in short supply, but are key complementary inputs to priority economic development strategies. Because both strategies and skills availability can differ, what is 'strategic' at any time in a given economy varies. Core skills are those occupational skills which are in demand across sectors. Many of these are traditional 'vocational' occupations such as secretary, electrician, craftsman and auto mechanic. Postwar societies may have opted for a development strategy implying the demand for certain strategic skills. Ex-combatants who have acquired such competencies should be identified in order to achieve an optimal utilization of these scarce skills.

## 4.2   Application of skills and utilization of human resources

When ex-combatants possess marketable skills, the important question is under what conditions these competencies are actually applied in civilian occupations. Very little evidence is available as to the degree of the actual transfer of skills acquired in the military into civilian applications. Data on South Korea reveal that many skills acquired by soldiers were not utilized productively and therefore were of no benefit to the economy. This case shows that, even where the potential exists for transferring skills, the transfer may not happen automatically (Ball, 1988).

Several preconditions are required for the actual use of skills. First, available skills of ex-combatants can be used productively only if there is a demand for these skills, and employment opportunities are provided in the relevant occupations in the civilian sector. Second, the former soldiers must feel the motivation and incentive to work in the particular occupation. The process by which individuals decide to implement changes and to actually utilize their capabilities is influenced by future expectations and past experience. The expectancy theory (Vroom, 1964) postulates that a certain action will take place as the result of behaviour and the desire for a particular outcome. The outcome may relate to monetary or to non-monetary motivation since moral incentives such as recognition or work ethics can be as powerful as monetary motives (Prokopenko, 1989). Furthermore, the individual's history is assumed to play a significant role in the decision to change behaviour, apply skills and make use of information (Campbell and Pritchard, 1976).

Third, even where employment opportunities exist and former soldiers are motivated, various obstacles may prevent them from applying their skills. Individuals may have less control over their own behaviour than they would like to. The obstacles may be cultural attitudes or expected negative feedback, such as jealousy and resentment. Particularly for those who start their own enterprise, the lack of access to complementary resources such as credit and physical inputs, or legal constraints, may be barriers. Ex-combatants looking for paid employment may lack job-search skills. There is evidence that veterans may find it difficult to obtain information on job opportunities (World Bank, 1993).

Finally, complementary training may be required to facilitate the transfer of skills. There may be important differences even between similar occupations in military and civilian sectors which militates against the easy transfer. Many civilian occupations, particularly in skilled trades, demand a much higher skill level than is required of a soldier in counterpart military occupations. Skills and knowledge required may differ markedly because of differences in equipment, organization and methods. For example, a mechanic responsible for maintenance of tanks is not necessarily the same as a civilian auto mechanic (Ball, 1988).

## 4.3   Policies for effective utilization of human resources after demobilization

Effective utilization of existing skills, abilities and competencies requires supportive policies and complementary measures helping ex-soldiers to make use of their skills in civilian life. These measures and policies refer to both the supply and demand side of the labour market. On the supply side of the labour market, skill verification for former soldiers who have acquired marketable skills enhances their competitiveness. In Ethiopia, for example, certificates were issued to those who had acquired skills during military service. Certification of skills would provide information to potential employers on the person's type and level of experience. The certification should be done in such a way as to ensure credibility in the private sector (Colletta *et al.*, 1996a).

Job placement and counselling programmes may help veterans

find existing jobs. It appears that few of the governments in African postwar countries have established formal mechanisms for assisting veterans to find employment in the private sector (World Bank, 1993). Furthermore, there is evidence that the ambitions, aspirations and preference patterns of ex-combatants cannot always be met by opportunities. Counselling can assist individuals in becoming aware of and accepting the limitations, adjusting preferences to opportunities, and taking initiatives.

On the demand side of the labour market, the issue of creating jobs must be faced where jobs are unavailable. The economic situation in conflict-affected countries is generally not conducive to employment, making the total employment task a challenge. On top of that, structural adjustment and economic reform programmes implemented by governments in many postwar countries tend to increase unemployment, at least in the short term. Programmes to create jobs and paid employment for a large number of ex-combatants may in particular be created in employment-intensive infrastructure construction and rehabilitation (ILO, 1995d). Furthermore, self-employment in small and micro-enterprises is considered an important option in creating income opportunities for a large number of demobilized soldiers within a short period of time (ILO, 1995d). Those who plan to start their own enterprise may require access to complementary inputs, such as basic management or vocational training, counselling, credit, land or equipment. Business opportunity identification surveys are important in matching the preferences of the combatants with opportunities. Little attention appears to be given to business opportunity studies during the demobilization process. Consequently, the choice of small enterprise activities made by the ex-combatants appeared to be only weakly related to market opportunities (ILO, 1995e).

If these measures contribute successfully in utilizing available qualifications and competence, the benefits may be substantial. Effective utilization of human resources contributes to economic integration and rehabilitation of the economy, to social reintegration and the peace-building process. It is essential to manage available human resources effectively, to assist in job placement and to facilitate direct employment creation or increase the ability of ex-combatants for self-employment.

## 5 Human resources development and reintegration

Formation of human resources is expected to play an essential role in achieving the objectives of the demobilization process. The importance of training is recognized in most reintegration strategies (ILO, 1995a, b; Srivastava, 1994). Most education and training for ex-combatants aims at facilitating economic and social integration. Training may address former combatants who have very few or no marketable skills. Refresher or up-grading courses may be provided to those who had been trained prior to military service, or training may assist ex-combatants complementing skills acquired during military service. Special attention should be given to the initial training needs of former child soldiers and young ex-combatants. This target group is in particular need of education and training since most had no access to school and lack vocational and professional opportunities (ILO, 1995c). Post-conflict training strategies should also be developed with an eye on long-term national development. In most countries, unemployment and underemployment exist side by side with a shortage of skilled workers, middle and higher level technicians and professionals (Srivastava, 1994). In particular, strategic skills, which are required for the successful implementation of development strategies, should be developed.

### 5.1 Training for economic integration

A major short- and medium-term objective of human resource development in the demobilization process is to integrate ex-combatants into civilian life. Training aims at endowing ex-combatants with relevant skills, knowledge and information so that they will be able to find productive employment or start and manage successfully a micro-enterprise or small farm.

#### 5.1.1 The impact of training

The analysis of the process by which participation in training programmes is transmitted into benefits allows for impact at the level of the individual, enterprise and economy. Training may have a strong impact at the level of the individual. Human capabilities are created in individuals at the cognitive, affective and motivational levels. Human capital theorists highlight the relevance of increased cognitive abilities (Becker, 1975). Affective effects of education and training are related to important socialization effects shaping attitudes, values, norms and behaviour. Finally, training may have a strong impact in the psychological and motivational domain (McClelland, 1961). The training event itself, and the fact of being selected and given attention, may induce substantial motivation in participants. The development of these various capabilities and competencies in ex-combatants constitutes one important side of human development. Human capabilities help to remove barriers to economic, social and political opportunities (Haveman and Wolfe, 1984), and to foster empowerment so that ex-combatants can take advantage of existing opportunities.

The development of human capabilities and their effective use results in economic effects which are highly desirable in postwar countries. First, individual competence is positively related to the physical productivity and technical efficiency of labour. It enables increased output with given quantities of input through the efficient use of given resources (Jamison and Moock, 1984). Welch (1970, p. 42) labels these the 'worker effect'. Developing countries, and in particular postwar societies, are characterized by an environment where goods and factor markets are not well established and where relevant aspects of the production technologies and processes are not completely known. Relevant training improves the ability of entrepreneurs to cope with fragmented markets, to promote product quality and maintenance which results in higher technical efficiency.

Second, human capabilities contribute to higher allocative efficiency. This helps the manager in allocating the firm's resources in a cost-efficient manner, choosing which outputs and how much to produce, and in what proportions to use inputs in production (Jamison and Moock, 1984). Welch (1970, p. 42) calls this the 'allocative effect' of education and training. The allocative or entrepreneurial capacity (see Section 4.1.3) is of little value in static societies. However, when changes in economic conditions occur and disequilibria arise, the allocative ability has high productive value (Schultz, 1975). Consequently, these abilities tend to be highly relevant in postwar countries.

Third, human resources formation tends to have positive effects on the supply of entrepreneurial activity and enhances the capacity and the willingness to invest, innovate and imitate by applying new discoveries and ideas. The availability of technical skills is an important factor in technology choice and utilization. Furthermore, since employment opportunities in postwar countries are rare, most ex-combatants have to turn towards self-employment in the informal sector. In order to start a small enterprise, individuals must be motivated, have a positive attitude towards self-employment and should possess entrepreneurial and managerial capacities. These variables tend to be positively related to training.

Finally, job mobility and the ability to move into higher productivity sectors and occupations are related to the level of qualification. Those individuals who are endowed with marketable skills increase their employability. They will be more flexible in adjusting to changes in economic structures and can take advantage of employment opportunities.

### 5.1.2   *Training design for effective economic integration*

Training may be a solution in achieving economic integration of ex-combatants. However, not all problems can be solved through an increase in the level of skills and knowledge. Analysis must demonstrate and identify the role for training as part of the solution to a given problem. Usually, the supply of skilled labour does not create its own demand. Pre-employment training for entry into the formal sector and the large supply of vocationally trained graduates in many developing countries resulted in high rates of graduate unemployment, underemployment and low rates of human resource utilization where other factors and conditions were not present (Lauglo and Närman, 1988; Mingat *et al.*, 1989). Consequently, training of ex-combatants for direct employment has to be based on labour market studies and should be strictly demand driven (ILO, 1995d).

Training for self-employment in the informal sector requires analysis of markets. Feasibility studies must demonstrate potentials for self-employment. If there is a market, training aiming at facilitating entry into self-employment can be effective (McLaughlin, 1989; Boomgard, 1989).

Once a role for training is identified, the specific training needs have to be analysed. Training needs analysis involves three steps. First, the skill requirements of occupations or tasks have to be analysed. Second, the level and extent of existing skills among former combatants need to be identified. Relevant knowledge levels and qualifications can be identified through aptitude tests, interviews or recruitment procedures. Third, the skills and standards inherent in the training need to be identified.

Inadequate planning of training without hard data on needs and market demand is cited as a major problem in several postwar countries. When skills training programmes started in Ethiopia, there was insufficient time to make advance plans for training based on market demand. It was originally planned that a survey would be conducted to determine the training needs of demobilized soldiers reintegrating in urban areas. However, this could not be done due to time constraints (ILO, 1995a).

### 5.1.3 Target group selection and trainee specification

Effectiveness requires that participants of training programmes apply what has been learned. Therefore, training should be provided to those who demonstrate a positive long-term aptitude in the practice of the particular skills. Training programmes for small-enterprise development have to ensure that only those ex-combatants are selected who are motivated to start their own business. In this context it is important that training is the only motivation to participate in training courses. Some programmes pay training allowances where participation in training seminars may become profitable. Paying training allowances may contribute to attracting the wrong people, resulting in low effectiveness.

The design of training programmes has to be attuned to the socioeconomic and educational characteristics of the targeted ex-combatants. Trainees with little formal knowledge and literacy skills need specific teaching methods and much more attention may be focused on the motivational and psychological aspects of training. Female ex-combatants tend to face gender-specific obstacles and constraints both in finding employment and self-employment. They tend to have little access to knowledge, skills, information and resources. Gender-differentiated use of time gives them less flexibility, as they face social and cultural restraints on productivity and limited access to higher income-generating activities. Training programmes should address these issues and take constraints into account in their design. In addition, scheduling of training programmes should consider time constraints of women due to their multiple tasks.

Studies on demobilization programmes in African countries conclude that the short-term approach adopted in the reintegration programmes resulted in a lack of coordinated programmes for special groups of demobilized combatants, such as women, children and disabled persons. Studies on Mozambique and Uganda view the lack of attention to the needs of various target groups a major shortcoming in demobilization (ILO, 1995a).

### 5.1.4 *Minimalist versus multi-package approach*

Training alone may not always be effective. Additional assistance may be required in order to achieve effectively the objectives of training. Pre-employment training may require further assistance to ensure successful transfer between training and work. Job placement or counselling may be important in particular after institution-based training, where vocational education is not aimed at meeting specific employment needs of particular organizations.

There is evidence that training micro-entrepreneurs in management skills may be rather effective when the objective is to improve performance of an existing enterprise. However, if the objective is to start an enterprise or to transform into higher value-added products, training alone may not be very effective. Start-up programmes tend to require a complex package including technical and management-training, credit, technical assistance, etc. This is particularly important when programmes address disadvantaged pre-entrepreneurs without access to resources (McLaughlin, 1989).

The majority of demobilized combatants will have to turn to self-employment in the informal sector. Assistance packages for this target group should, however, not be too complex, for two reasons. First, the costs may become very high, resulting in low cost-effectiveness. Second, implementing organizations may have difficulties in handling complex packages, also contributing to low cost-effectiveness of programmes (Tendler, 1989).

## 5.2 Training for social integration

Most studies discuss education, training and work experience in the context of economic integration. The previous discussion on human resources and human development has shown that education and training is more than endowing people with marketable skills for productive purpose. The formation of human capabilities and the training process itself may induce favourable effects which are desirable after demobilization.

### 5.2.1 *The impact of training*

Training is expected to contribute to social integration of former combatants in different ways. First, the possession of skills that are of immediate appreciable value to the community, and the capacity and willingness to work, will facilitate acceptance of ex-combatants by the community and foster social integration.

Second, training facilitates social integration through its socialization effect. In many cases the ex-combatants spent many years in combat and have been socialized according to military rules and hierarchical structures. Attending schools or participating in training allows them to learn or relearn norms and practices of civilian society (ILO, 1995b). This is particularly true for ex-child soldiers; they have often lost cultural values, which is very serious given that they were in the crucial stages of development. Training is therefore considered important for their rehabilitation and social integration. Such action 'is part of a process in the life of the child, and not something "done" to the child that can be separated from his/her experience in the military or prior to recruitment, or from the present situation' (ILO, 1995b, p. 8).

Furthermore, military training makes soldiers follow orders without asking too many questions. As a consequence they often tend to be reluctant to seek explanations or participate actively in demobilization and reintegration programmes. In Zimbabwe, training in participatory approaches to planning and decision-making was provided, helping ex-soldiers to overcome this attitude (ILO, 1995a).

Third, training helps in finding a new identity and empowerment. Training settings can contribute to developing a sense of identity that is not linked to the previous roles in the military. Education and vocational training can do a lot to build self-confidence and respectability, to redirect the individual's energy in useful ways and to build hope for the future (ILO, 1995b). Furthermore, training can be therapeutic and helps to reduce trauma caused by the loss of family members and friends. Ex-soldiers begin to recover from their experiences, and find a new identity during the training process.

Finally, regaining lost education and training opportunities avoids frustration among ex-combatants and facilitates integration. Freedom fighters fought for their ideals and often built up great expectations beyond victory (Klingebiel *et al.*, 1995). They may be easily frustrated when changes and possibilities do not occur as they had expected, and feel bitter and betrayed. In particular, they may become disappointed about their restricted economic opportunities when looking at the more qualified people who have fled the country or stayed behind and were able to continue their education and training.

## 5.2.2  *Training design for effective social integration*

Training for social integration is assumed to be most effective when it is provided in mainstream programmes and when training is linked to the working world. First, social integration of special groups is enhanced when training is not provided in separate courses, but rather in mainstream programmes. Studies on training for women (Goodale, 1989), former child soldiers (ILO, 1995b) as well as training for disabled persons (ILO, 1995c) strongly suggest not treating these groups as a separate group in programmes for vocational training, but rather placing them into courses with other trainees. This will ensure their assimilation and acceptance and will work towards conflict resolution. Vocational training is seen as an integral component of social reintegration, and efforts should be made to avoid marginalization (ILO 1995b). Furthermore, training in mainstream programmes avoids ex-combatants being perceived as privileged by the receiving community, which is considered important for successful integration (Kingma, 1996).

Nevertheless, demobilized groups have particular experiences and may have special needs, which will have to be addressed outside of mainstream programmes. There may also be a case for separate training when young ex-combatants hesitate to attend school classes with much younger children, or where attitude towards education is very negative (ILO, 1995b). A study in Uganda reports that civilian schools were reluctant to accept former child soldiers, and they expressed reservations that they could manage the behaviour of the children (ILO, 1995b).

Second, training enhances social integration when it is linked to work. The needs of former soldiers not only for vocational training *per se*, but also for basic education and training in life skills, is best met when training is not provided in isolation. Education with production is a model where education is linked to productive life to create a foundation for adult life, providing better opportunities for former child soldiers to integrate with other children and allowing the young soldiers to relearn the norms and practices of civil society in a natural and progressive manner.

Apprenticeship provides the opportunity for young people to be trained by craftspeople and local entrepreneurs, and in some cases even become members of the family for the duration of the training. In particular, traditional apprenticeship is open to most young people and activities are relevant to the local situation (Fluitman, 1989). Family-based training is carried out within the family to enable the children to learn skills traditionally associated with providing for the family's economic security. This provides an opportunity to support existing income-generating skills and improves the family's capacity to care for the child (ILO, 1995b). One can conclude that those training settings tend to be most effective in assisting in social integration which avoid marginalization of special groups and isolated training. Hence, training should be provided in mainstream programmes and work-related settings whenever possible.

## 6 Evaluation of human resource management

Human resource management devotes scarce resources to measures such as general and vocational education, formal or informal training, job placement, skills verification and certification, counselling and assistance in establishing a micro-enterprise. The scarcity of resources available for demobilization and development assistance poses high opportunity costs on any particular intervention. Projects chosen should be most effective in terms of objectives and achieve efficiency in terms of costs and benefits. Studies on demobilization and reintegration highlight the fact that benefits, costs and effectiveness of interventions and projects are hardly evaluated. Reasons for the lack of project evaluations may be time pressure, lack of funds, lack of experts to undertake the evaluation studies, or methodological or practical difficulties. Projects are evaluated, if at all, in terms of money spent as predicted or programme implemented as planned. It is simply assumed or hoped that implementation will bring the expected benefits to the target group.

Human resource management projects implemented in the context of demobilization may be evaluated with different methodologies. This part presents several evaluation approaches and discusses their appropriateness.

### 6.1 Cost–benefit analysis

Cost–benefit analysis evaluates projects and interventions in order to measure their profitability by comparing costs and benefits where both are measured in monetary terms (Levin, 1983). In principle, cost–benefit studies can be performed at the private, corporate and social level, measuring costs and benefits to the individual, to the implementing enterprise or organization, and to society, respectively (Metcalf, 1984). Cost–benefit analysis involves four steps. First, the project's relevant costs and benefits must be identified. Economic benefits can be defined as all goods and services made available to the economy by the effect of a project or intervention. Direct benefits occur to the immediate users of the project's output, while indirect benefits, or positive external effects, refer to the outcome of a project such as spillover effects or the creation of further employment. These indirect effects result in a net gain to society, but not to a direct gain to the individuals who acquire the project's output (Dasgupta *et al.*, 1972). In addition to the economic benefits, additional objectives of a society such as equity or environmental objectives may be achieved by the intervention which, in principle, should be identified and specified.

Costs are treated in analogy to benefits. They are defined in terms of opportunity costs, which is the maximum alternative benefit forgone. By devoting resources to a particular use, society has to sacrifice the benefits that could be obtained from using them for other purposes (Dasgupta *et al.*, 1972).

In a second step, costs and benefits must be given a value in order to be comparable. Market prices are used to assess a private investor's prospects, and social prices to assess the project from society's point of view. Third, costs and benefits must be compared over time by discounting those occurring in future periods. Finally, benefits have to be related to costs so that different projects can be compared. Different evaluation criteria may be applied such as pay-out period, benefit–cost ratio, net present value or the internal rate of return to investment (Roemer and Stern, 1974).

### 6.1.1 Benefits from effective human resource development and utilization

Effective human resource management may induce a variety of social effects which are highly desirable in a postwar country. They contribute directly to the short-, medium- and long-term objectives of demobilization strategies. Formation and effective use of human resources results in enhanced economic development and productive value by increasing allocative and technical efficiency, increasing the supply of entrepreneurial activities and fostering the willingness and ability to invest, innovate and imitate, and by enhancing the ability to move into higher-productivity sectors and occupations. Furthermore, effective human resource management also contributes to achieving social objectives such as reduced inequality. Social integration and cohesion of various groups with different socioeconomic, religious and cultural background is positively affected. Equal access to education and training, as well as access to employment opportunities for each of these groups, are considered essential in this context.

Providing ex-combatants with effective and well-designed education and training for rural employment either as farmers, as farm workers, or as rural entrepreneurs might motivate them to stay in their rural community instead of migrating to urban areas. Reduced rural–urban income differences and employment opportunities will contribute to a better balance between rural and urban development. These economic and social effects are considered critical in terms of political stability, security and peace. In the long term, economic, social and political effects of human resource development and utilization will thus foster human development.

### 6.1.2 Cost analysis of human resource management

Private cost analysis refers to costs borne by the trainee and his family or by an organization or enterprise, whereas social cost analysis includes all costs incurred on society. Analysis of the direct costs of the project starts with the 'net input' defined as 'the goods and services withdrawn from the rest of the economy that would not have been withdrawn in the absence of the project' (Dasgupta *et al.*, 1972, p. 53).

Cost components of human resource management programmes typically relate to labour costs, facilities, equipment and materials. Small-enterprise development programmes may require credit, machines, access to imported inputs, etc. (Levin, 1983). An important cost element is the productive value forgone as a consequence of the intervention. Ex-combatants who undergo training are not available for productive work and therefore may incur a loss of earnings. In many African countries soldiers in civil wars tend to be engaged in a variety of activities in agriculture, production and services.

All resources should be identified and included that are required to produce the benefits that will be captured in the evaluation. The degree of specificity and accuracy in listing cost components should depend upon their overall contribution to the total cost of the intervention.

In addition to direct costs, indirect costs of the intervention may be identified. Indirect costs may occur through crowding-out effects. Demobilized soldiers finding employment may simply substitute employed labour. Training to assist in small-enterprise development increases performance of participants, but may reduce the income of competitors. Such negative external effects would substantially reduce the net benefits.

Additional costs may be incurred when further socioeconomic objectives such as equity and income distribution are affected in a negative way. This would be the case when funds are withdrawn from projects targeting low-income groups. Employment-creating projects such as construction of physical infrastructure may induce costs by negatively affecting the natural environment or by consuming irreversible natural resources. Some indirect and additional costs of projects may be very difficult to identify, quantify and value. Dasgupta *et al.* (1972) maintain that such evaluations are not always worth making, since errors due to inaccurate measures may be greater than the errors that result from neglecting certain indirect effects.

### 6.1.3 *Value benefits and costs in monetary terms*

The main difficulties in cost–benefit analysis are converting all relevant benefits and costs into monetary terms. Traditional cost–benefit analysis restricts evaluation to tangible and quantifiable indicators (Roemer and Stern, 1974). Valuing the benefits and costs of human resource formation and utilization tends to be much more complicated. In the framework of the human capital concept the economic contribution of education and training is usually measured in terms of labour market outcomes. Indicators relate to earnings at the individual level and to increased profit at the enterprise level (Metcalf, 1984). There are, however, some critical issues at the theoretical, empirical and methodological level in applying earnings and profits as indicators for measuring the benefits of education and training programmes (Maglen, 1990). In addition, in an informal sector or small-scale agriculture, it is usually extremely difficult to obtain reliable data on income and profit.

It is even more difficult to place a monetary value on non-economic benefits and costs. The specification of benefits has shown that training results in empowerment of people which contributes to human development. These effects can hardly be valued in monetary terms. In addition, there are no fully acceptable methods of determining the monetary value to society of less tangible effects such as social integration and cohesion, nation-building, reduced inequality, increased security or political stability. In the light of the theoretical, empirical and methodological difficulties of valuing all costs and benefits in monetary terms, traditional cost–benefit analysis does not appear to be the most appropriate evaluation methodology for human resource management projects in postwar countries.

## 6.2 Effectiveness study

The effectiveness approach aims at assessing the degree to which a programme affects variables of interest (Stone, 1982). In contrast to cost–benefit analysis, the effectiveness approach is objective and target-oriented. Success or failure of a human resource management project is assessed by the extent to which given objectives and goals have been achieved. This approach does not require placing monetary value on benefits. Effectiveness studies involve three steps.

First, the variables of interest, i.e. the objectives of interventions have to be determined. In the context of demobilization, the relevant objectives of human resource management programmes may be economic and social integration, political stability, rehabilitation and human development. These objectives are abstract variables which are not directly measurable. Since empirical research can deal only with observable and operational variables, indicators have to be identified which can validly index the degree of success in terms of objectives.

Second, a construct has to be defined allowing the identification of appropriate and workable indicators. The analysis of benefits provides an appropriate framework and approach for identification of indicators. Indicators for evaluating effectiveness of training for micro-entrepreneurs may relate to the level of competence achieved, the extent to which enterprises are established, employment created or the business performance.

Third, effectiveness has to be assessed by quantifying the degree to which standards of success or failure have been achieved. The evaluation study has to make sure that the effects observed were caused by the intervention. In other words, the research design has to ensure that the outcomes measured are the 'true' programme effects, and that observed changes, which are caused by other factors, are not taken as programme effects (Stone, 1982). Control groups and a pre-test/post-test design comparing the observation of chosen indicators before and after the intervention imply a rather high degree of validity. The strength of the effectiveness approach is that it evaluates the success of human resource management programmes directly in terms of a variety of objectives. However, it does not consider costs.

### 6.3  Cost-effectiveness study

The cost-effectiveness study combines the effectiveness study with costs. It usually starts from one particular objective or goal and compares several alternative projects. Cost-effectiveness studies involve three steps. First, the intervention's objective has to be determined, together with an appropriate indicator to measure effectiveness. Second, the effectiveness data of several alternatives have to be compared with their costs in order to provide a cost-effectiveness evaluation. Third, the alternative has to be selected, which provides the maximum effectiveness per level of cost or which requires the least cost per level of effectiveness (Levin, 1983).

In contrast to cost–benefit analysis, cost-effectiveness studies free the evaluator from many requirements and methodological problems by enabling a more direct measure of impact in terms of the effectiveness of the intervention (Levin, 1983). The outcome does not need to be converted into monetary values and therefore permits the assessment of the outcomes in their own terms. In the context of demobilization, training programmes endowing unemployed ex-combatants with marketable skills can be assessed directly in terms of the percentage of trainees employed after a certain period of time. Those programmes should be selected that achieve the highest effectiveness in terms of employment for a given level of cost.

The cost-effectiveness approach is suggested as an appropriate tool for evaluating human resource management programmes, in particular if there is only one outcome or benefit to be considered. Cost-effectiveness studies face problems when there are several variables of interest and more than one outcome of the intervention is to be taken into account. It may turn out that the best or most cost-effective alternative for one outcome is a poor choice to effect a different outcome. The challenge of multiple outcomes is to ascertain how one can set criteria to make cost-effective choices that take account of all of the important outcomes.

### 6.4  A modified cost–benefit approach

In light of the strengths and weaknesses of traditional evaluation methodologies, an alternative approach has been developed to evaluate training projects. The approach has been successfully tested and applied in several African countries in the framework of an ILO project providing management training courses for micro-entrepreneurs in the informal sector (Nübler, 1993).

Efficiency of projects is determined by comparing benefits with costs. The discussion on cost–benefit analysis has shown that the identification and valuation of costs of training programmes usually do not face major problems. The difficulties arise when evaluating the benefits. This challenge has been met through the development of a modified approach to evaluating the benefits of training programmes.

The modified approach is based on the willingness-to-pay concept. The willingness to pay reveals the marginal value individuals attach to goods produced. Traditional social cost–benefit analysis deals with the evaluation of physical outputs and services. These tangible outcomes are to be valued with the consumer's willingness to pay. It is expected that willingness to pay precisely reflects expectation of satisfaction. Under conditions of perfect competition, the marginal value of a private good is equal to its market price (Dasgupta *et al.*, 1972).

The outcomes of training projects, however, are not physical products or services, but outcomes such as cognitive, affective and motivational changes in individuals, behaviour and changes in business performance. The modified approach does not attempt to place value on each of these outputs of the training project. Rather, the training itself is treated as the project's output. As a consequence, the training project can be evaluated by revealing a participant's willingness to pay for a similar type of training seminar. It is assumed that the value attached to another training seminar is based on the expectation of satisfaction which is determined by the benefits that participants derived from the previous training experience. The total value attached to the seminar, i.e. the benefit derived by all participants, is determined by adding all participants' willingness to pay (Nübler, 1995).

It should be kept in mind that willingness to pay only reflects the direct benefits of the training project, i.e. benefits accrued by participants. Furthermore, empirical evidence shows that costs borne by the participants during the first seminar were taken into account in deciding the contribution. Therefore, the indicated willingness to pay has to be considered as the net benefit expected from another seminar. Consequently, costs borne by participants should be added to the willingness to pay when undertaking the cost analysis.

The modified cost–benefit approach allows for evaluation of both costs and benefits and provides information on the efficiency of training projects. This approach proved to be appropriate and feasible in an informal sector environment and therefore appears to also be an appropriate methodology in evaluating human resource development programmes in a demobilization context.

### 6.5 Selecting the appropriate evaluation methodology

The nature of the analytical task represents one important criterion that will determine the appropriate evaluation methodology. In the context of human resource management projects, cost–benefit analysis tends to be problematic. In contrast, cost-effectiveness analysis can be applied for a wide variety of analytical tasks, and is considered an appropriate methodology in evaluating human resource management projects in the demobilization context as long as only one outcome is considered. Problems tend to arise when multiple outcomes have to be taken into account. Effectiveness studies provide relevant information on the degree of success or failure of human resource management programmes with regard to several objectives. However, since costs are ignored, alternative interventions cannot be compared in terms of cost-effectiveness. The combination of an effectiveness study with a modified cost–benefit analysis appears very appropriate since information can be obtained on both the effectiveness and efficiency of human resource management programmes, even in an environment where practical and methodological difficulties tend to be high.

Furthermore, the evaluation approach itself has to be cost-effective. If the project and the expected impact are small, then only a small investment in evaluation would be merited. However, when the value of an intervention can be very great, it may be worth making a large investment in evaluation and analysis. Anandarup (1984, p. 7) concludes that 'practical analysts must learn how to use the limited resources at hand most effectively, avoiding excessive detail and spurious precision and employing proxies and shortcuts suitable for the projects, with which they are concerned'.

## 7 Conclusions

The relevance of ex-combatants and their capabilities during a demobilization and reintegration process may be analysed in the framework of human capital theory, human resource approach and the human development concept. The human capital theory provides a rather narrow framework allowing mainly for analysis of human competencies for productive purposes. The human development concept is considered too broad for the task it should perform. The human resource approach is considered the most appropriate and useful concept to analyse issues related to demobilization and reintegration in Africa. Human resource management relates both to the effective utilization and the development of human capacities. Both components play an important role in achieving the objectives of demobilization and reintegration, such as economic and social integration, political stability and security, social cohesion, and economic and human development.

The human capital concept may be considered as one facet of the human resource concept and at the same time the human resource approach may be considered as an integral part of the human development concept. Within the human development concept, enlarging people's choices with respect to economic, social and political dimensions constitutes the ultimate objective of development. In this sense, human development as the ultimate objective sets the norms, standards and goals to be achieved by human resource policies.

Policies for effective utilization of human resources during reintegration may relate to the supply and demand side of the labour market such as the certification of skills, job-placement measures, counselling, creation of employment, assistance to establish small enterprises, etc. Planning of policies and design of effective projects need to be based on data on existing skills, competencies, qualifications and experience of ex-combatants. Skill analysis should take a broad view and identify skills acquired at the cognitive, affective and psychomotor level. Furthermore, formal and traditional skills as well as strategic skills should be identified and the relevance of skills should be analysed. In particular, it must be assessed to what extent the skills acquired in the military can be applied in civilian occupations. Furthermore, information is required on the motivation, expectations and ambition of ex-combatants in order to match their plans with opportunities. Finally, particular attention should be given to the needs of special groups of the demobilized.

The development of human capabilities is the second important element of human resource management in demobilization strategies. The formation of skills, knowledge and competencies contributes to (re)integration. Economic integration is fostered by training for (self-)employment. Training for direct employment needs to be demand-driven and based on training-needs analysis. Inadequate planning without data on the needs and market demand is considered as a problem in reintegration strategies. Training for enterprise creation in the informal sector can be effective, if feasibility studies have identified markets and demonstrate potentials for self-employment. Social integration tends to be promoted most effectively in training schemes that avoid isolation of ex-combatants. Whenever possible, training should be provided in mainstream programmes. However, ex-combatants have special needs which should be addressed outside of mainstream programmes. Social integration is fostered by schemes that link training to work such as apprenticeship, education in production, and family-based training. These tend to be particularly relevant for young ex-combatants.

Training policies in postwar countries have to meet the challenge of providing skills for integration in the short and medium term and to develop and rehabilitate the training system. Promotion and use of all appropriate formal, non-formal, informal and traditional training modes is suggested in order to meet training needs during the reintegration process. The rehabilitation, adjustment and long-term development of the training system should build incrementally from this existing base of institutions. Thus, the reintegration of ex-combatants offers the opportunity to rehabilitate and develop the training system, and to increase effectiveness and efficiency.

Measures, interventions and projects for human resource management should be effective in terms of objectives, and efficient in terms of costs and benefits. So far, little effort is made in the demobilization process to undertake evaluations. Such information, however, is highly relevant for policy makers in order to allocate funds to activities, policy measures and projects, where effectiveness and efficiency can be high. Demobilization and reintegration strategies tend to focus mainly on aspects of human resource formation – with less attention for effective utilization. A broader view in skills and competencies might, however, reveal some skills and qualifications possessed by ex-combatants that can benefit the individual and society.

Methodologies in evaluating interventions during demobilization and reintegration must be appropriate in light of the task, time and resources available. Traditional evaluation methodologies such as cost–benefit analysis tend to be rather difficult to apply. However, cost-effectiveness studies appear to be appropriate, in particular when different projects are to be compared with respect to one objective. Furthermore, a modified cost–benefit approach, that evaluates benefits of training programmes on the basis of participants' willingness to pay for further training, appears to present an appropriate approach. If this is combined with an effectiveness study, then data on effectiveness and efficiency of projects can be obtained.

We conclude that the design of effective human resource management programmes requires a minimum of analytical and research activities such as skills analysis of ex-combatants, data on their expectations and plans, training needs analysis and analysis of labour and goods markets. Such analysis has often been neglected, due to time pressure, lack of funds or experts. Demobilization strategies should give much more attention to analysis and strengthen their research component.

## Note

1   An earlier, slightly longer, version of this chapter was published by BICC in 1997 as 'Human Resources Development and Utilization in Demobilization and Reintegration Programs', BICC Paper 7 (Bonn: BICC).

# 4
# Trends in Armed Forces and Demobilization in Sub-Saharan Africa

*Kees Kingma and Garry Gehyigon*

## 1  Military data

The purpose of this chapter is to provide an overview of the trends in the armed forces, demobilizations and military expenditures in Sub-Saharan Africa, since the early 1980s. For the aggregate data on the armed forces presented here the same database is used as compiled for BICC's annual Conversion Survey (BICC, 1998). The initial source for 1981–93 data on armed forces personnel was the US Arms Control and Disarmament Agency (ACDA). These figures have subsequently been compared with data from a variety of other sources, including the International Institute for Strategic Studies (IISS) and additional publications relevant to the topic. When support existed for a non-ACDA estimate, this was used. Data for 1994–6 stem from a variety of sources, including IISS, country studies and press clippings. Regular armed forces refer to government forces, excluding reservists, whether stationed within the country itself or abroad. Paramilitary troops, civilians employed by the armed forces are not included; also opposition forces are not included. The estimates are for the average size of the armed forces in the relevant year, but in many cases it is difficult to assess whether or not data conform to these definitions.

For military expenditures the data are in line with the estimates of the BICC Conversion Survey (BICC, 1998). The definition of what is included in military expenditure is as much as possible in line with the one accepted by the North Atlantic Treaty Organization (NATO), because it is the broadest of the established definitions.

ACDA data in constant US dollars terms have been used as the initial source for 1983–93. The figures were compared with other sources, such as from the Stockholm International Peace Research Institute (SIPRI) and press articles. In cases in which sufficient support for deviation existed, the more appropriate figures were substituted. Figures are preferably based on data in constant national currencies at 1993 prices. (Exchange rates are also those of 1993.) Figures for 1994–96 are own BICC estimates, using a variety of sources with a preference given to trends found in the SIPRI Yearbook (SIPRI, 1997).

As shown in the Annex Tables A.1 and A.2, several gaps still remain in the data on armed forces and military expenditure. To reach more accurate estimates for the (regional) aggregates presented in Table 4.1 and 4.2, these gaps have been filled with interpolations or extrapolations to calculate the aggregates.

Regarding all conclusions drawn from the statistical data presented, a strong word of caution is appropriate. All data on armed forces and military expenditure should be treated with great prudence. Military expenditure data in general show serious weaknesses as a result of conceptual and definitional inconsistencies, non-availability, inter-temporal inconsistencies, currency conversion and deflation problems (Brzoska, 1995). One should therefore always be very cautious comparing them between countries, as well as over time. Armed forces data also show problems because national governments are often reluctant to report – particularly in times of war or political crisis – and definitions of what personnel should be counted are not always used clearly and consistently.

Several organizations mentioned above, such as ACDA, IISS and SIPRI, collect military data and publish global data sets. All of them, however, experience difficulties in obtaining the data. The sets therefore contain several gaps and, when published, they are often still unreliable. Data provided by national sources might be incomplete or even purposely misleading, since military information is often considered sensitive. The staffing and capacity of these organizations is actually very small and this allows them to do only limited cross-checking and standardization (Brzoska, 1995). The above problems, and this call for caution, apply for all military expenditure and armed forces data in general, but even more so in Africa.

## 2  Trends in armed forces and military expenditure

As shown in Table 4.1, levels of military personnel in Sub-Saharan Africa fluctuated since the early 1980s. From 1981 to 1990 there was an increase from 1.13 million to 1.47 million, while the number dropped to 1.12 million in 1996. The level around 1996 was again similar to that of the early 1980s.

The decline over the early 1990s was more or less in line with a global trend in armed forces personnel. The total number of armed forces world-wide reached its high of 28.8 million people in 1987. Subsequently it decreased to an estimated 22.7 million in 1996. To put the relative size of the armed forces in Sub-Saharan Africa in a global perspective, the regular armed forces in Sub-Saharan Africa account for about 5 per cent of all the soldiers in the world, while the population is about 10 per cent of the world population.

The decline in the number of armed forces in Africa set in initially in West Africa in 1985, mainly due to the reduction of the Nigerian armed forces from about 144 000 in 1984 to about 76 000 in 1992. The overall decline in the number of forces in Africa in the early 1990s is largely due to the demobilizations undertaken in a number of countries, especially in Southern and East Africa. As we will see in this chapter, the numbers of combatants involved in the demobilizations were particularly high in Ethiopia and Mozambique, but throughout the region there were also some upward movements, for different reasons. One example is the increase in the forces in South Africa due to the integration of seven armed forces of the apartheid era into the new South African National Defence Force (SANDF).

Keeping in mind the difficulties in obtaining accurate data, the information available with regard to military spending in Sub-Saharan Africa indicate that between 1983 and 1990 there was an increase in military expenditure from US$8704 million to US$10 675 million (in US$ of 1993). Subsequently, expenditures on the military declined to US$7717 million in 1996 – below the level in the early 1980s.

The regional military expenditure pattern is heavily influenced by spending in South Africa. Between 1989 and 1996, South Africa almost halved its military spending from US$4938 million to US$2500 million. Although South Africa's share in the total region reduced from 46 per cent in 1989 to 32 per cent in 1996, its reductions were decisive in the downward trend in the region since 1990. Overall, we see that levels of spending in Central and West Africa were in

**Table 4.1  Armed forces in Sub-Saharan Africa (in thousands)**

|  | 1981 | 1982 | 1983 | 1984 | 1985 | 1986 | 1987 | 1988 | 1989 | 1990 | 1991 | 1992 | 1993 | 1994 | 1995 | 1996 |
|---|---|---|---|---|---|---|---|---|---|---|---|---|---|---|---|---|
| Central Africa | 115 | 109 | 111 | 136 | 139 | 135 | 144 | 151 | 154 | 170 | 201 | 172 | 172 | 175 | 187 | 197 |
| East Africa | 478 | 483 | 480 | 457 | 458 | 515 | 523 | 533 | 648 | 718 | 350 | 487 | 464 | 448 | 421 | 418 |
| Southern Africa | 265 | 241 | 239 | 267 | 272 | 303 | 319 | 350 | 359 | 344 | 384 | 343 | 343 | 289 | 323 | 307 |
| West Africa | 274 | 279 | 281 | 292 | 282 | 271 | 277 | 230 | 234 | 238 | 236 | 206 | 206 | 200 | 195 | 198 |
| *Totals* | 1132 | 1112 | 1111 | 1152 | 1151 | 1224 | 1263 | 1264 | 1395 | 1470 | 1171 | 1208 | 1185 | 1112 | 1126 | 1120 |

*Source*: BICC database (see section on military data, above, and appendix tables).

**Table 4.2  Military expenditure in Sub-Saharan Africa (in millions of US$)**

|  | 1983 | 1984 | 1985 | 1986 | 1987 | 1988 | 1989 | 1990 | 1991 | 1992 | 1993 | 1994 | 1995 | 1996 |
|---|---|---|---|---|---|---|---|---|---|---|---|---|---|---|
| Central Africa | 635 | 630 | 636 | 884 | 881 | 874 | 814 | 804 | 905 | 840 | 905 | 684 | 676 | 681 |
| East Africa | 747 | 767 | 1111 | 1223 | 1389 | 1664 | 1784 | 1809 | 1507 | 1600 | 1527 | 1467 | 1531 | 1507 |
| Southern Africa | 5783 | 5669 | 5216 | 5698 | 6359 | 6452 | 6670 | 6655 | 5836 | 4979 | 5148 | 4449 | 4179 | 4086 |
| West Africa | 1539 | 1532 | 1560 | 1462 | 1208 | 1327 | 1363 | 1407 | 1380 | 1291 | 1361 | 1467 | 1466 | 1443 |
| *Totals* | 8704 | 8598 | 8523 | 9267 | 9837 | 10 317 | 10 631 | 10 675 | 9628 | 8710 | 8941 | 8067 | 7852 | 7717 |

*Source*: BICC database (see section on military data, above, and appendix tables).

1996 similar to the levels in the mid-1980s, while in East Africa they are considerably higher. A clear downward trend is visible only in Southern Africa.

## 3   Opposition forces

It should be noted that particularly in Africa the resources absorbed by military activity are not only those organized by the state. Rebel groups and other opposition forces take up a sizeable number of people and use considerable resources. Opposition forces refer to organized groups of people with political agendas who are using – or threatening with – violence against an established government. They might be operating from outside or within a given country, usually using guerrilla tactics. They are also referred to as informal forces, irregular forces, militia forces or guerrilla.

We estimate that the total number of armed opposition fighters in the mid-1990s in Sub-Saharan Africa might have been over the 150 000; thus over 13 per cent of the estimated size of the regular forces. The National Union for the Total Independence of Angola (UNITA) and the various factions of the Sudan People's Liberation Army (SPLA) probably accounted for about two-thirds of the total opposition forces. Clearly, these armies are very difficult to assess or measure. Numbers fluctuate with the beginning or ending of wars, or even (seasonal) offensives. Some fighters can be considered as part-timers. Recruitment is either carried out by force in territories gained or by voluntary means. In some instances people join opposition forces for revenge against government forces. This makes it difficult for even the leadership to know the exact numerical strength.

Most opposition forces receive their financial and logistical support from sources which are often not made known to the public. They have in the past been largely dependent on external support. Increasingly, however, they draw on local resources. Among those are natural resources, such as timber, ivory and diamonds. Renamo forces in Mozambique, UNITA in Angola as well as the forces of Charles Taylor in Liberia, provided examples. Several sources indicate that UNITA received about US$600 million a year from illegal diamond sales; that would be about 8 per cent of the estimated total military expenditure in the whole of Sub-Saharan Africa.

The relationships between guerrilla movements and the local population differ from case to case, as will be shown in the country studies in this book. In Eritrea, for example, the Eritrean People's

Liberation Front (EPLF) ran parts of the county virtually like a benevolent government, while in Mozambique, Renamo relied largely on plunder and extortion. Various cases have been reported in which armed opposition forces exploit relief aid to run their armed struggle. This has sometimes even reached the point – for example in Liberia and Sudan – that commanders of armed groups have purposely held groups of hungry people in their vicinity in order to obtain access to international relief goods.

## 4   Demobilizations

This section provides an overview of the main characteristics of the demobilizations in Sub-Saharan Africa, at various points in time over the past decade – and with different degrees of success. As defined in Chapter 2, demobilization is the process that significantly reduces the number of personnel in the armed forces. We will see that Eritrea, Ethiopia, Mozambique, Namibia and Uganda conducted significant demobilizations in the first half of the 1990s. The first three of the above-mentioned demobilizations will be dealt with in special case studies (Chapters 5–7) in this book. The section on Uganda in this chapter is somewhat longer than the other demobilizations outlined, since it will also be part of the comparative analysis in Chapter 8.

### 4.1   Angola

The first attempted demobilization in Angola, following the 1991 Bicesse Accords, failed mainly because of a lack of political commitment. Both the government and the opposition force of UNITA were unwilling to cooperate with each other and maintained secret armies in violation of the accords. Following the elections held in 1992 the war broke out again, in even more violent and destructive ways than before.

In line with the peace accord signed in Lusaka in November 1994, about 76 000 combatants of the Angolan Armed Forces and UNITA were to be demobilized. Initial progress was made in 1997 in terms of encampment and demobilization. By April 1998 almost 50 000 had formally been demobilized, according to UN data. These people found themselves in very difficult circumstances, in a country which was actually still at war. Of those registered about 26 000 left the quartering areas before formal demobilization.

Despite the fact that UNITA joined the government of national unity in 1997, it was delaying the implementation of the measures agreed in the 1994 Lusaka Protocol. Some UNITA groups were in the capital, Luanda, while others continued to threaten with (and actually apply) the military option. By mid-1998 UNITA officially split into different groups. The actual fighting forces were still controlled by Jonas Savimbi, who refused even to come to Luanda. Fighting was renewed in several parts of the country and by December 1998 the country returned to an all-out war. It is widely believed that many of those who left the demobilization camps and many of the UNITA fighters formally demobilized had continually been under UNITA command. Only about 11 000 of the former UNITA fighters have joined the new Angolan Armed Forces (*Reuter*, 10 July 1997). The total number of active UNITA fighters was by late 1998 estimated at about 30 000.

The war in the Democratic Republic of Congo worsened and complicated matters even more. Initially in 1997, many UNITA forces supported Mobutu's efforts to stay in power, in what was then still Zaire. Laurent Kabila's defence against rebel forces, that started in August 1998, is being supported by Angolan government forces, most importantly to make sure that UNITA does not receive support or find refuge in the Democratic Republic of Congo. On the other hand, UNITA forces are reported to support the Congolese rebels.

### 4.2   Djibouti

The 1994 peace agreement in Djibouti included the commitment to demobilize half of the 18 000-strong Djibouti armed forces. About 3000 soldiers were demobilized in 1994–96. The government hopes that many of the demobilized Issas would return to southwestern Ethiopia, from where they were recruited in 1991 (*Africa Confidential*, 6 June 1997, p. 7). In the Round Table donor meeting, in May 1997, donors pledged support of approximately US$15 million for the demobilization packages of about 8500 soldiers. The World Bank, the European Union and the French government are providing assistance to the government to support the reintegration of the ex-combatants.

### 4.3   Eritrea

The government of newly independent Eritrea demobilized about 54 000 of the 95 000 EPLF liberation fighters between independence in 1993 and 1997. The first group of 26 000 was demobilized in June 1993. The second group of 22 000 longer-serving fighters was demobilized in 1994–95. Another 6000 fighters were progressively demobilized in 1995–97. Many of the fighters (8000–10 000) were first assigned to temporary public-sector jobs, replacing Ethiopians who had left. Eritrea received relatively little support from the international community in the process of demobilization, resettlement and reintegration. The ex-fighters are playing a very important role in the establishment and development of the new state. (See case study in Chapter 5.) In 1998, due to tensions and fighting with Ethiopia, the number of people in the army was boosted, which included the remobilization of large numbers of ex-EPLF fighters.

### 4.4 Ethiopia

In Ethiopia the army of the military Derg regime, of almost half a million soldiers, was totally demobilized in 1991, following its defeat. It was replaced by the army of the Ethiopian People's Revolutionary Democratic Front (EPRDF), which was subsequently renamed the Ethiopian National Defence Force (ENDF). By 1997 it numbered about 120 000 soldiers. Between 1992 and 1994 another 22 200 fighters of the Oromo Liberation Front (OLF) were demobilized, after the OLF left the government coalition and fought with government troops. The new government also released about 20 000 ENDF soldiers (mainly Tigrayans) in 1995 in the process of restoring the ethnic balance of the forces. However, since it replaced them with members of other Ethiopian nationalities, it should not be perceived as demobilization – despite the fact that the reintegration challenge and support was quite similar. (See case study in Chapter 6.) In 1998, due to conflict with Eritrea mentioned above, the active Ethiopian armed forces grew quickly. It has been reported that many soldiers of the demobilized Derg forces have been recruited.

### 4.5 Liberia

After several failed peace accords in Liberia, disarmament and demobilization of 20 332 fighters of six fighting factions were eventually implemented between November 1996 and February 1997. Among the demobilized were about 4300 children. The average age of the demobilized was 24 years (CAII, 1997). Reintegration support is predominantly provided to communities as a whole, in order to reach all war-affected groups. There are questions to what extent the command structures of the former factions have indeed disappeared. However, now that the political situation in the country is stabilizing since the July 1997 presidential elections, the majority of the ex-fighters is most likely focused on creating a living through non-violent means. New national armed forces of about 5000 are being created.

### 4.6  Mali

About 9500 Touareg fighters were demobilized in 1995, following the overthrow of a 23-year-old military dictatorship in 1991 and a peace agreement between the government and the opposition forces in 1992 (Poulton and Youssouf, 1998). About 1500 other fighters were selected to be integrated in the uniformed services. In March 1996 a largely symbolic flame was lit, burning 3000 of the weapons that were handed in: the *Flamme de la Paix*. The reintegrating ex-fighters in the north of the country were supported by a UN programme, which provided among other things for training, credit and counselling.

### 4.7  Mozambique

Following the Rome General Peace Agreement of October 1992, between the government of Mozambique and the Renamo opposition forces, 92 890 combatants were demobilized in 1994, of which 70 910 government were soldiers and 21 980 Renamo fighters. The demobilized had a total of about 215 000 dependants. The ex-combatants received considerable resettlement and reintegration support from the government and the international community. A variety of forms of assistance was provided, most importantly 24 months of cash payments through a bank in the district of resettlement. A final payment of about US$50 was made to all ex-combatants in early 1997. The great majority of the ex-combatants resettled in rural areas, particularly the ex-Renamo fighters. (See case study, Chapter 7.)

### 4.8  Namibia

Before the UN-monitored national elections in November 1989 – leading to independence in March 1990 – about 49 500 combatants were demobilized in Namibia. These came from both sides of the conflict. About 26 000 of them came from the People's Liberation Army of Namibia (PLAN) and about 23 500 had fought for the South West African Territorial Force (SWATF) on the side of South Africa (Colletta *et al.*, 1996b). Of the two forces, about 7500 joined the new Namibian Defence and Police Forces. Reintegration support was not part of the mandate of the United Nations Transitory

Assistance Group (UNTAG). It was generally assumed that, with the excitement of independence, reintegration would simply happen. Subsequently, planning and programming started in reaction to the destabilization threat from some ex-combatants (Preston, 1994). Unemployment among the ex-combatants is still high and their frustration was reflected in protest marches and sit-in strikes in several parts of the country in 1997 and 1998.

### 4.9 Sierra Leone

Between the election of the civilian President Ahmad Tejan Kabbah in March 1996 and the military coup that overthrew his government in May 1997, demobilization and reintegration plans were developed. These were shelved after the coup. The military junta was again ousted in March 1998 by the Nigeria-led Military Observer Group (ECOMOG) of the Economic Community of West African States (ECOWAS), restoring the government headed by President Kabbah. The national army was disbanded and initiatives taken for the recruitment of a new national force. However, many different armed groups still operated in the country, involving thousands of child soldiers. By mid-1998 plans for demobilization and reintegration of up to 33 000 combatants, largely from the Civil Defence Forces, were again being detailed, and external funding raised (*Jane's Defence Weekly*, 26 August 1998, p. 18). However, in the light of the brutal war still fought in the country by late 1998 between ECOMOG troops and the remnants of the Revolutionary United Front (RUF) and forces loyal to the junta, the actual implementation is problematic.

### 4.10 Somalia

Despite the continuation of violence and the lack of a central government in Somalia, several limited demobilization efforts have been made over the past few years. After relative stability was attained following the Boroma conference in early 1993 in northwestern Somalia, the self-declared government of 'Somaliland' made partially successful efforts to reduce the number of arms and armed men in the country. A National Demobilization Commission encouraged and managed the disarmament and demobilization process with some outside assistance. There were initial successes, but also setbacks, due to fighting between former militias. Lack of resources to support reintegration, and the need to balance between the different groups, has however led to the absorption of most of the encamped militia men into the national army and police force of Somaliland.

In January 1993 the Unified Task Force (UNITAF) in Somalia experimented briefly with a 'food for guns' programme. It was, however, quickly terminated when it led to tensions between UNITAF command and relief agencies that had to provide the food. Demobilization efforts by the United Nations Operations in Somalia (UNOSOM) failed because of continued fighting among the warring factions. The expectation that the UN operation would not be able to see its disarmament programme through, and that power would continue to depend on military capability of the militias, made significant demobilization impossible. However, more recently, several limited efforts have been initiated to draw young men out of militias. By providing incentives, these men are encouraged to give up their weapons and start training or other activities. Most of these projects are being supported by major international development agencies and implemented by local and international NGOs.

## 4.11   South Africa

A 'defence transition' is part of the general post-apartheid reforms in South Africa. Starting in 1994, seven armed forces had to be integrated into the new South African National Defence Force (SANDF). Those forces were the old South African Defence Force (SADF), the *Umkhonto We Sizwe* (MK) – the armed wing of the African National Congress (ANC) – the Azanian People's Liberation Army (APLA) – armed wing of the Pan-Africanist Congress (PAC); and the armies of the four former 'homelands', Bophuthatswana, Ciskei, Transkei and Venda. This led to a temporary increase in the total numbers of armed personnel in the SANDF. At the outset of this integration process a group of MK and APLA fighters was demobilized straight away, because they did not meet the standards for integration or did not want to pursue a military carrier. By February 1997, 3770 people had been demobilized (Motumi and McKenzie, 1998). Meanwhile, a natural outflow is taking place. A further demobilization – or 'rationalization', as it is called in South Africa – of about 30 000 military personnel is planned to start in the second half of 1999.

## 4.12   Uganda

The current Ugandan armed forces originate in a guerrilla movement against the government of President Milton Obote. A small group of about 26 men, led by Yoweri Museveni, started their struggle 'in the bush' in early 1981 as the National Resistance Army (NRA).

After an increasing guerrilla warfare the NRA was, by January 1986, able to take the capital city Kampala and overthrow the military regime led by the brothers Bazilio and Tito Okello. At that time the NRA most likely numbered close to 20 000 fighters, predominantly from the southwestern and western parts of Uganda. The defeated government army was estimated to number about 15 000 soldiers.

In a quest for reconciliation the new National Resistance Movement (NRM) government invited members of the defeated national army and members of other opposition groups to join the NRA's ranks. Another reason to strengthen the armed forces was to fight insurgencies in the north and northeast of the country, that started quite soon after the NRM government came to power. Some members of the other former guerrilla forces and the defunct government army did join the NRA; others fled into neighbouring countries; while again others formed or joined rebel groups against the government. Meanwhile, the size of the NRA continued to grow – to about 90 000 soldiers in the early 1990s.

By 1992, while the NRM-led government was still struggling to reconstruct the war-torn country, it had become clear that it was no longer necessary to maintain such a large army. The government thus decided to implement a demobilization for – as it expressed it – budgetary, social and military reasons (Mondo, 1994). It was felt that the financial resources could be better used elsewhere, for the development of the country and its people. Some of Uganda's principal donors of development assistance also applied pressure in their dialogue with the government, arguing that the military expenditures in the country were on the high side, given the country's security concerns and development challenges. The government also had military reasons to demobilize. To deal with the remaining rebel groups in the country it felt the need to professionalize the armed forces, which would imply improving the equipment and working conditions of the soldiers, and raising their salaries. The manner in which the army had grown, by absorbing many irregular groups and untrained soldiers, implied that many of the NRA soldiers in the early 1990s were not well qualified to serve in a professional army. In addition, a large number of soldiers suffered from ill health.

The government set up a special organization to plan and implement the demobilization – in close cooperation with the armed forces and the donors who provided financial and technical assistance. The Uganda Veterans Assistance Board (UVAB), which was established for this purpose in 1992, fell directly under the Prime

Minister's Office. In a short period of time a pilot demobilization of about 400 soldiers (military police) was conducted, and UVAB prepared for the demobilization's first phase. The trial run was to identify unforeseen difficulties in the demobilization exercise. It helped in planning for practical matters, such as the number of dependants and amount of luggage per demobilizing soldier.

In the first phase of the demobilization exercise, between December 1992 and July 1993, 22 900 soldiers were demobilized. Another 9300 followed in a second phase in April–July 1994. The third and final phase of the demobilization was completed in 1995 – resulting in a total of 36 350 demobilized soldiers since 1992. The total number of their dependants was over 100 000 (Kazoora, 1998). The decision on who to demobilize was the sole responsibility of the NRA, which informed the UVAB. Disarmament of the soldiers to be demobilized was done in the barracks, before they were taken to the demobilization centres.

To avoid disruption, indiscipline, high costs and other difficulties in sustaining a large number of soldiers and their dependants in one place, the actual demobilization was carried out as quickly as possible. The soldiers who were to be demobilized, and their dependants, received pre-discharge briefings, providing them details on, for example, how to open a bank account, how to start income-generating activities, environmental and legal issues, family planning, and AIDS prevention. Upon receiving their discharge certificate and completing the orientation, the veterans and their dependants were discharged and transported to their home districts.

Resettlement was supported by a cash and in-kind package for the first six months, provided by UVAB. The package included, among other things, provision of shelter, food, clothing, health care and the payment of school fees for veterans' children. The content of the resettlement support changed between the three phases on the basis of lessons learned.

The demobilization exercises in Uganda received substantial financial and technical support from bilateral and multilateral donors (Colletta *et al.*, 1996b). The World Bank played a major role in fund-raising and coordinating between the various donors and the government. According to UVAB data the external assistance to demobilization and resettlement amounted to US$39.9 million – 89 per cent of the total costs. Besides direct support to the demobilization exercises and the resettlement packages, donors supported several reintegration support initiatives. Reintegration was, for example, supported through health-care programmes, vocational training, agricultural tools and technology, feeder road construction, and small credit schemes. Most of these reintegration support schemes, however, covered only specific regions or districts.

When the ex-soldiers returned to the areas in which they intended to integrate, they received assistance from District Veterans Assistance Officers, whose responsibility it is to administer and advise veterans as well as provide data for monitoring and evaluation. District Veterans Assistance Committees were also established to handle resettlement issues, such as land allocation and disputes in the communities. Reception of ex-soldiers in the rural areas was initially met with some reservation and suspicion, but this attitude usually disappeared over time. The reception of those demobilized in the third phase was already considerably better than in the first phase. According to Kazoora (1998), about 90–95 per cent of the returned veterans could be considered as being socially integrated.

Economic reintegration faced more difficulties, because the level of skills of the ex-soldiers was generally low and their expectations often too high. The success of reintegration also depended on the region. Most of the soldiers who returned to rural areas were found to be involved in agriculture quite quickly after their demobilization (Colletta *et al.*, 1996b), but there remain questions about to what extent they are really able to support themselves without help from the community (Kazoora, 1998). The death rate of demobilized soldiers has been rather high. By July 1995, 1696 veterans (5.3 per cent) were reported to have died. It is believed that one-third of these deaths was due to AIDS (Colletta *et al.*, 1996b).

The demobilization, and particularly the demilitarization aspect of it, started facing setbacks in 1996. Around that time the government felt the need to increase military expenditures again, due to increasing threats posed by several insurgencies – by then also in western parts of the country. Not only was equipment purchased, the number of soldiers was also increased again – including the remobilization of several thousands of demobilized soldiers. Uganda's active involvement in the war in the neighbouring Democratic Republic of Congo (earlier Zaire) over the past few years is also likely to have added to pressures to raise the number of soldiers again.

### 4.13   Zimbabwe

Zimbabwe experienced a demobilization in the early 1980s – right after liberation. At that time about 40 000 combatants were demobilized. This demobilization is beyond the scope of this study, but it is relevant to note that the demobilization still plays an important role in the country, in political as well as economic terms. The veterans, organized in the Zimbabwe National Liberation War Veterans' Association, staged protests in mid-1997 – 17 years after the end of the war. Revelations had come out that several high-ranking members of the ruling party had plundered the War Veterans' Fund. Veterans are still rather influential and much respected, particularly in rural areas. In August 1997 the government eventually gave in to the veterans' demands and agreed to one-off compensation packages of Z$50 000 (then about US$3800) each, with subsequent monthly pension payments of Z$2000. Based on an assumed 75 000 recipients, the one-off package would cost the government Z$3.75 billion (about US$290 million at November 1997 exchange rate), while the pension would cost about Z$1.8 billion per year. The total commitment, including other benefits, was estimated at the time to cost about 3 per cent of GDP in the 18-month period until the end of 1998 (*Financial Times*, 8 October 1997, p. 8). The financial commitment has thus added to many other current economic problems in the country. Zimbabwe has reportedly reduced the size of its armed forces over the last five years by 16 000 because of these economic problems (*Jane's Defence Weekly*, 25 March 1998, p. 25).

## 4.14   Other countries

In several other countries minor or attempted demobilization has taken place in the past decade. In Chad, for example, 15 000 soldiers were demobilized in 1992–94. Subsequent to the signing of a peace agreement between the government and several rebel movements, the number of forces was reduced from about 30 000 to about 20 000 in 1997 (*Radio Nationale Tchadienne*, 29 April 1997. Also Rwanda announced the demobilization of part of its armed forces in September 1997 (*Radio France Internationale*, 29 September 1997). About 5000 soldiers were to be in a first group to return to civilian life. The reason given was that the armed forces had become too expensive for the country. However, given the war that continued in 1998 – inside and outside the country – it is unlikely that it concerns a significant reduction of the armed forces.

# Part II
# Case Studies

# 5

# 'Leaving the Warm House': the Impact of Demobilization in Eritrea

*Eva-Maria Bruchhaus and Amanuel Mehreteab*

> *We have convinced them to be ready to die; why shouldn't we be able to convince them to work for themselves?*[1]

## 1  Introduction

Strategies of demobilization and reintegration depend to a large extent on their specific context. This refers not only to the type of war in which the combatants were fighting, and the way in which the conflict ended, but also to the historic period of its implementation and the degree of autonomy that national actors enjoy. All these aspects combined make demobilization and reintegration in Eritrea a particularly interesting, if not a unique, case.

The three decades of war with Ethiopia ended in May 1991 with the victory of the Eritrean People's Liberation Front (EPLF). In December 1992 the Provisional Government of Eritrea decided to reduce the number of combatants of the newly established army to 40 per cent of the total number of EPLF fighters[2] at the end of the war, and thus to demobilize 57 000 fighters. Eritrea received relatively little support from the international community in the process of demobilization, resettlement and reintegration. Characteristic for the Eritrean exercise is also that, right from the beginning, the plans for reintegration were based on the principle of 'self-help support'.

Section 2 of this chapter will outline the context in which Eritrean demobilization took place when, after three decades of the war, the Eritrean government – composed of not-yet-demobilized fighters – demobilized about 60 per cent of their comrades and started to facilitate their reintegration into a new nation. Section 3 of the chapter will describe the national strategy and the institutional set-up, the process itself and the measures initiated to achieve sustainable results. Section 4 will assess the impact of demobilization and reintegration on the micro-level of the ex-fighters and the macro-level of the country's socioeconomic development. This is followed by conclusions in Section 5.

## 2   Background

### 2.1   The roots of the conflict

Eritrea is a new nation, but an ancient country. Prior to Italian colonization, and over many centuries, the area which became Eritrea had been subject to waves of migration from the Ethiopian plateau and the Arabian peninsula. Its peoples had many different cultural and political experiences, part of the impact of which would underpin twentieth-century social and political divisions. Migration and mixing of peoples with different languages and religions has produced a complex pattern of ethnic, religious and linguistic groups. Loosely organized empires succeeded each other, took various political forms and extended over different geographical areas. These empires extracted tribute from subject peoples when they had the military and administrative capacity to do so. For long periods, parts of Eritrea maintained their autonomy. In the pre-colonial period the Sudanic Funj Kingdom, the Ottoman Empire, Egypt and several Ethiopian empires ruled over different parts of the land that became Eritrea after the establishment of Italian rule (Pole, 1982).

The basis for the modern State of Eritrea was laid in 1890 by the Italian invaders who set up an administrative system of, in effect, *apartheid*. In 1941 they were defeated by the British who replaced the Italian military and civilian administration under mandate of the United Nations (UN) (as they did in Somalia and Libya) and dismantled the economic infrastructure the former rulers had built, but leaving most of the Italian workforce in place. Under the British mandate the ground for future sovereignty was laid. Political parties, parliament, trade unions, and even a flag were established. But before decolonization was achieved, Eritrea, unlike other Italian colonies, was sacrificed for the strategic benefit of the winners of the Second World War – particularly the US – which secured bridgeheads in strategically important areas such as the Red Sea coast. Against the repeatedly and openly expressed opposition of the Eritrean people the country was federated to its neighbour Ethiopia in 1952 through UN Resolution 390A/V.

Ironically, the delegates of the Soviet Union and Czechoslovakia pointed out that in fact the UN had not carried out its responsibility of respecting the right of the Eritrean people to self-determination and predicted that this union of unequal partners would eventually lead to conflict. Not only representatives of the Eastern Bloc were aware of that risk, John Foster Dulles, the then Secretary of State of the USA, also admitted: 'From the point of view of justice, the right of self-determination of the Eritrean people has to get due consideration, but for the interest of the United States and stability in the region, Eritrea has to be federated with Ethiopia'. Federation was thus replaced by open annexation in 1962. Eritrea became the northern province of the Ethiopian empire – and political opposition turned to armed resistance.

## 2.2 Thirty years of armed struggle for liberation

As history shows, the emergence of the Eritrean Liberation Front (ELF) in the early 1960s and later of the EPLF was not based on a sudden outburst of the Eritrean peoples' 'struggle'; it was the continuation of the sporadic uprisings for independence and historical resistance of the rural peasant population, together with the Eritrean workers and intellectuals (Gebremedhin, 1996, p. 5). Without their active participation the thirty years-long war – the longest of its kind in Africa – would not have been won or led to an independent and sovereign Eritrean State.

The ELF was initially the leading fighting force. After some of the members became dissatisfied with the ideology (which was mainly based on traditional religious and ethnic divisions) and the pro-Arab bias of the movement, another group was formed with the name of Eritrean People's Liberation Front (EPLF). This coincided more or less with the overthrow of the Ethiopian emperor Haile Selassie and the coming to power of a military junta called the Derg, proclaiming itself obedient to Marxist–Leninist principles. The Soviet Union and her allies sensed their historical chance to obtain a new foothold on the African continent, after the regime of Siad Barre in Somalia drifted more and more 'westwards'. With massive military support and assistance in setting up an East German-type intelligence service, the Derg seemed in a position to defeat the Eritrean liberation forces which at that time were fighting each other. The double pressure led in 1978 to the so-called 'strategic retreat' of the EPLF into the northern part of the country, the core region of the liberated areas.

By 1981 the EPLF had become the only force in Eritrea, joined by those of the ELF fighters who wanted to continue the fight for independence after their movement had split into several factions with most of their members leaving the struggle for exile abroad, mainly in Sudan. For ten years the EPLF held the front line of the fighting at Nacfa, in northwestern Eritrea. During that time the EPLF fighters in the rear worked in harmony with the local population, building feeder roads, setting up primary health care and school education, but also organizing the population to govern their own affairs at village level. The EPLF gained the respect and support of the civilian population through the provision of services to the community, but also through interacting respectfully with them in all aspects of life.

The East–West conflict played an important role in the annexation of Eritrea by Ethiopia but the Eritrean freedom fighters never received the benefits which other guerrilla movements obtained from the superpower confrontation. They stood alone and fought against all odds. About 30 000 fighters – in the end 95 000 – beat by far the largest African army of up to half a million soldiers. The defeat of the Derg – the military junta ruling Ethiopia (see Chapter 6) – coincided more or less with the end of the Cold War, and the reduction of military support which Ethiopia had received from the former Soviet Union since the mid-1970s. The termination of military aid to Ethiopia contributed to speeding up the victory of the EPLF.

Despite the superior military strength of the heavily armed Ethiopian army (sometimes one EPLF fighter stood against ten or even more soldiers of the Derg) it proved impossible to annihilate the Eritrean resistance. In 1988 the EPLF moved forward to capture the town of Afabet, which had previously been the stronghold of the Ethiopian army. This battle was one of the turning points in the war; another was the capture of Massawa on 10 February 1990. The EPLF moved steadily forward until 24 May 1991, when the fighters entered the capital Asmara. Liberation did not yet mean direct independence, which was not officially achieved until two years later, with the vast majority of the population approving it in a referendum. Official independence came on 24 May 1993.

## 2.3 The postwar socioeconomic situation

The price of freedom was high. It is estimated that 150 000 fighters and civilians were killed; 70 000 fighters and civilians were disabled; 90 000 children of fighters and civilians were orphaned; one-third of the total population was displaced; between 300 000 and 500 000 had fled to Sudan; and 80 per cent of the country's infrastructure had been destroyed. Maybe the biggest loss the country has experienced in 30 years of war and occupation is – apart from the lives of fighters and civilians – the exodus of about one-third of its population, mainly people of working age and a high percentage of them well-trained.

Eritrea's annual GDP is estimated at US$960 per capita (World Bank, 1994). The annual growth rate was 6 per cent in 1995 and 7 per cent in 1996. About 16 per cent of GDP is produced in agriculture, 22 per cent by the industrial sector and 62 per cent by services. However, the relatively small contribution of agriculture to the country's production hides the fact that 85 per cent of the Eritrean population live in rural areas and exist on rain-fed subsistence agriculture and pastoralism (ERRA, 1994).

With about half of the country's population, the highlands, covering about one-quarter of the country, are the most densely populated area. The complicated land tenure system, overpopulation and overuse of the soil limit further agricultural expansion. Therefore increased agricultural development can take place only in the lowlands where most of the land is government-owned. Even if at present the contribution of agriculture to the GDP is small, it holds considerable potential for development. The country's marine resources represent another potential growth sector, as due to war and lack of resources the fishing sector was neglected until independence.

Historically, Eritrea has been a nation of skilled people with a wealth of experience in entrepreneurship, commerce and international trade. At the end of the 1930s some 730 companies producing industrial goods existed in Eritrea. In addition, some 2200 trading companies were active. During this period Eritrea also became a successful exporting nation. At the time of the Second World War, when imports from Europe to the East African markets were disrupted, Eritrean industries stepped in to supply these markets (World Bank, 1994). After independence, due to neglect during the period of Ethiopian occupation and war-time destruction, only 38 companies were minimally operational – functioning with old and dilapidated equipment (*Eritrean Profile*, 23 September 1995).

Given the present socioeconomic situation, employment creation is one of the country's priorities. Preliminary ILO estimates in 1994 indicated that:

- the level of underemployment in the agricultural sector was of the order of 35 per cent;
- urban unemployment was probably higher than 15 per cent (35 000–40 000 people);
- about 250 000 of the 500 000 refugees were predicted to come home;
- between 50 000 and 60 000 demobilized fighters would have to be reintegrated; and
- the estimated number of new entrants into the labour market was 25 000–30 000 each year (Srivastava, 1994).

It appears that in the short term the rural sector, including agriculture and non-farming activities, and the urban informal sector are likely to remain the most promising with regard to their potential for labour absorption. Wage employment opportunities within the formal sector, including government services and modern industry, will probably remain extremely limited. Self-employment is hoped to absorb the main part of the present and future labour force.

Eritrea has also inherited obsolete institutions and weak instruments for managing its economy. When part of the still centrally planned Ethiopian economy, the provincial administration in Asmara had little autonomy and no policy-making capacity. However, during the liberation struggle the EPLF had already developed an effective administrative structure in the liberated areas, which provided the basis for a civil service able to serve a peacetime economy. Furthermore, local community structures and self-help traditions had remained intact in many parts of the country (Bruchhaus, 1994). The government of Eritrea has now set up administrative structures on national, regional (formerly provincial) and local levels, and aims at the development of a democratic system based on political pluralism. It has entrusted a national commission to draft the country's constitution. After two years of discussion the constitution was adopted in May 1997.

Without being pressed by a debt burden like other countries in the region, the government is implementing a Recovery and Rehabilitation Programme for Eritrea (RRPE), emphasizing rehabilitation of physical infrastructure, the development of productive public enterprises and human resources development. At the same time the government is seeking to stimulate the process of nation-building, and reintegration of returnees, displaced people and ex-fighters into the multi-ethnic society. The government is trying to address the development of agriculture and fishing, leading to the goal of self-sufficiency and self-reliance. The government has also initiated a wide range of economic reforms, including market liberalization, privatization and export orientation.

## 3 Planning and implementation of demobilization and reintegration

### 3.1 Decision and objectives

Long-term objectives of demobilization are usually to enhance economic and human development and to foster and sustain political stability, security and peace. These certainly apply to the Eritrean case. It should be noted however that, despite heavy physical destruction and social disruptions, the situation in Eritrea in 1991 seemed to offer a number of important positive conditions for successful demobilization and reintegration.

Because of the political implications of Eritrea's independence, demobilization had to wait until Eritrea had officially become independent. Unlike other liberation struggles, independence was not achieved directly with victory over the occupation army. It had to be confirmed by an internationally controlled referendum. As early as December 1992 President Isayas Afeworki announced that Eritrea would have to demobilize about 60 per cent of its armed forces. A special committee was set up by the Department of Defence (DoD), composed of representatives of the Labour Office, the National Union of Eritrean Women (NUEWn), the Eritrean War Disabled Fighters Association (EWDFA), the Eritrean Relief and Rehabilitation Agency[3] (ERRA) and of various departments of the then Provisional Government of Eritrea. Its task was to study the procedures of the demobilization and reintegration process, and to prepare a survey in order to obtain a general picture of the EPLF fighters. Immediately after the referendum the President's Office published a 'Brief Summary of the Policy of Demobilisation of the Government of Eritrea', explaining that the country's meagre resources should be spent on reconstruction and development rather on defence and armaments. This was also meant as a signal for the neighbouring countries that they had nothing to fear from the newcomer on the African political scene.

### 3.2   The profile of the EPLF fighters

The above-mentioned survey in 1993 covered all 95 000 EPLF fighters and was conducted by the DoD. An additional survey was carried out with a sample of 1130 people. The overall survey was completed in July 1993, but because of problems with data entry it has not yet been completely analysed. When demobilization started, the main characteristics of the EPLF fighters were the following:

- 80 per cent had a rural background;
- 64 per cent were Tigrinya from the highlands, and 24 per cent Tigre from the lowlands;
- with 80 per cent having completed one to five years of schooling, the educational level of the fighters was higher than that of civilians;
- more than 80 per cent had no professional qualifications; and
- 94 per cent wanted to work; the remaining 6 per cent answered they could not, because of a disability.

When asked whether they wanted to stay in the army, 64 per cent of the fighters answered positively, 9 per cent said that they did not want to stay, and 27 per cent stated that they did not see any other alternative than to be demobilized.

### 3.3   Demobilization – approach and process

Designing and implementing demobilization is influenced by a distinct political and socioeconomic context. In the case of Eritrea, defeat of the Ethiopian army paved the way for effective demobilization. Despite absence of outside financial support the process in Eritrea was implemented as planned.

### *3.3.1   Approach*

The provisional government had decided to conduct the demobilization in two phases. The first phase – starting in June 1993 – concerned about 26 000 fighters, mainly young people, who had joined the 'struggle' after the Battle of Massawa (February 1990). It was expected that the majority of them would go back to their families and continue their studies or work. The 22 000 so-called 'veteran fighters' having stayed in the field for a longer time – mostly between seven and 20 years, or more – were demobilized from June 1994 onwards. In addition, 4000 fighters were demobilized within the streamlining of the public service in 1995 during which altogether 10 000 civil servants were laid off. Another 2000 fighters were progressively demobilized between 1995 and 1997. All in all,

Eritrea has demobilized 54 000 fighters since June 1993 – of which 13 500 were women. About 8000–10 000 not yet demobilized fighters were assigned to work in the public sector, mainly replacing former civil servants from Ethiopia, but also in institutions transferred from the liberated areas to Asmara. They were paid 'pocket money' of birr 100–200, according to the duration of their EPLF service.

The decision whether or not a fighter would be demobilized depended on several criteria, mainly health status and the situation of his or her family: whether parents had lost more than one child in the 'struggle', or whether the fighter was the only child of her or his parents. Disabled or pregnant fighters were not allowed to be demobilized. It was mainly the vulnerable part of the target group which feared more disadvantages than advantages from the new condition: people with little education and no or few skills, with heavy family burdens – for example single women with children – and those with poor health. This applies particularly to the fighters who had been totally taken care of by the EPLF during their life in the field.

In order to facilitate integration, those demobilized in the first phase were given between birr 1000 and 5000 (according to the length of their stay in the EPLF) in addition to food rations for six months. The 'veteran fighters' each received food rations for one year and a standard amount of birr 10 000 to be deducted from their service payment of US$30 per month of service which was to be paid later. Former prisoners of war who had been fighting with the EPLF were asked whether they wanted to continue in the regular army. Around 400 replied that they wanted to go home and were given all their severance money at once, which cost the government around birr 4 million. The ELF members who joined the front after independence were given birr 10 000, like the other veteran EPLF fighters.

### 3.3.2 Process

The demobilization itself was a fairly easy procedure. Since the ELF had been defeated by the EPLF in the early 1980s, and some of its fighters had joined the EPLF, the new government had to deal with the demobilization of only one very disciplined armed force. After the end of hostilities the fighters had continued to stay in their barracks and camps, and the EPLF ensured their livelihood as before. In order to prepare the fighters for demobilization, meetings were held to inform them about the procedure and the help they

could expect. Those to be demobilized left for their chosen destination, after having collected their demobilization money and first
food ration. They left their weapons behind, which were registered
and therefore could be controlled. Disarmament, demobilization and
the creation of a downsized military force went smoothly and according to schedule, managed by the DoD and carried out with the
support of other departments and institutions, such as the ERRA.

Within ERRA most of the work was done by the Department for
Demobilisation and Reintegration of Ex-combatants, set up in December 1992. In order to express the concept of self-help support,
which it was supposed to offer, it was called *'Mitias'* after a traditional mutual-help system in which the community gives a helping
hand to someone starting a new life, for example after marriage.
All positions of responsibility in *Mitias* were filled with veteran fighters. They were believed to be best suited for this task, as they and
their target group belonged to the same community of freedom-
fighters. *Mitias* handed out the demobilization money and the
certificate of service and assisted demobilized fighters in their
reintegration.

### 3.4  Integration and reintegration

Demobilization and reintegration are closely linked. The payment
of demobilization money is already meant to help the fighters start
their reintegration, and in many cases it effectively serves this purpose. Many experiences show that successful reintegration depends
on appropriate demobilization measures. On the other hand, all
positive effects of timely and properly managed demobilization could
be spoilt by the – often long-term – negative effects of inappropriate
reintegration efforts.

#### 3.4.1  The Eritrean concept

The Eritrean concept aimed from the beginning at the double objective of demobilization and reintegration. It was obvious that the
government did not have the means to launch large-scale assisted
reintegration programmes. These would also have been in contra-
diction to the policy of self-reliance which had governed the EPLF
in war times and which continued to be applied after independence. Emphasis was therefore put on helping the ex-fighters to
reintegrate themselves, on 'weaning them off' and on encouraging
them to take their life into their own hands, helped by their families and the communities. The demobilization money – or at least

part of it – was meant to serve as investment. Furthermore, the belief was that war-hardened ex-fighters, after having been able to cope with the tribulations and hardships of the struggle, could become the primary agents of development in society; and it was expected that the respect which they had earned by their commitment to the national cause would be an asset in finding a job, setting up a business opportunity, or participating in training.

### 3.4.2 *Mandate and set-up of* Mitias

According to this concept, *Mitias* was set up to offer the demobilized fighters a foundation which would help the individuals to pass through several stages of adjustment, especially from dependence to independence, through burden-sharing during the transition period. *Mitias'* mandate is as follows:

- to carry out studies and investigations concerning the situation of fighters (demobilized and not yet demobilized) with the aim of obtaining data to be used for support measures;
- to raise funds for training programmes, loan schemes and settlement projects;
- to look for appropriate areas of training and settlement sites; and
- to provide services to ex-fighters to facilitate reintegration into civil society.

The head office of *Mitias* is in Asmara, with about 20 staff members. Nearly 100 staff members are working in the branch offices in all ten former provinces. (There are now six administrative regions.) An Advisory Committee composed of representatives of ministries, public institutions and national organizations, such as the NUEWn, the National Union of Eritrean Youths and Students (NUEYS), EWDFA, the Labour Union, ERRA and the Office of the President was set up to advise *Mitias*, to ensure the commitment of their institutions and to shoulder responsibility for support required. In order to study the viability of projects and prepare the ground for settlements in targeted areas the Committee was entitled to set up task forces composed of experts from the ministries concerned and other institutions when needs arise (ERRA, 1994, pp. 3–5).

In April 1996 ERRA and the Commission of Eritrean Refugee Affairs (CERA) were merged into the new Eritrean Relief and Refugee Commission (ERREC). The new Division for Rehabilitation and Reintegration is now in charge of both ex-fighters and returnees. *Mitias* has thereby been reduced to a unit within this division – dealing especially with the ex-fighters.

### 3.4.3  Mitias *support activities*

In the ERRA setting, as well as in the new ERREC structure, the reintegration of ex-fighters is supported by a variety of activities: credit schemes, job placement, on-the-job training, settlements and agricultural activities, assistance in administrative matters, assistance in starting income-generating activities, psychosocial counselling, and special support to female ex-fighters. Among the wide range of support activities, training, loans and agricultural settlements reached the greatest numbers of ex-fighters. This does not mean that the other components are of minor importance, but the number of beneficiaries and their impact is more difficult to assess. In certain cases *Mitias* acts as implementing agency, in others its role is to participate in the conception of measures and to facilitate their implementation.

*(1)  Training measures.*   About 9300 ex-fighters have benefited from on-the-job training – nearly one-third of them women. The main partner of *Mitias* in training is the German NGO Otto-Benecke-Stiftung (OBS), which has been organizing training programmes since 1993. These were initially only for returnees, but increasingly included ex-fighters. Minor partners in training were – and partly still are – ACORD (Agency for Cooperation and Research in Development), ISCOS (Instituto Sindicale di Cooperazione per Sviluppo) and the GTZ (German Agency for Technical Cooperation).

Whereas at the beginning most of the training courses were conducted on-the-job – mainly in private enterprises – the trend is towards more formalized programmes in training centres. The training is both practical and theoretical. The duration of the courses is from three to nine months – in some cases up to 12 months. The trainees receive birr 400 per month in order to enable them to support themselves and their families while undertaking the training. The choice of courses is not based on detailed studies of the labour market, but according to estimates of job opportunities or – in certain cases – answering special needs (for example training civil aviation staff). There is a great variety of skills covered, from masonry and carpentry, to catering, driving and telephone operating (mainly for women). In a study based on interviews with 100 graduates from OBS courses, Koester and Pape (1996) found that most of the interviewed former graduates were self-employed. The masons, and in second place the carpenters, could be considered the most successful. The overwhelming majority in these trades were men, earning between birr 500 and 800 per month (for carpenters) and birr 1500 and 3000 per month (masons). Most women – mainly those trained in tailoring and handicrafts – could not survive only with the income earned with their new skill (birr 50–100 per month). The few women having participated in training courses in welding, carpentry and masonry had difficulties finding a job, and even if they happened to get a job they were usually considered to be less competent than men. The courses in commerce and typing were not very successful either. They were too short and the educational background and job experience of most of the women were too limited. Nevertheless, there have been cases which proved successful, for example the tile-laying course for five women in a private enterprise.

*(2) Credit schemes.* *Mitias* grants loans or facilitates access to loans, coupled with technical and administrative assistance, with the aim of helping demobilized fighters to carry out economically viable activities. There are two types of loans: special Commercial Bank (CB) loans for ex-fighters, and the Revolving Loan Fund (RLF) managed by the Credit Unit of *Mitias*. Altogether, 68 staff members – most of them (not yet demobilized) fighters – manage and implement the loans. They consist of:

- 50 'barefoot bankers' at sub-zone level (each responsible for one sub-zone),
- 16 credit officers (each responsible for three sub-zones), and
- 2 credit officers at headquarters' level.

The so-called 'barefoot bankers' – half of them female ex-fighters – are the backbone of the system. They help assess the viability of the project for which the loan is requested. They help and advise the loan takers when need arises, but they are also in charge of following up the repayment. In order to enable them to fulfil their tasks they have taken several training courses organized by ACORD, which has also worked out the rules and procedure of the RLF, following more or less the example of the Grameen Bank in Bangladesh.

The CB loans started in autumn 1995. They run for one to five years, with interest rates of 8–12 per cent. The RLF goes back to 1994, when a number of ex-fighters participated in a small pilot loan scheme run by ACORD in Seraye province. At the end of 1995 the total amount of the loan scheme had reached over birr 2 million – benefiting from a GTZ grant. The maximum loan per person was birr 5000, with an interest rate of 12 per cent. According to an evaluation carried out in February–March 1997 in 42 places all over the country, 1791 ex-fighters (or 3 per cent of all demobilized fighters) had benefited from one or other type of loan by December 1996. Male ex-fighters represented 83 per cent of the total number receiving loans and received 88 per cent of the total amount of birr 13 million, whereas women represented only 17 per cent and their share was only 12 per cent of the total amount. The gap is even wider for CB loans, of which only 14 per cent of the recipients were women, receiving only 9 per cent of the total amount.

Comparing the CB and RLF loans, the latter have proved to be much more effective with 1176 clients in only four months, whereas the CB has only been able to provide loans on a monthly average of not even 50 ex-fighters. The main reason for this difference is the bureaucratic procedure and lack of interest of the CB staff in relatively small loans (averaging birr 18 982). Nevertheless the maximum amount of the RLF loans per person is considered as too small, and the procedure of setting up a collateral has to be adapted.

The loan schemes – especially the RLF – can be considered as one of the main instruments for economic reintegration – together with training measures – even though the available funds are too limited to have a noticeable impact. According to the findings of the evaluation they have to be considerably increased, especially if the target group is to include returnees (which would logically be the case after the merging of ERRA and CERA and the integration of the two target groups in the OBS training programme).

*(3) Settlement.* Agricultural settlement projects play a major role in the reintegration strategy. They make it possible to relocate a great number of people, to ensure their livelihood, and raise agricultural production, both of food and cash crops. It is expected that it will be possible to settle altogether about 10 000 ex-fighters in high-potential agricultural areas. In the past, returnees and ex-fighters were dealt with by different agencies (CERA and ERRA) and in most cases were settled at different sites. From the beginning *Mitias* has tried to mix ex-fighters, returnees and local peasants, as far as possible – that is, unless the funds are meant to serve only one target group.

When the first settlement was established in Ali Gider in 1994, and as it was not possible to find enough ex-fighters to reach the target of 2500 settlers, returnees were invited to fill the gap. However, in the meantime more than 5000 ex-fighters – among them many single women – have registered with *Mitias* for places in future settlements. To date, altogether five settlements have been implemented, mainly in the Western Lowlands, for a total of 3000–3500 settlers,[4] with financial and technical support from the Eritrean government and various foreign (mainly German) aid agencies:

- Ali Gider (irrigated cotton farm) for 2500–3000 settlers (Gash plain),
- Gahtelalai (irrigated vegetable farm) for 50 settlers (Eastern Escarpments),
- Sabunai I (rain-fed food crop production) for 300 settlers (Gash plain),
- Sabunai II (former Jemmel, rain-fed food crop production) for 220 settlers (Gash plain),
- Gefate (rain-fed food crop production) for 300 settlers (Gash plain).

A number of smaller farms on the Gash and Barka plains are worked by ex-fighter groups numbering among three and 20 people – altogether more than 100. Usually, the settler family gets two hectares of land (if the husband and wife are ex-fighters they are entitled to two hectares each), shelter, kitchen utensils, beds and blankets, and food rations until the first harvest. Clearing and land preparation is done with the help of the Ministry of Agriculture, which also provides seeds. According to a study carried out by CERA in 1996 (Woldegiorgis, 1996), there are no problems in the relations between returnees and ex-fighters, as well as with the surrounding local farmers, which is partly explained by the fact that the ex-fighters are educated. Many ex-fighters in settlements have benefited from RLF loans, mainly used to pay for agricultural labour at harvest time. About one-quarter of the settlers are single women, usually with small children. No special provisions are made for them when they arrive in the settlements. Nevertheless, they are given priority as regards permanent housing. Their work in the field is often hampered by the presence of small children, and in a few settlements efforts have been made to establish day-care centres and to create off-farm income-generating activities.

*(4) Job placements.* Between mid-1993 and the end of 1995 an average of 750 people came to the *Mitias* offices per week in search of advice and/or a job. In some cases they could be helped. In the

early stages it was relatively easy to find jobs in ministries and public enterprises. However, with the streamlining of the public sector in 1995 and growing competition on the labour market (25 000– 30 000 school-leavers each year), it became increasingly difficult. Nevertheless, in some cases ex-fighters have been given preference by a few Eritrean employers as well as by foreign aid agencies. A group of 1200 ex-fighters – having completed the OBS training – have been assisted in getting a job with a South Korean construction company, building houses in Asmara and Massawa.

*(5)  Counselling.*   Many ex-fighters have come to *Mitias* for help in administrative matters. Altogether *Mitias* has helped more than 500 ex-fighters to obtain a business licence, a piece of land, or to become demobilized. Other services rendered were, for example, referral of disabled fighters to health services, securing financial help from husbands for families from which they were living apart, and helping to solve quarrels with employers or superiors. All in all, *Mitias* defends the interests of the ex-fighters.

Much more difficult to handle are those cases in which psychosocial help is required. Even after ACORD had trained 20 *Mitias* staff members in counselling, there was still a lack of qualified staff, both in headquarters and at provincial level. More than half of those coming with psychosocial problems are women. They show more or less pronounced symptoms of stress and depression, mainly due to economic and family problems, such as unemployment, lack of understanding by the husband or his family, lack of appropriate child-care possibilities, but also work and land issues. Certain problems arise because the society does not always show sympathy towards the female ex-fighters when they refuse to return to the traditional role and submissive behaviour expected of them, as is frequently the case.

*(6)  Special support to women ex-fighters.*   As women form a particularly vulnerable group among the ex-fighters, special efforts have been made to help them to obtain a fair share in all measures. In order to make these efforts more efficient a special Gender Unit has been established at *Mitias* headquarters, working closely with the provincial delegations and trying to find ways and means of enhancing the women's self-help potential, for example by promoting saving clubs and discussion groups.

(7) *Business start-ups.* With various different kinds of support, about 1000 ex-fighters have been assisted in starting their own businesses – mainly in the informal sector. It should be noted, however, that the support received from the extended family is often the critical factor for success in starting a business. Most of the new businesses are small restaurants, shops of all kind, bakeries, bicycle and motor-car repair workshops and so on. In order to open new fields of activity *Mitias* has implemented a series of pilot projects, mainly with support of NGOs, benefiting female ex-fighters, for example a T-shirt printing workshop for ten women ex-fighters in Asmara, and a toy workshop for disabled fighters (eight women and one man) in Massawa. Other projects were possible because the government practised 'positive discrimination' towards ex-fighters. A total of 310 ex-fighters (three-quarters of them women) received a licence for distribution of beer and liquors. Another example is the Gemel Public Transport Corporation, set up with support of *Mitias* and the DoD. The government sold 49 mini-buses on credit to a company of 208 shareholders, composed mainly of female and war-disabled fighters. The company created jobs for 250 people – mainly ex-fighters – as drivers and conductors.

*(8) Training measures for not yet demobilized fighters.* Training courses have been carried out for not yet demobilized fighters in public service, in most cases without external funding: the Ministry of Construction for technical skills; the Ministry of Justice for 250 legal advisors at provincial level and 45 persons preparing their diploma at Asmara University; the Ministry of Education for about 300 teachers, school directors and inspectors; technical training for more than 200 disabled and other fighters; the Ministry of Health has various courses for about 500 former 'barefoot doctors'; NUEWn short-term and long-term training within Eritrea and scholarships for studies abroad for 150–200 women fighters. Altogether up to 1500 people have benefited from these measures. As all these fighters will be demobilized sooner or later – many of them staying on as civil servants in the same institution – this should be seen as an important contribution to human resources development in the country.

*(9) Eritrean War-Disabled Fighters Association.* Apart from a few exceptions the war-disabled fighters have not yet been demobilized. They receive a small amount of money (birr 350–400 per month)

plus some help in kind. The EWDFA has been set up to defend their interests and conceive and implement income-generating projects, mainly for groups. A bakery has been opened in Nefasit, a mill in Segeneiti, compressed-earth blocks production in Agordat, an artists' workshop in Asmara, etc. EWDFA has at present about 4000 members.

*(10) Bana Share Company.* The Bana Share Company was set up in 1995 by demobilized and not yet demobilized female fighters who wanted to invest their demobilization money and at the same time provide training and employment mainly for unskilled single mothers. Up to now *Bana* has about 1000 shareholders and has provided training for over 200 women in driving, carpentry, catering, fish-processing, computer and construction skills. *Bana* has helped some who had completed training to set up group ventures such as a fish market and a laundry. It also tries to find jobs for its members in various different factories and enterprises, with the help of the Labour Office.

### 3.5 External assistance

At the Paris meeting of the main bilateral and multilateral donors in December 1994, the Eritrean government presented its views in a statement which can be summarized with the following essential points (Government of Eritrea, 1994b):

- *On partnership*: 'The country being assisted . . . plays a focal role in articulating and prioritizing the problems and in designing and implementing their solution.'
- *On technical assistance*: 'Ideally, funds earmarked for technical assistance should be directly transferred to the concerned country as budget support for it to decide how to spend it to build its capacity.'
- *On delivery of external assistance*: 'External assistance is usually delivered in tied forms. . . . Funds should thus be transferred directly to the government concerned.'

Clearly, the long-term objective of the government is to help the country and its people to disentangle themselves from chronic dependency. The government has therefore developed a policy in which programmes are carried out by the country itself. International organizations were asked to provide technical services and financial resources when needed, but not to substitute local capacities. Indeed, this policy is nothing less than a reorientation of the usual development aid pattern: cooperation based on partnership and mutual responsibility, rather than the classical unequal donor–recipient relation. Unfortunately, this view was not shared by some representatives of the donor community. It is thus not surprising that less than US$12 million was pledged for the reintegration of ex-fighters, instead of the US$48 million, which was the lowest estimate of requirement. In the end, the total amount of financial and technical assistance received was even lower than that pledged: about US$10 million (as shown in Box 5.1).

---

**Box 5.1  Overview of foreign assistance to reintegration in Eritrea**

**Germany:** About US$4 million, mainly for institution-building, training, revolving loan fund (RLF) and agricultural settlements (partly with EU funds);

**Italy:** US$2.4 million, mainly for shelter of settlers in Ali Gider and training measures (partly with funds from the EU);

**USA:** US$2 million, in the form of tractors;

**Others:** US$1.5–2 million, mainly from NGOs co-funded together with the EU, for various small projects, mainly benefiting women.

---

## 4  Impact of demobilization and reintegration

In order to create a total picture the impact of demobilization and reintegration has to be measured at both the micro- and macro-level. What is the socioeconomic situation of the ex-fighters four or five years after demobilization? How do they perceive their situation, compared to their expectations, and compared to others? At the same time it is necessary to assess the impact of demobilization and reintegration in the general context of the country, taking into consideration security, finance, development and social cohesion.

### 4.1  Impact on the micro-level: survey results

A sample of 238 ex-fighters was interviewed in February–March 1997 with the help of a questionnaire.[5] One-third (34 per cent) of the ex-fighters interviewed were women – corresponding to the proportion of women in the armed struggle. Of the sample, 37 per cent belonged to those demobilized during the first phase, 43 per cent to those of the second phase, 15 per cent were demobilized in 1995, and 5 per cent were demobilized after 1995. The sample was

**Table 5.1  Sample of ex-fighters**

|        | Urban | Semi-urban | Rural | Total |
|--------|-------|------------|-------|-------|
| Female | 39    | 11         | 32    | 82    |
| Male   | 70    | 35         | 51    | 156   |
| Total  | 109   | 46         | 83    | 238   |

selected with the assistance of the *Mitias* offices in the regions. There was random selection within quotas according to the membership per office.[6] It was also ensured that 33 ex-fighters from the sample had started their business without *Mitias* assistance. In addition to the survey, more than 30 in-depth interviews were conducted in April 1997, mainly with self-employed ex-fighters. Even though the sample and the questionnaire are different from the ones used for the July 1993 survey, it is possible to compare the data on some of the issues.

### 4.1.1  Profile

Two-thirds of the ex-fighters interviewed were younger than 32 years; 28 per cent ranged between 32 and 45 years; only 5 per cent were older than 45. Regarding their health condition, 85 per cent declared themselves to be satisfied and 15 per cent complained about health. A little more than one-third said they suffered from some disability[7] but did not consider themselves disabled since they were able to work. Of the sample, 65 per cent resided in towns or semi-urban areas, only a little more than one-third lived in the countryside. If we compare this result to the 1993 survey, according to which 80 per cent of the ex-fighters interviewed had a rural background, it shows that most of the demobilized fighters had settled in and around towns. It is interesting to note that the tendency to live in towns was even stronger among women, and that the proportion of women in rural areas was also higher while comparatively less women lived in semi-urban areas. It was concluded that the female ex-fighters either preferred to go to larger towns in order to find a job and/or escape the control of their family, or to return home to their villages and the protection of the family.

More than half of the individuals in the sample were married, more than a quarter were single, and almost one-tenth were divorced. In the 1993 survey less than half were married. The women especially seem to have 'caught up'. Many of the recent marriages have been between fighters. The qualities ascribed to (ex-)fighter

**Table 5.2   Marital status, by sex**

|           | Female        | Male          | Total          |
|-----------|---------------|---------------|----------------|
| Single    | 11 (13.4%)    | 56 (35.9%)    | 67 (28.2%)     |
| Married   | 46 (56.1%)    | 91 (58.3%)    | 137 (57.6%)    |
| Divorced  | 15 (18.3%)    | 5  (3.2%)     | 20  (8.4%)     |
| Separated | 7  (8.5%)     | 1  (0.6%)     | 8  (3.4%)      |
| Widowed   | 3  (3.7%)     | 1  (0.6%)     | 4  (1.7%)      |
| Total     | 82 (34.5%)    | 156 (65.5%)   | 238  (100%)    |

**Table 5.3   Level of education**

| Years of schooling | Female        | Male          | Total          |
|--------------------|---------------|---------------|----------------|
| 0–5                | 39 (47.6%)    | 47 (30.1%)    | 86 (36.1%)     |
| 6–8                | 29 (35.4%)    | 45 (28.8%)    | 74 (31.1%)     |
| 9–12               | 14 (17.1%)    | 52 (33.3%)    | 66 (27.7%)     |
| > 12               |               | 12  (7.6%)    | 11  (4.6%)     |
| Total              | 82 (34.5%)    | 156 (65.5%)   | 238  (100%)    |

spouses are: better understanding of problems, comradeship, flexibility, and speaking the same language. 'Fighters are always fighters', as one of the interviewees put it. Among the 81 married to a fighter or ex-fighter, 58 per cent are female. Male ex-fighters clearly have more opportunity to marry civilians than female ex-fighters do. There is a significant difference between male and female ex-fighters in the proportion of divorced, those living in separation and widow(er)s.

Three-quarters of the interviewed ex-fighters had their own household, 54 per cent lived with their spouse, or with their spouse and children. The subcategories of those living alone (18 per cent) and those living with their children (4 per cent) are mainly composed of women. In 1993 only 25 per cent of the sample had between one and three children. This group has now increased to 58 per cent. The overwhelming majority (80 per cent) of the children are younger than four years; this reflects the postwar 'baby-boom'. The relatively small number of children per family indicates that fighters generally did not want to have many children (usually two or three) and that they practise family planning.

Concerning the educational level of the ex-fighters, more than one-third had less than six years of school education but only one man had never been to school! Only 5 per cent had finished 12th

**Table 5.4  Rank and file, by length of service**

|  | 0–5 years | 6–10 years | 11–15 years | >15 years | Total |
|---|---|---|---|---|---|
| Unit leader | 3  (3.7%) | 8 (17.1%) | 8 (20.0%) | 11 (17.2%) | 30 (12.6%) |
| Platoon |  | 3  (6.4%) | 6 (13.6%) | 18 (28.2%) | 27 (11.3%) |
| Company |  |  | 1 (2.27%) | 9 (14.1%) | 10  (4.2%) |
| Battalion commander |  |  |  | 2  (3.1%) | 2  (0.8%) |
| Ordinary | 79 (96.34%) | 36 (76.6%) | 29 (65.9%) | 23 (35.9%) | 167 (70.2%) |
| Total | 82  (34.5%) | 47 (19.7%) | 44 (18.5%) | 64 (26.9%) | 238 (100%) |

grade (end of secondary education). The average education of male ex-fighters was clearly higher than that of their female colleagues. Of the men, 41 per cent had more than eight years of education; of the women only 17 per cent. But we have to note that the overwhelming majority of the women were educated in the field.

It is not possible to compare the skills between the samples of 1993 and 1997. In the 1993 survey the question was geared to 'professional qualifications' – 85 per cent answered that they had none; whereas in our questionnaire they were asked what 'skills' they had, and the answers gave a much more positive picture: only 30 per cent said they had no skills. The others named a wide range of skills: carpenters, metal workers, 'barefoot doctors', drivers, traders, radio operators, tailors and dressmakers, artists, teachers, secretaries and other office workers.

Table 5.4 shows that more than one-quarter of the sample had spent over 15 years in the field (18 women and 46 men). About one-fifth had served between 11 and 15 years; another one-fifth between six and ten years; and one-third had participated in the 'struggle' less than six years (mainly demobilized in the first phase); 70 per cent had served as ordinary fighters; 13 per cent were unit leaders; a little less than that platoon leaders; and the remaining 5 per cent had been able to rise to the levels of company and battalion leaders.

### 4.1.2  *Economic and social integration*

One of the essential questions asked after demobilization is how the ex-fighters earn their living (see Table 5.5). At the time of the interviews 24 per cent of our sample (28 per cent of the women and 21 per cent men) were without a job; 12 per cent had found employment (11 per cent of the women, 12 per cent of the men);

**Table 5.5 Current occupation, by year of demobilization**

|  | 1993 | 1994 | 1995 | After 1995 | Total |
|---|---|---|---|---|---|
| In training | 14 (16.1%) | 9 (8.7%) | 2 (5.7%) | 1 (7.7%) | 26 (10.9%) |
| Employment | 13 (14.9%) | 12 (11.7%) | 1 (2.9%) | 2 (15.4%) | 28 (11.8%) |
| Self-employed | 40 (46%) | 56 (54.4%) | 25 (71.4%) | 5 (38.5%) | 126 (52.9%) |
| Unemployed | 20 (22.9%) | 26 (25.2%) | 7 (20%) | 5 (38.5%) | 56 (23.5%) |
| *Total* | 87 (36.6%) | 103 (43.3%) | 35 (14.7%) | 13 ( 5.5%) | 238 (100%) |

11 per cent were participating in training schemes (11 per cent of women and men); and 53 per cent were self-employed (50 per cent of the women, 55 per cent of the men).

From the 12 per cent of the sample who had found employment, one-third were employed by the government, more than half worked with private companies and those remaining had a job with a contractor. Nearly two-thirds had found their job without outside intervention, one-third had been helped by *Mitias* or by their family and a few had been helped either by a friend or by *Bana* or ACORD. More than half of the people in this group were not satisfied with their situation; most found their salary too low. More or less the same number had tried to find another job but so far without success.

With 53 per cent the self-employed were by far the largest group. Most of them (77 per cent) worked alone. More than half had started their business without any support. Among those who were helped (45 per cent), the majority received support from their families, the remaining from *Mitias* (11 per cent), comrades in ministries, friends, or their spouse's parents.

Twenty-four per cent of the sample had not been able to find a job, training opportunity or to become self-employed. In this group we find relatively more women than men. Less than one-third of the unemployed rely on their family, nearly half of them sustain themselves by working occasionally and 18 per cent have participated in food-for-work programmes. Most of them said that they thought they could find a job if they had the appropriate training; 18 per cent stated that they would like to start a business if they could find the necessary funds. Most of them were of the opinion that the government should pay special attention to their problems, either by creating jobs, giving loans, or even by reversing the decision to demobilize them.

Apart from the ex-fighters who were jobless and needed help from their families, and those participating in training measures, many of those employed and self-employed were able to help their families. Among the employed ex-fighters a little more than half said they were able to help their families financially, but only one-third were able to do so on a regular basis. The percentage of self-employed giving financial help to their parents (and other close relatives) was higher: 58 per cent, and more than 90 per cent of them did this regularly. This is a clear indication that self-employment should generally not be considered as disguised unemployment, but is often a solid ground for sustaining the livelihood of the ex-fighters.

Eighty-six per cent of the interviewees said they visited their families living apart from them, more than 25 per cent regularly. Visits and financial help were not the only links. Nearly half of the interviewees (49 per cent) asked family members for advice, mostly in business matters, and a smaller number in personal problems. In turn, they gave advice to family members, mainly in personal matters. Less than one-third felt competent to give business-related advice.

Sixty-four per cent of the people in the sample said their best friend was an (ex-)fighter, 17 per cent answered 'a civilian'. The ratio is similar for the answer to the question which group of friends is bigger. Asked whether they shared their skills with others (a very important principle of the EPLF during the war) 45 per cent were affirmative, 54 per cent gave a negative answer. They cited 15 different skills, mainly traditional trades, such as metalwork and carpentry. Concerning the usefulness of military experiences for communal activities, three-quarters thought they were useful. The qualities or values, acquired in the war, most often mentioned were:

- knowledge of the culture of the different peoples composing the Eritrean nation (26);
- self-reliance and self-confidence (29);
- perseverance and hard work (30);
- ethics, discipline, motivation, group work, taking care of others (39);
- medical knowledge and related skills (28); and
- capacity to solve conflicts, to be an example for others, sense of initiative (14).

Nevertheless, more than half (57 per cent) did not participate in communal affairs. One-quarter (26 per cent) were engaged in activities of the People's Front for Democracy and Justice (PFDJ – successor of the EPLF), 18 per cent in local administration, 17 per cent in environmental protection and those remaining in mass organizations such as NUEWn and NUEYS. These activities cover a wide spectrum: construction of dams, churches, grain stores, and roads; afforestation; soil conservation; social activities; football; saving clubs, etc. One-fifth of those participating in communal activities were also involved in decision-making. The following positions were cited: PFDJ group leader, NUEWn group leader, member of local council ('baito'), and chairman of a sports club.

According to the survey the attitude concerning demobilization has changed considerably. Asked whether they had welcomed the decision to be demobilized, a little more than half of the interviewees answered 'yes'. Among those who had not been happy about it were comparatively more female ex-fighters. However, when it came to the question how they found the situation in comparison to their expectations, many more women found it better than expected. In the 1993 survey the not-yet-demobilized interviewees were asked whether they wanted to stay in the army or to be demobilized. Nearly two-thirds said they would liked to stay, only 9 per cent preferred to be demobilized, and 27 per cent answered that they did not see any other alternative than to be demobilized.

Asked how they judged their current situation, three-quarters answered 'good' or 'medium'; the rest found it 'bad'. It is interesting to compare this judgement with the attitude concerning demobilization: among the women who had not wanted to be demobilized, 69 per cent judged their current situation as 'good' or 'medium'; 31 per cent considered it was 'bad'. If we compare the women's attitude with the men's, we notice that comparatively less male ex-fighters of the group which had a negative opinion about demobilization found the current situation 'good' or 'medium'.

### 4.1.3 Interpretation of findings

*Demobilization.* Those in charge of preparing the fighters for demobilization seem to have been aware of the fact that it would not be an easy exercise. As Fissum Teklebrhan put it in a parable during a sensitization seminar in 1994: 'When a mother bird notices that the wings of the young ones are well developed, she decides to convince them to leave the nest, even if she does not know whether the wings will be strong enough to carry them to a safe place. In the same way during the "struggle" the fighters have developed the necessary strength to overcome difficulties on their way. Now the EPLF has to demobilize them, not knowing whether all of them will be able to cope.' Nevertheless, he was quite confident about the following: 'We have convinced them to be ready to die, why shouldn't we be able to convince them to work for themselves?' For women and men alike it was a sharp transition from the difficult but protected life in the field to the peaceful but uncertain existence as an individual civilian. Female fighters were more afraid of leaving the EPLF which had replaced their family. Nevertheless, it seems that most found that, after all, they were able to cope with the new situation.

*Marital and family situation.*  Eritrea had a high share of women in the armed forces, and many marriages between fighters. However, there was still an imbalance between the two sexes, as women represented only one-third of the total number. In most cases the married couples did not live together, as they were usually assigned to different units in different places and only spent between a couple of days and one month together, during common leave. It is also noteworthy that there were no material problems they had to bother about. Even if it was not much, the EPLF took care of this. After liberation, when the couples came home, they suddenly had to cater for their livelihood. Problems with in-laws also started. Whereas the fighters had learned to disregard ethnic and religious differences, their civilian relatives had not reached that stage. They often rejected sons- and daughters-in-law, because they did not belong to their own ethnic or religious community. Another fact should not be neglected: in cases where the wife was demobilized and the husband remained in the new army, he usually had to join his unit far away from their residence, and she was expected to follow him. In many cases she refused to do so. Considering all these circumstances, it is actually astonishing that there are still many happily married (ex-)fighter couples.

The fact that 80 per cent of their children were born after liberation is not surprising. If a couple had a child (or children) during the 'struggle', it was usually not planned; they saved their wish to have children for postwar times. It is also of no surprise that only 13 per cent had more than four children, and about two-thirds one to three children. In general, fighters are very concerned about the future of their children, especially about their education. Since their time in the field, most of them practise family planning.

There is a rather high percentage of women who have to raise their children alone – be they widows, divorced, separated or single. This is a heavy burden. Unlike during the war when children were totally taken care of by the Front, in postwar Eritrea kindergartens are rare, especially in small towns and villages. Many female ex-fighters cannot go for training or take up employment, because they do not have anybody to take care of their children – who as we have seen are mainly one to five years old. This is one of the reasons why women with children prefer to live in bigger towns and why *Mitias* built a kindergarten in Keren, where we find a concentration of female ex-fighters with children.

*Length of service and rank in the military.* Among the interviewees having served less than six years, women are relatively under-represented – even more so among the fighters having joined after the battle of Massawa (1990). Among the ex-fighters having spent more than five years in the field, we find proportionally more women than men. But again, those having served more than 15 years constitute 22 per cent of the women and 30 per cent of the men. At the beginning of the armed struggle only a small number of women had joined the ELF, and they mainly performed auxiliary tasks. From 1974 onwards, when the EPLF came in and proclaimed equal representation of men and women, the situation changed slowly and the female population in the liberated and semi-liberated areas progressively got ready to both liberate their country and defend their interests. We can see that the women joined in the hardest times of the liberation struggle, when the Ethiopian army was five to eight times stronger than the EPLF; whereas in the end, when victory was at hand, more young men decided to give a helping hand in the final blow.

*Educational level, skills and work experience.* The findings of the survey confirm that ex-fighters are better educated than their civilian counter-parts, of whom at least 80 per cent are illiterate. More than one-third of the sample went to school between one and five years, nearly one-third completed 6th to 8th grade, but only a small percentage of the sample reached 12th grade or more (4 per cent). However, these findings require to be differentiated. As far as fighters with a rural background were concerned (sons and daughters of peasants and herders and 80 per cent of the EPLF) their educational level was certainly much higher than that of those who had stayed be-hind. But if we look at children with an urban background – of families which were intellectually and economically better off – who had spent more than ten years in the EPLF, we note that they suffered a severe setback concerning their education. At their present age it was usually difficult to overcome this handicap. On the labour market they had to compete with young university graduates and returnees who were able to study – often with scholarships – and who had gathered professional experience in exile. The same applied to those who had left a business behind, or a well-paid job: when they came back the job was often held by a civilian. However it should not be forgotten that the *formal* grade achieved does not necessarily say enough about the *real* capacity. If we look, for example, at one of the in-depth interviews, the ex-fighter had completed 4th grade when he joined the EPLF; twenty years later he still considered himself as '4th grade' although he had worked in different sections which demanded a much higher level of knowledge and skill, such as logistics, relief work and radio communications.

Not every fighter was sent to the front. According to capacities, skills and health condition, they might have been assigned to the rear, taking up civilian tasks. They may have worked as 'barefoot doctors', teachers, secretaries or in local administration, public relations. During offensives of the Ethiopian army they were mobilized to reinforce the front line. Moreover, between liberation and demobilization they were involved in a wide range of civilian tasks. The experience they had been able to collect during and after the 'struggle' should not be disregarded. Therefore, the percentage of interviewees who answered that they had no skills (30 per cent) seemed too high. It can be assumed that many interviewees in this category just did not recognize what they had learnt and practised during the war as skills, even though the EPLF had handed out certificates confirming their participation in training courses. The list of skills named seems to confirm this. It includes mainly conventional skills such as carpentry, tailoring and dressmaking, and does not mention, for example, the work of public officers, who were quite numerous.

The sample indicates that the proportion of men and women going for further education was the same. However it might not be representative in this case. The authors found that among those who go to evening classes there were more female than male ex-fighters. It is interesting to note that among the members of this group relatively more are satisfied with their current situation than in the other categories.

*Labour potential and economic activities.*   Concerning the age of the interviewees, we notice that the overwhelming majority are of working age. Most of them are younger than 32 and can thus still be considered as not lagging too far behind their civilian counterparts. They certainly represent a valuable labour potential for the development of the country. For those veteran fighters who joined the 'struggle' at the age of 20 and who are at present 40 years and older, it seems difficult to start a new life without professional experience – in a country where the average life expectancy is 46 years. The majority of the interviewees say they are in good health. On the other hand, without being recognized as disabled, many of the ex-fighters still suffer from various injuries. Some of them have been wounded several times, but most of them would never complain, and as long as it does not hinder them in doing their job they will not mention it.

The fact that more than half of the interviewees are self-employed (some of them as employers) confirms the limited possibilities of the labour market. As already mentioned, the self-employed help their families more than those who have found employment, and are also more satisfied with their situation. This high proportion can also be interpreted as a clear sign of self-reliance and initiative. This is also confirmed by most of the in-depth interviews. The fact that the overwhelming majority feel qualified for the business and only a small number (7 per cent) admit that they need more skills can be seen as a sign of self-confidence, but also of ignorance concerning the necessary prerequisites for successful business management. In the in-depth interviews nearly all ex-fighters who had started their own business complained about the attitude of their civilian colleagues. Used to solidarity and mutual help, they felt bitter about the unwillingness of the others to share their knowledge and experience even if they also understood that this belonged to the 'rules of the game' in a capitalist system.

*Various indicators for successful social integration.* We may conclude from the survey that the social fabric of Eritrean society is still strong. Communities and families generally feel responsible for those of their members who need help. Especially in the in-depth interviews we were told many stories about the support the returning fighter received from his or her parents and friends, and sometimes even from outsiders. This attitude is fostered by the respect and trust people have for and in the fighters, which would not exist without the good relationship fighters and civilians had developed during the 'struggle'. Nevertheless, it is obvious that friendship between civilians and ex-fighters often ends where business – that is competition – starts. For the ex-fighters who have learned to share, not only material things but also knowledge and skills, this means not only a change in attitude, but also a departure from some of what they called 'the values of the struggle'. Some have developed strategies aimed at harmonizing the two worlds, like the owners of the glass workshop in Keren who invite neighbouring business people in to socialize one afternoon a week.

The results also show that the main pillar of reintegration is the fighters' family. Links between ex-fighters and their families as a whole are fairly close and contacts quite frequent. Only a small percentage (14 per cent) never visit their families and it may be that they live too far away. The close links are also illustrated by the fact that it seems natural for most of the interviewees to ask the family for advice, mainly in business-related matters. The advice of ex-fighters is appreciated in personal matters, which is probably due to the fact that they are known to have developed certain human qualities which are not so common in the civilian society, such as conflict resolution.

In most cases the capital needed to supplement the initial demobilization money to enable the ex-fighter to start his or her own business was given by the family. The moral support of the family is also of key importance. Fighters also feel responsible for their family. The in-depth interviews provided many examples of ex-fighters – men and women – who shouldered the responsibility for an entire family after return. As with the three trainees in brick-making and -laying interviewed in Keren, one of the reasons why they participated (two women, one man) in the course was to obtain a job which would enable them to take care of their families. Their feelings of bitterness were caused by the fact that during their absence they were not able to shoulder these responsibilities; and now that they were back they often did not have the means.

During the war the EPLF had replaced the family for the fighters. As we were told during one of the in-depth interviews, in a very touching way: Gebriela B.B. came back home to find her father dying and became aware that she was not able to mourn him in the way she had mourned her martyred comrades: 'I discovered that for me comradeship had replaced kin- and friendship.' So the biological family is only one leg on which the demobilized fighters stand, the other is the fighter's community personified by very close comrades: the best friend of nearly two-thirds of the interviewees is an (ex-)fighter, and most of them move mainly among (ex-)fighter friends of equal economic condition.

Initially it was perhaps surprising that more than half of the ex-fighters interviewed did not participate in communal affairs. But if we consider that they had been demobilized for only a relatively short time, and thus were newcomers to the community and in civil society, having to overcome many problems before they became settled, it seems even astonishing that more than 40 per cent had indeed engaged themselves in communal affairs – mainly as members of the PFDJ and local councils. Nineteen per cent of them participated in decision-making – again mainly in the PFDJ.

## 4.2 Development impact on the macro-level

As already mentioned, it is very difficult to measure the impact of demobilization and reintegration in Eritrea at the macro-level. One reason is that the context in which these operations have been carried out had a major influence on the results. As we have seen, in Eritrea this context was quite favourable. Even the comparatively insignificant financial contributions from outside can be considered as a blessing in disguise: if they had been larger, it might have been impossible to avoid outside interference.

The weight of factors which cannot be measured should also be taken into consideration. For example: What is the value of the respect or disrespect that the civilian population show for demobilized combatants? Yet it has had a tremendous influence on reintegration. The same applies to certain social changes which the combatants went through, such as the change in gender roles, or the examples of discipline, tolerance and commitment many fighters give. Other factors are difficult to assess because we lack the necessary indicators, for example to appraise the impact of demobilization on development. It would also need precise figures to quantify the impact on certain economic sectors. At this stage of the process it is less difficult to assess the impact of demobilization, be it in general terms, than to measure the effects of reintegration at the macro-level, especially in the social and cultural field.

*Financial implications.* The total cost of demobilization and reintegration support of about US$100 million (a little under US$2000 per demobilized fighter) is a heavy burden for the small and devastated Eritrean economy. The severance payments cost the government a total of US$60 million. Reintegration support and some additional demobilization activities cost US$40 million, of which about US$10 million was funded from external funds. A much bigger amount would still be needed if the government were to fulfil its promise to pay each fighter US$30 per month of service: if one assumes an average of ten years of service per ex-fighter, this would amount to another US$100 million. In comparison, the total annual government budget is estimated at US$350–400 million.

Initially the government had to spend between birr 330 and 340 million (about US$50 million) to cover the cost of demobilization. After having tried in vain to obtain external funding for the demobilization, the government decided to take a loan from the state-owned Commercial Bank (CB). The whole demobilization process left the government with a debt of about birr 432 million (about US$65 million) by the end of 1996. In 1997 it was still not clear how the government wanted to raise the necessary money for the US$30 per year of service, mentioned above. Although this large payment has not yet started, it was decided to use the government promise as collateral for the loans that each fighter could take from the CB.

The implementing agency, *Mitias,* was not very costly and worked without significant outside support (GTZ and Cooperazione Italiana have funded some cars, computers, office equipment and part of the salaries; GTZ contributed an advisor for two years). The contribution of ERRA in the form of offices, telephone and other facilities, as well as the help of the various ministries in the form of technical expertise and machinery has been important for *Mitias'* work, but in financial terms it was not much. The staff consisted mainly of fighters receiving the usual pocket money until 1995 and salaries between birr 500 and 1650 per month during the following two years.

The government has been able to save considerably by using ex-fighters, receiving only pocket money, as civil servants. It has sometimes been argued that they have been more of a burden than a help. This might be true for some, but not for the majority. Most have compensated their lack of professional qualification and experience by a much higher level of commitment and discipline than the average civilian. Of course, it is difficult to assess the financial benefit. Assuming that for three years the government has saved an average of 800 birr per person by employing fighters instead of civilians, and taking an average number of 7000 fighters (between 4000 after and more than 10 000 before the reduction in summer 1995), the government appears to have saved at least birr 200 million.

*Peace dividend.* In a narrow sense the term 'peace dividend' can be used for funds made available for non-military activities through the reduction of military expenses. In the case of Eritrea it is not possible even to estimate how much this amounts to, as the budget of the EPLF armed forces is not known. It is worth mentioning that, at the 1994 EPLF congress, President Isayas estimated the contributions of the Eritrean Diaspora to the war effort (women contributed more than men!) to be US$20 million. One also has to bear in mind that most of the weapons used during the 'struggle' were captured from the enemy. The amount of money used for armaments was thus reduced by an 'Ethiopian contribution in kind', whereas the Eritrean government now has to buy its arms. Personnel costs have also increased, even though the armed forces have been reduced by about 60 per cent. The freedom fighters did not receive any pay (but were instead promised US$30 per month of service to be paid after the war). However, the soldiers of the current regular national army are being paid. Thus the military expenditure has not declined compared to the cost during the liberation struggle, but on the contrary has increased sharply.

In a broader sense the 'peace dividend' includes the increased production and consumption per capita. In Eritrea – where production had nearly come to a standstill at the end of the war, where trade and communication were made impossible by continuous fighting and the nearly total destruction of infrastructure and where the civilian labour force was highly demotivated – it can be assumed the 'peace dividend' defined thus would reach a considerable amount if it were possible to assess its value in financial terms.

In monetary terms there is thus no clear 'peace dividend' in Eritrea. In non-monetary terms, however, peace in the country and freedom of the people are in the eyes of the people – especially the fighters – the only results which count. A firm basis for economic growth and human development has been laid by establishing relative security within the new country. The hard-won peace and stability that is prevailing at the moment has been achieved through the coming together of all human and material resources depending mainly on self-reliance. It is the social capital which played, and is still playing, the most important role.

### 4.3  Security impact

As shown in Chapter 2 of this volume, various types of security can be distinguished. To assess the impact of demobilization on security we will try to use some of these categories. The military security of Eritrea has not been affected by demobilization and reintegration. The new national army consists of the best fighters (using military criteria) and is filled up annually by young people who have completed their national service and are willing to join the armed forces. Despite growing tension in relations with Sudan, and intermittent friction with Yemen across the Red Sea, Eritrea is considered strong enough to cope with intensifying confrontation. Additionally, a high percentage of the demobilized fighters can be considered as a reserve army, ready to take up arms if there is a serious threat to the country's sovereignty and stability.

Neither has demobilization had negative impact on the national security of the country, as, apart from a few exceptions, the ex-fighters identify themselves with the government formed by veteran EPLF fighters. This also applies to former ELF fighters who were demobilized on the same conditions as the EPLF fighters. Nevertheless, it cannot be excluded that the situation could deteriorate suddenly as a result of increasing destabilization by fundamentalists operating from Sudan and trying to antagonize the Muslim population in the Western Lowlands – the core region of former ELF.

The Red Sea region always was – and still is – of major strategic importance, even if military bases do not play the role they did fifty years ago. Thus tensions in one country have repercussions in the entire region – and beyond. At present the drive of the fundamentalist Islamic forces ruling Sudan – but also spreading from as far as Pakistan – is a clear menace to peace and stability in the region. Unclear boarder conditions on land and sea, uncontrolled movement of people and goods, disintegration of political and administrative structures, as in Somalia, all these affect the fragile balance of power and peace in the region. Eritrea is actively participating in the Inter-Governmental Authority on Development (IGAD), attempting to strengthen its stabilizing influence in the region.

Most observers would agree that since independence human security in Eritrea is among the highest in Africa. It has rarely been greater in any other period of the country's history. The demobilized fighters constitute one of its components, and they certainly contribute to human security, both in the short and long term. Despite certain feelings of uncertainty and frustration, this group has more of a stabilizing than of a destabilizing influence on other groups in society. Using some of the criteria listed in Chapter 2, it is clear that:

- demobilization has contributed to lessening tensions in the region;
- demobilization has not led to an increase of the number of un-controlled small weapons in society;
- demobilization has had no negative impact on the crime rate in the country;
- concerning the improvement of civil–military relations, it has to be kept in mind that it is the first time in history that Eritrea has its own armed forces, and that the population still identifies these forces with the liberation movement;
- there is no known impact of demobilization on the environment, neither positive nor negative; and
- demobilized fighters certainly do not deal more violently with potential conflicts than any other group of people.

## 5  Conclusion

Among African countries which have recently gone through demo-bilization and reintegration Eritrea is not typical. It has benefited from a series of specific conditions:

(1) The struggle for independence was not a civil war, even though in some periods in the 1970s the fighting between the EPLF and ELF caused as many victims as the fighting against the Ethiopian army. The liberation movement achieved its aim without having to compromise with a rival faction, and it was backed by the overwhelming majority of the country's inhabitants.

(2) The war ended with a military victory: there was no peace agree-ment which would have meant a compromise of principles. The fact that the defeated troops left the country immediately was also positive; as well as the fact that it was in reality a double victory, because at the same time the allied Tigrayan People's Liberation Front (TPLF) defeated the Derg with the help of part of the EPLF.

(3) There was no significant outside assistance either with troops or weapons. Therefore the new state had neither financial nor political debts to pay. This was also important for the morale and the self-confidence of government and fighters.

(4) Much more than in any other guerrilla war in Africa (apart maybe from the TPLF) the fighters of the EPLF had not only military but also civilian tasks to fulfil. They had to act accord-ing to values based on solidarity, respect, self-reliance and discipline. They had ample time to start building the new society

in the liberated areas, for the benefit of and in co-operation with the local population. This can be considered as an important investment into postwar Eritrea, as it is the capital on which the trust of the people in the government and the ex-fighters is based.

Nevertheless, the postwar situation had its own constraints. For a society having lived in isolation for two to three decades, contacts with the outside world – which has changed in the meantime – are not easy, mainly for the following reasons:

(1) The country's infrastructure was in such a state of destruction that everything had to be rebuilt simultaneously: establishing an administration; repairing roads, bridges, schools and hospitals; rehabilitating agricultural and industrial production; and last but not least demobilizing 60 per cent of the fighters, under time pressure and without sufficient means and know-how.

(2) There were great expectations on all sides – on the part of civilians as well as the fighters. This is a general state of mind in times of change. It happened when the African countries became independent, and these expectations are probably even greater after the victorious end of a war. For the fighters the expectations concerned as much material improvements as societal changes, which were of no, or much less, concern to the civilians.

(3) During the war Eritrean society had split into many different sections. After the war these had to be reintegrated, and reintegration did not only affect the fighters' and civilian society. There are as many different civilian societies which had developed separately during war and exile, which had affected between one-third and one-quarter of the country's population.

(4) Eritrea happened to achieve its independence when the world was undergoing a significant mutation towards economic globalization, which has not yet come to its end. In this new world order, the values of the 'struggle' which are still shared by many, if not all, fighters seem not only obsolete – they become counterproductive. But maybe this is too short-sighted a judgement; maybe this is the last – and best – weapon in the fight for complete independence.

All in all, demobilization went well, has made a major positive impact on security and has contributed to an environment conducive to development in Eritrea. The 'peace dividend' is the atmosphere of peace that Eritrean society is enjoying.

# Notes

1 Senior EPLF fighter during demobilization.

2 In this chapter we speak of 'fighters' as this term is used by the Eritreans (*tegadelti* in Tigrinya), and the word 'combatants' means both guerrilla fighters and soldiers (see Chapter 2).

3 Formerly the Eritrean Relief Association.

4 As the number of settlers in a settlement always fluctuates, especially in Ali Gider, it is not possible to give a precise figure.

5 This field research was part of the work for Amanuel Mehreteab's MA (1997) at Leeds University, UK.

6 The sample shows an unintended imbalance concerning the distribution of the different ethnic groups: with nearly 88 per cent (compared to about two-thirds in the EPLF forces) Tigrinya are over-represented. This is because a large percentage of ex-fighters of the other ethnic groups returned to their original (remote) rural areas and could not be reached by the interviewers. It is thus likely that the sample has some urban bias.

7 Overall, about one-fifth of the EPLF fighters were perceived to have some kind of disability after the end of the war.

# 6

# 'From the Gun to the Plough': the Macro- and Micro-Level Impact of Demobilization in Ethiopia

*Daniel Ayalew and Stefan Dercon*

## 1 Introduction

After decades of armed conflict, during the first part of 1990s, about half a million ex-soldiers were demobilized in Ethiopia. This chapter provides an analysis of the consequences of this demobilization. It looks at the impact on the ex-soldiers, on their households and on society at large. After looking at the context in which demobilization took place, the second section presents a profile of the ex-combatants, the assistance that was provided, and the impact of the assistance on the ex-soldiers. It also looks at the government expenditure and security consequences of the demobilization. In a third section, micro-level evidence from ex-soldiers who returned to rural areas is presented, to assess the welfare effects of the demobilization.[1]

Ethiopia has a poor agricultural economy. The country has faced unprecedented events in the last three decades. It has been highly affected by recurrent drought, famine and civil war. The military government, after the 1974 revolution,[2] undertook rapid social and institutional transformations. First, the military junta nationalized land and major industrial, agricultural and service enterprises in order to build socialist Ethiopia under a policy of command economy. Second, it committed a significant amount of scarce resources to public campaigns to eradicate illiteracy and expand school enrolment and health facilities. Finally, it carried out immense military campaigns against external aggression and internal turmoil under the slogan of 'everything to the war front' especially in the late

1980s and early 1990s. The war had, therefore, increased the nation's commitment of resources to the defence sector and threatened the country's political and economic stability.

In this regard Collier (1994a) identified two interrelated detrimental effects of warfare on income: directly through the diversion of resources into military activity and disruption of production and indirectly by reducing capital stock. Accordingly, in Ethiopia (i) the war had consumed a bulk of the national budget and productive manpower at the expense of the other sectors of the economy; (ii) it disrupted agricultural production, transportation and trade, and demolished crops and villages including physical assets, which exacerbates the problems of the country's poor; (iii) it destroyed infrastructure, including railways and ports, a large number of schools and health establishments; and (iv) its effect on human beings in the form of death and disablement should not be overlooked (see Eshetu and Makonnen, 1992; and Getachew, 1994).

In spite of this, in 1991 the Tigrayan-led forces of the Ethiopian People's Revolutionary Democratic Front (EPRDF) emerged as winners from the civil war, establishing authority over most parts of the country, while Eritrea effectively seceded under the Eritrean People's Liberation Front (EPLF) (see Chapter 5). The EPRDF forces inherited a war-torn economy and a country shattered by political conflicts, recurrent drought and inappropriate policies. The victorious party and different political groups, then, signed a Charter to form the Transitional Government of Ethiopia (TGE), which immediately decided to formally demobilize the defeated Derg soldiers as they were a threat to the country's internal security and stability. The war-torn economy of Ethiopia was not able to support a large army, and beyond that there was no further need for such a large force (ILO, 1995a). As clearly indicated by Eshetu and Makonnen (1992), the demobilization of the former army had posed challenges on the process of transition from war to peace, testifying its importance in the establishment of genuine peace in the country. Consequently, the TGE established the Commission for the Rehabilitation of Members of Former Army and Disabled War Veterans on 14 June 1991. The Commission was made responsible for the registration, disarmament and formal demobilization of combatants and for facilitating their social and economic reintegration into peaceful, productive and self-sustained lives.

After the defeat of the Derg army and the downfall of the regime, almost half a million Derg soldiers were to be demobilized.

Most of them initially returned to their homes by themselves while some went to neighbouring countries (Sudan, Kenya and Djibouti) without formal demobilization and often with their weapons – except those captured by the EPRDF or EPLF. Later, in July 1991, the Commission called upon Derg soldiers to report for formal demobilization at nine discharge centres all over the country. In response to the announcement, 455 000 ex-combatants including returnees from refugee camps reported for registration and pre-discharge reorientation in two batches. The repatriation of about 132 000 ex-soldiers (mainly from Sudan and Kenya) was undertaken by UNHCR in collaboration with the International Red Cross Societies (IRCS) and the Ethiopian Red Cross Society (ERCS). About 50 000 did not report to the Commission.

In addition, the Oromo Liberation Front (OLF), one of the political factions to sign the transitional Charter, withdrew from the TGE and started armed struggle with the EPRDF forces in the summer of 1992. EPRDF won the conflict and captured 22 200 OLF fighters in June 1992. These were detained in military camps for reorientation like the Derg ex-soldiers. Finally, the TGE disbanded up to 30 000 EPRDF soldiers (mainly Tigrayans) in 1995 in the process of restructuring the Ethiopian National Defence Force (ENDF) to keep ethnic balance by recruiting members of various nationalities with proportional compositions. It is, however, reported that several thousands of these demobilized EPRDF fighters have been incorporated into the police force with even a rise in their pay (*Africa Confidential*, 22 September 1995).

In total, the Commission was responsible for the demobilization and reintegration of about 509 200 ex-combatants. The high number made it a difficult exercise in terms of management, accommodation, transportation, etc. To start with, the discharge centres lacked the necessary facilities. Hence the first task of the Commission was to bring them up to the required standard. Besides, there was insufficient food, clean water and shelter in the centres, which endangered the lives of the ex-soldiers. In this regard the participation of NGOs in the provision of humanitarian assistance was important. Finally, the management and transportation of ex-soldiers in the discharge centres were conducted by ICRS and ERCS in collaboration with the TGE and EPRDF (Commission, 1994).

To understand the consequences of the large-scale demobilization, the changing economic environment is relevant. Simultaneous with the demobilization, the TGE introduced economic reform

measures to curb the downward trends in the economic performance and to stabilize macroeconomic imbalances, to eventually
transform the country from command- to market-oriented economy.
The TGE launched a Structural Adjustment Programme (SAP) supported by the Economic Rehabilitation and Reconstruction Programme
(ERRP) in October 1992. New measures also included retrenchment
of public-sector workers. The demobilization programme was thus
an integral part of the economic rehabilitation efforts and the peace
process in the country. As noted in Chapter 2, demobilization is a
complex exercise. The socioeconomic reintegration process is open-
ended – taking several years.

This chapter will try to examine the impact of the demobilization
and reintegration process in Ethiopia, using a variety of published
sources and data from a rural household survey conducted in 1994–
95. Section 2 will present an overview of the demobilization in
Ethiopia. It provides the *macro* picture of the demobilization: who
were involved and what was its impact on the ex-soldiers, their
families, society at large and the government finances. First, the
profile of the ex-combatants will be discussed, followed by an overview
of the support programmes for the ex-soldiers by government and
other organizations (Section 2.2). In Section 2.3 a general discussion of the likely impact of the programmes is presented. In Section
2.4 the focus is on the financial aspects of demobilization and the
issue of a peace dividend from demobilization. Section 2.5 presents
some preliminary conclusions. In Section 3 the emphasis is on the
*micro*-level consequences of demobilization: what happened to these
ex-soldiers and their families after they were discharged. A detailed
analysis of data collected in the context of the Ethiopian Rural
Household Survey (ERHS) is presented. After a presentation of the
data (Section 3.1), the characteristics of the ex-soldiers are discussed.
In Section 3.3 the actual assistance given is evaluated. In Section
3.4 some welfare indicators are given to provide an analysis of
reintegration. The key findings are summarized in the conclusions.

## 2 Demobilization in Ethiopia: an overview

### 2.1 Profile of ex-combatants

In this section we discuss the characteristics of the ex-soldiers at
the time of demobilization. The Commission has collected socioeconomic data in the discharge centres consisting of information
on, among others, education, skills and work experience which would

have helped to acquire better understanding of the target group during the resettlement and reintegration processes. However, the data, which are expected to contain comprehensive information about the characteristics and background of ex-combatants, have not yet been analysed and reported for public use, perhaps due to time constraints and limited capacity. The following generalizations are extracted from secondary sources concerning Derg and OLF ex-combatants (Colletta *et al.*, 1996b; Wilde and Anteneh, 1996).

*Age and sex.* Most of the ex-combatants from both Derg and OLF were found to be below the age of 25 at the time of demobilization. Only about 3–5 per cent of the Derg soldiers were female – about 10 per cent in the case of OLF ex-fighters.

*Marital status.* Around 50 per cent of the Derg ex-soldiers were married and slightly over 50 per cent had children to support. The results indicated that the rate was higher in the rural areas than urban centres. Similar information on the OLF captives is not available.

*Educational background and skills.* Most of the Derg soldiers did not attend beyond primary school (over 50 per cent). Close to 10 per cent never attended any schooling. In contrast, about 38 per cent of the OLF captives had not gone to school and 44 and 16 per cent attended primary and secondary school, respectively. The rest reported that they had some kind of vocational training, diploma or degree. While these levels of schooling may appear low even for African standards, this is actually considerably higher than those reported for the country as a whole. The 1994 Census results reported much lower levels of education: preliminary results[3] suggest that less than 10 per cent of the population beyond the age of 10 has more than primary education completed, while 74 per cent has no formal education whatsoever. In urban areas educational levels are higher: about 24 per cent has no formal education, but in rural areas more than 82 per cent has no education. Other evidence is consistent with these findings: the ERHS found that only 10 per cent of male adults between the age of 15 and 45 had primary education or more.[4]

Despite the relatively high level of formal education, concern has been expressed that most of the ex-combatants had no marketable skills or had low levels of skills (or no formal profession), which could enable them to participate in the labour market or engage in income-generating self-employment activities. The Commission and the World Bank (Colletta *et al*., 1996b) reached the conclusion that most of the ex-combatants came from poor families and hardly any had the necessary resources to start a new life. However, data are scanty to examine thoroughly what type of human capital building has taken place in the armed forces.

Some implications about the skills of ex-combatants can be derived based on the activities that they end up doing after demobilization. Out of the total number of demobilized soldiers only 3.8 per cent (6000) with special technical skills were included in the new defence force. Among 158 710 urban settlers, 1400 (0.9 per cent) were employed by the Ministry of Health as health practitioners. Another 9.6 per cent of the urban settlers (15 150), who were employees of different organizations before their conscription into the former army, were supported by the Commission to repossess these jobs. Note that the latter group had acquired their skill (profession) before they joined the armed forces. Finally, the Commission also issued skill certificates for about 5 per cent of urban settlers (7908), who had obtained marketable skills in the armed forces in the form of technical, electrical, driving and construction professions. These figures imply that only a few acquired saleable skills in the armed forces which can be used in civilian life. The same is true for the OLF captives. Only 12.5 per cent stated that they had marketable skills, mainly driving, tailoring, mechanical repair, carpentry, masonry, music, accounting and health care services.

*Duration of stay and health status.*   As the civil war in Ethiopia was severe and prolonged, most of the Derg soldiers had been enrolled in the armed forces for many years. The figures from the World Bank study (Colletta *et al*., 1996b) showed that only 15.4 per cent (70 162) served less than 18 months in the armed forces. Most of them were malnourished and in poor physical condition at the time of demobilization, mainly due to prolonged years of services. But their general health condition was good irrespective of their duration of stay, as most of them were young. On the other hand, most of the OLF captives joined the rebels after the defeat of the Derg army. Hence about 72 per cent of them had served less than 18 months.

Furthermore, more than 8 per cent (37 536) of Derg ex-soldiers were disabled at the end of the war – of whom almost half were moderately or more severely impaired. In the case of OLF captives only 2.6 per cent were disabled. More strikingly, recent statistical reports indicate that ex-soldiers form an exceptionally large percentage of AIDS patients in the country (CRS, 1994).

## 2.2 Demobilization programme

In Ethiopia the transition from combatant to civilian was classified into three stages:[5] demobilization, resettlement[6] and reintegration. Resettlement is a short-term phenomenon from six to 12 months after demobilization while reintegration refers to a relatively long period of time from 12 months to two years, until ex-combatants start to lead a 'normal civilian life' both in economic and social terms. In order to finance the costs of the three stages and achieve the objectives set for the Commission, the TGE called for help from the international donor community and other organizations. At the initial stage of demobilization the response of donors was not satisfactory and the burden was solely on the TGE. Eventually, different multilateral and bilateral donors and NGOs participated in the process, which eased some of the encumbrance of the Commission.

Under the resettlement programme the Commission provided a 'transitional safety-net' package to overcome the immediate problems of ex-combatants during the return to their localities. This package, which was designed based on the environment and on the needs of specifically vulnerable subgroups, consisted of cash and in-kind assistance. The cash assistance was birr 137 per ex-soldier in terms of transitional allowance, and a monthly stipend of birr 50 for the urban settlers only. The in-kind assistance was in the form of food ration cards up to a maximum of 12 months, depending on the target groups. Other assistance, such as free health services, land for construction of residential houses in rural areas and six-month rent allowance for the moderately disabled, were also provided (Colletta *et al.*, 1996b). The same type of resettlement assistance was applicable to OLF captives and ENDF ex-soldiers (Commission, 1994). However, ex-soldiers covered under a pension scheme or placed in any of the public offices did not qualify for cash payments.[7]

Finally, the TGE introduced a socioeconomic reintegration segment using the 'minimalist approach' to reinstate ex-combatants and their families into 'normal life'. That was simply the provision of basic needs. This programme was restricted to those who served for more than 18 months and to the disabled. The exclusion was based on the assumption that ex-soldiers, who served less than 18

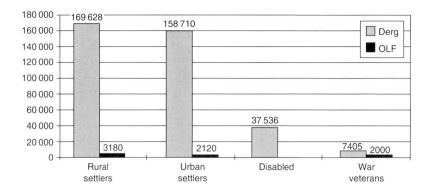

**Figure 6.1** Ex-combatants categorized under socioeconomic reintegration package

months, required less orientation and support to start a civilian life (Commission, 1994). The Commission then classified ex-combatants into four categories for the socioeconomic reintegration package, namely, (i) rural settlers; (ii) urban settlers; (iii) disabled ex-combatants; and (iv) war veterans covered under a pension scheme (see Figure 6.1.) Distinct programmes were designed and implemented for the four target groups based on their needs.

*Rural settlers.* Around 167 628 Derg ex-soldiers (45 per cent of the eligible) and 3180 OLF captives (44 per cent of the eligible) were registered as rural settlers with a desire to live as farmers. The Derg ex-soldiers were also further classified as crop (predominantly maize) producers (114 594); permanent crop (predominantly coffee) producers (42 447); and pastoralists (12 587). Most of the rural settlers of OLF captives were crop producers. Hence, rural settlers are primarily engaged in subsistence sedentary agriculture and pastoralism (Commission, 1994).

In the process the Commission extended material and technical assistance to help ex-combatants engage in subsistence agriculture. The support provided in the rural reintegration programme included: (i) provision of a plot of land; (ii) provision of basic agricultural inputs such as tools and implements, seeds and fertilizers; and (iii) supply of plough oxen and heifer to the most vulnerable among crop producers and pastoralists, respectively (Commission, 1994). Almost all the rural settlers received basic agricultural tools and implements and those involved in sedentary agriculture also obtained seeds and fertilizers. The Commission claimed that almost all the ex-combatants returned to the rural areas obtained land for cultivation. Due to resource constraints only one-third of them received oxen/heifer, although the initial plan of the Commission was to distribute one plough ox or heifer to all those returning to rural areas. In Section 3 of this chapter we will compare these findings with results of the ERHS.

*Urban settlers.* Around 158 710 Derg ex-soldiers (43 per cent of those eligible) settled in the urban areas. In addition, 2120 OLF ex-fighters (29 per cent of those eligible) applied to be included in the urban reintegration programme. This group included those who initially originated from the urban areas and those who served for a relatively long period in the armed forces and were hence used to urban life. In this case the Commission introduced various reintegration schemes, namely: (i) assisting those conscripted from their job to resume their former employment and those with some skills to obtain employment in civil organizations; (ii) issuing of skill certificates for those who acquired skills in the form of technical, electrical, driving and construction works during their stay in the armed forces; (iii) provision of vocational training in marketable skills in collaboration with vocational training schools; (iv) establishment of a revolving credit fund scheme, with soft loans; and (v) facilitated entrance and application formalities for those who wanted to continue their formal education. The reintegration of the urban target group was relatively 'complex and difficult' for the Commission due to the 'tightness of the labour market' and lack of saleable skills (Colletta *et al.*, 1996b).

Using the above-mentioned schemes the details of the actual implementation are given as follows. Consequently, 15 150 resumed their former jobs in both public and private organizations (note that the organizations were paying their salaries to their families while they were in service), 39 330 had been employed by the Ministries of Agriculture and State Farms on a contractual basis in agricultural and construction activities and 1400 were hired by the Ministry of Health as health practitioners. Furthermore, around 6000 Derg soldiers were incorporated into the new ENDF. Second, around 7908 obtained civilian certificates to help them find employment or start their own businesses. Likewise, 6130 ex-soldiers acquired training and skill upgrading courses for similar reasons. Third, 295 micro-projects, which were designed to reintegrate 6828 ex-combatants, were financed through the revolving loan scheme. The

Commission claimed that the credit scheme was generally a success from the socioeconomic point of view, although USAID concluded that it was not 'economically viable but self-depleting' (Colletta *et al.*, 1996b). Finally, the Commission created conducive conditions for 7500 college and university students from Belate training camp and 8522 OLF captives who wanted to pursue their formal education at various levels. Totally around 98 766[8] ex-combatants have been supported from the urban settlers.

*Disabled ex-combatants.* This group was categorized into three subgroups based on the severity of their disabilities. Accordingly, less severely disabled ex-combatants (20 000) were provided with necessary medical and paramedical rehabilitation and then included in the other reintegration programmes. Second, 15 208 moderately impaired ex-combatants were covered under the pension scheme after receiving the necessary medical treatment and vocational training. Those who participated in the training programme were also provided with materials, such as machinery, tools, raw materials and household utensils, to start their own self-supporting activities. Finally, 2328 more severely disabled ex-combatants were initially receiving institutional care. Later some of them have joined their families after getting vocational training and financial assistance which could help them to embark on sustainable income generating activities (Alemayehu, 1996).

*War veterans under pension scheme.* In addition to disabled ex-combatants, Derg ex-soldiers and OLF ex-fighter who are 45 years or older are covered under the same pension scheme. The Commission claimed that 7405 Derg ex-soldiers and approximately 2000 OLF ex-fighters are receiving pension income from the government treasury. Around 300 soldiers and their families held a demonstration in April 1996, requesting government to keep its promise of pension payments, or otherwise to refund their cash contribution during service (*The Horn of Africa Bulletin*, no. 3, 1996).

### 2.2.1 External assistance

Bilateral and multilateral organizations and NGOs, in collaboration with the Commission, have participated in the reintegration support. The main organizations were the German Agency for Technical Co-operation (GTZ), Catholic Relief Services (CRS), the World Bank and OXFAM (UK/Ireland).

*GTZ-Reintegration Programme.* The GTZ-Reintegration Programme (GTZ-RP) was established in February 1992. The programme was initially targeting Derg ex-soldiers. Later its task was expanded to include OLF captives, displaced persons and returnees from neighbouring countries with the objective of promoting employment and income opportunities. The GTZ-RP used the following instruments: (i) food and/or cash-for-work projects; (ii) provision of agricultural inputs and hand tools; (iii) training programmes in different marketable skills; (iv) small-scale income-generating projects using credit and/or grants; (v) a salary subsidy scheme; and (vi) low-cost house construction for disabled war veterans (GTZ, 1994; Wilde and Anteneh, 1996). In total around 20 639 ex-combatants benefited from the GTZ-RP schemes (Colletta *et al.*, 1996b).

*Catholic Relief Services – rehabilitation grant fund.* Catholic Relief Services (CRS) initiated small-scale credit schemes for micro-enterprise activities targeting a limited number of ex-combatants. The rehabilitation grant fund supported only about 300 ex-combatants.

*Ethiopian Social Rehabilitation Fund (ESRF).* The social rehabilitation fund has been one of the major components of the ERRP, initiated by the World Bank. The objective of the social rehabilitation fund is to assist community-based income-generating activities for displaced people, demobilized soldiers and other poor socioeconomic groups. The ESRF benefited around 5617 demobilized soldiers (Getahun, 1996).

*OXFAM (UK/Ireland).* OXFAM also directly participated in reintegration support for demobilized soldiers, mainly through rural development programmes. It has supported ex-soldiers and their families, but the coverage was not significant (Colletta *et al.*, 1996b).

## 2.3 Impact of demobilization

In general, the Ethiopian demobilization and reintegration process was considered as a success by the government and the donors. The programmes undertaken by the Commission and bilateral and multilateral NGOs reached a notable number of ex-combatants as to the published sources. At least 332 435 ex-combatants, or about 70 per cent of the number of Derg and OLF ex-combatants at time of demobilization, benefited from the various programmes. On average the cost of the reintegration programme per demobilized soldier was estimated to be birr 398 (about US$60), but there are significant differences across the distinct programmes (see Table 6.1).

**Table 6.1  Reintegration programmes and beneficiaries (Derg and OLF)**

| Promoter | Programme | Amount in millions (birr) | Beneficiaries | Per-capita costs (birr) |
|---|---|---|---|---|
| Commission | Rural reintegration[a] | 52.00 | 169 628 | 307 |
| | Urban reintegration | 46.40 | 98 766 | 470 |
| | credit projects | 14.40 | 6 826 | 2 110 |
| | Disabled | 20.00 | 37 536 | 533 |
| | Pension | n/a | 24 600 | n/a |
| GTZ | Reintegration programme | 8.12 | 20 639 | 393 |
| | credit projects | 1.82 | 1 038 | 1 750 |
| CRS | Rehabilitation grant | 0.24 | 300 | 800 |
| OXFAM | | | | |
| (UK/Ireland) | Reintegration support | 0.16 | n/a | n/a |
| ESRF | Credit and training | 5.46 | 5 566 | 982 |
| | credit projects | 5.04 | 5 192 | 982 |
| Total[b] | | 132.38 | 332 435 | 398 |

*Source*: Colletta et al. (1996b).
  [a] Derg ex-soldiers only. They received multiple support.
  [b] Excluding pension scheme and OXFAM (UK/Ireland), and assuming no overlap among different programmes.
  n/a Not available.

The exchange rate during this period was about 6–6.30 birr per US$. Moreover, the Commission and the country report of the World Bank claimed that most rural ex-combatants were in the same or even a better economic position than civilians after the first harvest, although the empirical basis for this statement is very weak. Lack of inputs and problems in securing land were constraints to the reintegration of rural settlers. Some of them, who returned into resource-constrained communities and areas affected by natural calamities, remained below the living standard of the average rural Ethiopian.

On the other hand, the reintegration programmes in the urban areas have had a dissatisfactory impact because of lack of skill and a depressed labour market. This may provide some explanation for why around 15 per cent of ex-combatants were effectively unemployed in 1994/95 (Colletta *et al.*, 1996b). This figure seems quite small in a country where urban unemployment affects 40 per cent (ILO, 1995a) of the urban labour force. This may be due to the fact that those urban ex-soldiers temporarily employed by the Ministry of States Farms were considered as if they were in a permanent job. It could also be a reflection of their relative poverty: in a country with only very limited social security provision the poor could not afford staying unemployed for any length of time, even if it means very low earnings from informal-sector activities.

As opposed to the above discussion, IMF and World Bank staff estimates also disclosed that ex-combatants earn birr 642.7 per person per annum, which is far less than the per-capita GDP of Ethiopia's working population (birr 1161). This implies that ex-combatants may be in a difficult situation as compared to their civilian counterpart.[9] This result appears not to be consistent with the reported condition of rural settlers after the first harvest. The other alternative argument is that the living standard of the urban settlers remained much lower than the living standard of their civilian counterpart. Given the poor empirical basis for these estimates we need to be very careful with these conclusions.

Almost all the benefits accrued to ex-combatants were not extended to their dependants in particular and to the community in general. The reintegration support was mainly targeting ex-soldiers alone, due to financial constraints. Spouse and children received minor assistance in the form of free health services and support for school fees and materials (Colletta *et al.*, 1996b).[10]

Female ex-combatants were part of the main reintegration programmes. The Commission believed that economic reintegration was easier for female ex-combatants than for their male counterpart as they were holding positions such as musicians, secretaries, radio operators and cooks. Not everybody shares this view. The CRS (1994) notes that the involvement of female ex-combatants was very low due to the insensitivity of the responsible agencies towards women.

The situation of former child soldiers was the worst, both economically and psychologically, as there was no special programme for them. Their situation has been exacerbated by lack of marketable skills and a low level of education (most of them have not completed primary school).[11] Likewise disabled ex-combatants were given very little attention as their impact on the security situation of the country was insignificant. Most of them were left to struggle by themselves with minimal assistance (CRS, 1994; Wilde and Anteneh, 1996).

Finally, ex-combatants who failed to participate in the reorientation programme of the Commission were not able to find any formal assistance from the Commission and donor agencies. Hence they were the most marginalized group among ex-combatants. However, this does not mean that ex-combatants were unable to get assistance from their communities, friends and relatives. Communities are very sympathetic to the destitution of any of their members. As a result we could expect that ex-combatants had received important assistance from their communities, most notably from friends and relatives. For instance, ex-combatants could benefit from the traditional labour-sharing agreement which is a common practice in rural Ethiopia. It should also be noted that farmers were obliged to work – without pay – on the fields of combatants while they were in-service.

Beyond the direct impact on the ex-soldiers and their families, demobilization may have externalities. One hypothesis is that demobilization might increase crime rates. In the case of Ethiopia one could expect a serious problem in this regard as a lot of ex-soldiers went back with their weapons in disarray. Initially, there were incidents of theft and armed robberies, mainly rural banditry, organized by ex-combatants as reported by police and the press. The government then established mechanisms to collect weapons, namely, through a call in the media to return weapons and through searches by district-level security committees. The personal weapons of the ex-soldiers collected by the TGE are now in the possession of the ENDF. We do not have information about how many were collected. However, as far as evidence is available, there has not been a significant increase in the crime rates of the country since demobilization. The Commission as well as the Police Commissioner reached a conclusion that the incidents were insignificant as compared to the number of demobilized soldiers and the crime rates reported in neighbouring countries (Commission, 1994; Collier, 1994b).

There was also a flow of arms to neighbouring countries such as Kenya, Djibouti and Sudan, though information is scanty on this issue. This is expected as most of those who fled to these countries had gone with their weapons. Around 51 000 Ethiopian ex-soldiers in Sudan and 28 000 in Djibouti surrendered their weapons to authorities in the refugee camps (NGO Networking Service, 1995).

### 2.4 Cost of demobilization and peace dividend

The costs of the Ethiopian demobilization and reintegration programme were estimated by different institutions and experts, such as local and ILO experts and World Bank staff. The World Bank staff estimates complemented by data collected from the Commission and other concerned organizations are found to be the most comprehensive and reliable.

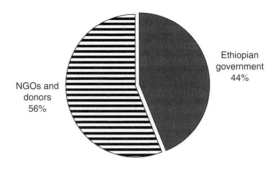

**Figure 6.2**  Cost breakdown of the demobilization exercise

The total costs of the three phases of the demobilization exercise were estimated at about birr 518.3 million, of which birr 170.4 million and birr 171.2 million were used for demobilization and resettlement phases, respectively. Second, about birr 132.4 million were spent on reintegration support to Derg and OLF ex-combatants. The remaining birr 44.3 million were used for local administrative expenses, mainly by the Commission. Interestingly enough, the administrative expenses were only 8.5 per cent of the total cost of the demobilization and reintegration, perhaps an indication for efficient utilization of the available resources.

About birr 227 million were covered by the government of Ethiopia. Donor and NGO assistance was estimated to be birr 291.3 million – out of which birr 186.3 million were for emergency relief assistance and transportation during the demobilization and resettlement phases by International Committee of the Red Cross (ICRC), UNHCR, the United States and the World Food Programme (WFP). These indicated that the reintegration phase, which was crucial for ex-combatants to return to a civilian life, was mainly the responsibility of the Commission. The cost breakdown in percentage terms is shown in Figure 6.2.

As indicated above, the Commission followed the minimalist approach in its assistance to ex-combatants. With this general targeting mechanism the Commission and other participants of the demobilization and reintegration process designed 'needs-based' programmes for different ex-combatant categories. As a result the cost per demobilized soldier was different across different categories of ex-soldiers and also across different programmes within the same category (see Table 6.1). In general, the per-capita cost for urban settlers was higher than for rural settlers. This was mainly due to the per-capita cost of the credit projects targeting urban settlers.

Now we will consider the expected 'peace dividend' from the end of the civil war. The transition from war to peace is generally expected to redirect significant amounts of resources from military to productive activities, i.e. a reduction in military expenditure which will allow an increase in public expenditure on other activities. In this regard Collier (1994a, 1996) argued that the diversion effect is less easily reversible. This implies that the peace dividend may not be realized instantaneously to increase productivity and, in turn, the level of output. The suggested reasons can be summarized as: (i) there will be a lag in the decline of military expenditure due to a delay in demobilization or even if the military size decreases substantially, the savings are often used to increase the salaries of the remaining army; (ii) there might not be an improvement in the fiscal position after the restoration of peace as the transition probably reduces government revenue due to collapse of the revenue-collection system, even if one assumes a fall in military expenditure; and (iii) there will also be a problem to increase productive public expenditures owing to fiscally unsustainable positions in the final years of war.

The first reason does not correspond to the situation in Ethiopia as demobilization of the former army took place immediately after the fall of the Derg regime. The other two justifications can be cases in point to some extent. First, domestic government revenue as a share of GDP declined from 18.4 to 15.2 per cent after the end of the war. This happened because the military regime was collecting funds for military and other emergencies even by using coercive measures which could not be applied during peace and the revenue-collection system collapsed. In addition, there was also a downward adjustment in the different tax rates due to the introduction of the SAPs. Second, there was also an increase in the fiscal deficit of the government in the last two years of the civil war (see Table 6.2) which led to an increase in domestic borrowing from the banking system to a rate that ranges from 85 to 90 per cent of domestic financing. As a result no significant change has been observed in the expenditure pattern of the government towards health and education services even if military expenditure as percentage of GDP declines significantly from an average of 9.5 per cent for the final five years of the war to an average of 2.6 per cent for the

**Table 6.2  Government expenditure at current market prices in millions of birr**

| Year | GDP | Total expenditure | Total revenue | Budget deficit | Health | Education | Health and education | Military |
|---|---|---|---|---|---|---|---|---|
| 1986/87 | 15501.2 | 4125.4 | 3742 | −383.4 | 146.3 | 416.3 | 562.6 | 1011.1 |
| 1987/88 | 15996.9 | 5058.1 | 4576 | −482.1 | 154.7 | 444.6 | 599.3 | 1540.5 |
| 1988/89 | 16873.4 | 5912.3 | 5446.8 | −465.5 | 169.7 | 482.0 | 651.7 | 2016.3 |
| 1989/90 | 17871.7 | 5367.0 | 4096.7 | −1270.3 | 175.5 | 491.5 | 667.0 | 1871.7 |
| 1990/91 | 19815.6 | 4913.8 | 3636.3 | −1277.5 | 163.2 | 486.4 | 649.6 | 1725.1 |
| 1991/92 | 20393.8 | 4183.6 | 3102.0 | −1081.6 | 190.4 | 534.4 | 724.8 | 751.8 |
| 1992/93 | 26056.7 | 5012.6 | 4342.5 | −670.1 | 236.3 | 606.6 | 842.9 | 696.9 |
| 1993/94 | 27396.8 | 7549.6 | 6761.5 | −788.1 | 422.0 | 990.3 | 1412.3 | 709.3 |
| 1994/95 | 34200.0 | 8253.4 | 6874.1 | −1379.3 | 402.7 | 1094.4 | 1497.1 | 672.5 |
| 1995/96 | 38414.3 | 8573.2 | 7824.0 | −749.2 | 445.1 | 1344.5 | 1789.6 | 761.6 |
| *As percentage of GDP at market price* | | | | | | | | |
| 1986/87 | | 26.6 | 24.1 | −2.5 | 0.9 | 2.7 | 3.6 | 6.5 |
| 1987/88 | | 31.6 | 28.6 | −3.0 | 1.0 | 2.8 | 3.7 | 9.6 |
| 1988/89 | | 35.0 | 32.3 | −2.8 | 1.0 | 2.9 | 3.9 | 11.9 |
| 1989/90 | | 30.0 | 22.9 | −7.1 | 1.0 | 2.8 | 3.7 | 10.5 |
| 1990/91 | | 24.8 | 18.4 | −6.4 | 0.8 | 2.5 | 3.3 | 8.7 |
| 1991/92 | | 20.5 | 15.2 | −5.3 | 0.9 | 2.6 | 3.6 | 3.7 |
| 1992/93 | | 19.2 | 16.7 | −2.6 | 0.9 | 2.3 | 3.2 | 2.7 |
| 1993/94 | | 27.6 | 24.7 | −2.9 | 1.5 | 3.6 | 5.2 | 2.6 |
| 1994/95 | | 24.1 | 20.1 | −4.0 | 1.2 | 3.2 | 4.4 | 2.0 |
| 1995/96 | | 22.3 | 20.4 | −2.0 | 1.2 | 3.5 | 4.7 | 2.0 |
| War average | | 29.6 | 25.3 | −4.4 | 0.9 | 2.7 | 3.6 | 9.5 |
| Postwar average | | 22.7 | 19.4 | −3.4 | 1.1 | 3.1 | 4.2 | 2.6 |

*As percentage of total government expenditure*

| | | | | |
|---|---|---|---|---|
| 1986/87 | 3.5 | 10.1 | 13.6 | 24.5 |
| 1987/88 | 3.1 | 8.8 | 11.8 | 30.5 |
| 1988/89 | 2.9 | 8.2 | 11.0 | 34.1 |
| 1989/90 | 3.3 | 9.2 | 12.4 | 34.9 |
| 1990/91 | 3.3 | 9.9 | 13.2 | 35.1 |
| 1991/92 | 4.6 | 12.8 | 17.3 | 18.0 |
| 1992/93 | 4.7 | 12.1 | 16.8 | 13.9 |
| 1993/94 | 5.6 | 13.1 | 18.7 | 9.4 |
| 1994/95 | 4.9 | 13.3 | 18.2 | 8.2 |
| 1995/96 | 5.2 | 15.7 | 20.9 | 8.9 |
| War average | 3.2 | 9.2 | 12.4 | 31.8 |
| Postwar average | 5.0 | 13.4 | 18.4 | 11.7 |

*Sources:* (1) Ministry of Economic Development and Co-operation; (2) the source for total government expenditure and revenue (1994/95–1995/96) is the National Bank of Ethiopia. Hence there is a need to be cautious for compatibility and consistency of the two data sets.

first five years of peace. Hence, we need to agree with the view
that 'the prolonged civil war may not produce a rapid peace dividend' (Collier, 1994a, p. 5).

## 2.5   Demobilization in Ethiopia: the macro-picture

In many ways it would be fair to say that demobilization was a far
more successful operation than many may have expected before-
hand. About 455 000 ex-combatants from the Derg army, probably
more than 90 per cent of the army existing at the time of their
defeat, went through a formal discharging procedure during 1991.
Later, a large number of OLF fighters and new government soldiers
were also formally demobilized. The logistical problem appears to
have been handled reasonably well. The lion share of costs was
borne by the government, although over time more donors provided assistance to help to complete the process. There is some
evidence to suggest quite an efficient use of resources. Administrative
costs appear to have been quite low, while leakage has probably
not been very large, at least on the basis of the existing evidence.

A large part of the arms of the ex-soldiers seems to have been
collected, even though no figures are available. It does not appear
that a large micro-level insecurity, in the form of criminal activity
by ex-soldiers, has followed the end of the war. After a few incidents the government forces' reaction appears to have been sufficient
to maintain relative security in most areas, resulting in positive
consequences for economic activity. The larger part of ex-soldiers
returned to rural areas, although it is unclear which percentage of
ex-soldiers who originated in rural areas actually returned to these
areas. The suspicion is that a not-insignificant part remained in
urban areas, adding to the rapid increase in urban population in
recent years. Labour markets are unlikely to have absorbed them
easily in urban areas: during the economic reform period, job opportunities in the formal sector have declined rapidly, while urban
labour market data suggest that there has been only limited expansion of private-sector employment. Although ex-soldiers appear to
be generally more educated than the rest of population, they do
not appear to have acquired a large number of useful business skills
to become successful in self-employment.

It has been suggested by some that those returning to rural areas
may have had an easier time than those in urban areas. Official
figures suggest that the levels of support appear to have been quite
high, although lower in per-capita terms than in urban areas.

Reintegration in rural communities may have been helped by community support. Nevertheless, very little evidence is available to obtain a complete macro-picture on living standards of the ex-soldiers and their families. In the next section we will try to fill in this gap by focusing on some ex-soldiers from different communities included in a rural household survey.

## 3 Impact of demobilization in rural areas

### 3.1 Data

As discussed in the Section 2, most of the demobilized soldiers were from rural areas and many decided to return to these areas. In percapita terms they received less help than the urban soldiers (see Table 6.1). Given that urban poverty is generally not higher than rural poverty (Dercon and Mekonen, 1997), this may result in a much higher relative vulnerability of rural ex-soldiers than the urban soldiers. Against this view, rural ex-soldiers may be able to return to communities in which reintegration is easier than in urban areas. As a result, the view that rural settlers soon became better off than their urban counterparts (see Section 2.3) may be correct. Nevertheless, the question whether rural or urban ex-soldiers are better off might not be the most important issue. More relevant for an assessment of the impact of the demobilization is whether ex-soldiers manage to get reintegrated within society at large and specifically within their own communities.

For this study we do not have access to comparative data on all different groups of ex-soldiers. However, we have access to an extensive rural data set. The Ethiopian Rural Household Survey (ERHS) was jointly undertaken by the Department of Economics of Addis Ababa University and the Centre for the Study of African Economies, Oxford University, in collaboration with the Institute of Development Research, Addis Ababa University. The survey covers 15 villages of the country and interviewed 1477 households over three rounds in 1994–95. The areas were chosen to reflect the different agro-climatic zones in the country, and include villages in Tigray, Amhara Region, Oromiya and SEPAR.[12] The households were randomly chosen within each village and the sample size in each village was proportional to the total population in the specific agro-climatic zone. The survey was multipurpose: data were collected on consumption, income, agriculture, health, nutrition, assets, fertility and many more topics. As a consequence it is suited to investigate welfare differences and the factors causing them.[13]

The survey was not specifically targeted to investigate ex-soldiers but was large enough so that 124 ex-soldiers were included following random sampling in each community.[14] This makes the data set unique: it allows the study of the ex-soldiers in relation to the rest of the communities in which they live. In particular it allows an evaluation of their reintegration: to what extent are they similar or dissimilar to the rest of the population. Questions that can be addressed include: Are they having a similar standard of living? Are they having access to similar resources and assets? What support did they get to help their reintegration?

The survey was not specifically designed to come up with extensive data on the process of demobilization and its impact on individuals and households in Ethiopia. Hence, one needs to be cautious in the interpretation of the findings as detailed information is not available on some of the important aspects. Nevertheless, a module had been included to provide at least some detail on these ex-soldiers, for example in terms of the support they received at the time of demobilization. The study is based on 124 demobilized soldiers, although detailed information is available only for 106 individuals, of which 92 belonged to the Derg army, eight to the EPRDF force, and one from another unspecified army. However, information is not available for the remaining ex-soldiers as to which army they belong, but they are likely to have belonged to the Derg army or to some other grouping which they did not wish to mention.

## 3.2   Characteristics of ex-soldiers

The data allow us to compute some of the basic characteristics of the rural ex-soldiers.

*Age and sex.*   Most of the ex-soldiers covered in the rural household survey were young, which is consistent with the overall profile of ex-soldiers. Around 70 per cent were between 17 and 35 years in 1994, that is almost three years after the fall of the Derg regime. Hence, most of them were at the age at which integration into productive life is very important. In addition, all of them were male (see Table 6.3).

**Table 6.3  Age distribution of ex-soldiers**

| Age in years | Frequency | Percentage |
|---|---|---|
| 17–19 | 3 | 2.8 |
| 20–5 | 31 | 28.4 |
| 26–30 | 25 | 22.9 |
| 31–5 | 17 | 15.6 |
| 36–40 | 13 | 11.9 |
| 41–5 | 5 | 4.6 |
| above 45 | 15 | 13.8 |

**Table 6.4  Marital status**

| Status | Frequency | Percentage |
|---|---|---|
| Married | 64 | 66.0 |
| Divorced and separated | 4 | 4.1 |
| Never married | 29 | 29.9 |

**Table 6.5  Relation to household head and family size**

| | Frequency | Percentage | Average family size |
|---|---|---|---|
| Head | 64 | 58.7 | 5.5 |
| Husband/partner | 3 | 2.8 | |
| Son | 36 | 33.0 | |
| Grandchild | 1 | 0.9 | |
| Brother | 3 | 2.8 | |
| Unrelated person | 2 | 1.8 | |

*Marital status and family size.* Reintegration of ex-combatants concerns the whole family, especially spouse and children when these depended on the income of the ex-soldier prior to demobilization (Klingebiel *et al.*, 1995). In this regard the survey data confirmed the estimation of the Commission and the World Bank working group (see Table 6.4). We found that 66 per cent were married and about 4 per cent were either divorced or separated while the remainder were single in 1994.[15] Close to 59 per cent were heads of households with a responsibility of supporting about 5.5 individuals on average. In general, ex-combatants live in a household where the average family size equals approximately seven persons (see Table 6.5).

**Table 6.6 Level of education**

| | Before joining the army | | After demobilization | |
|---|---|---|---|---|
| | Frequency | Percentage | Frequency | Percentange |
| No schooling | 27 | 22.0 | 27 | 25.0 |
| Literacy certificate | 9 | 7.3 | 5 | 4.6 |
| Primary and junior school | 77 | 62.6 | 70 | 64.8 |
| Secondary school | 9 | 8.1 | 5 | 4.6 |

Note: There is a discrepancy in the total number before and after demobilization. The discrepancy arises due to missing values in the case of the latter.

*Regional distribution.* The majority of ex-combatants covered in the survey were from the Oromia administrative region, followed by Amhara. The other important feature is that more than 75 per cent were from the four sites (Debre Birhan, Shashemene, Bule and Dodota) which are relatively near to urban centres. This suggests that recruiting was more effective near urban centres.

*Education.* The majority had had at least some education when they joined the army. We found that around 62.6 per cent had attended primary and junior school and another 8.1 per cent had attended secondary school. Besides, 7.3 per cent had an adult or other literacy certificate. Of the total, more strikingly, 20 per cent had been students before they joined the army. On the other hand, only 22 per cent had never had any form of schooling. This is much lower than in the equivalent age groups in the entire sample: more than 40 per cent of those men with a civilian background, and in the same age group as the ex-soldiers, had never any schooling.

Table 6.6 indicates that there is no change in the educational level of ex-soldiers included in the survey before and after demobilization, which clearly shows that they had not acquired additional formal education while serving in the armed forces. In addition, only 7.3 per cent resumed their education after demobilization. In general their educational level is better than their civilian counterpart. This may be due to the selection criteria of the Derg regime, i.e. one had to be able to read and to write to join the armed forces, especially before the final years of the civil war. Alternatively, schools may have been easy recruiting areas for activists, or easy targets for conscription programmes. Whatever the reason, this is an important finding, consistent with the evidence reported in Section 2. While Ethiopia has an extremely low educational attainment, the war was fought by a relatively educated army.

**Table 6.7  Effect on family labour**

|  | Frequency | Percentage |
|---|---|---|
| No effect | 41 | 36.3 |
| Hiring of extra labour | 22 | 19.5 |
| More intensive use of family labour | 30 | 26.5 |
| More intensive use of family labour and hiring extra labour | 19 | 16.8 |
| The entire household left | 1 | 0.9 |

*Health status.* About 80 per cent of the ex-soldiers reported that they did not suffer from any chronic or major disabilities. Among those with disabilities, one of the major disabilities is found to be mental illness – proportionately more than in the rest of the population. Otherwise, most were at least physically fit to work: more than 90 per cent of the sample reported they could easily hoe a field for a morning.

*Main activity.* Before joining the army most of the ex-soldiers (about 74 per cent) were farmers or sheepherders. Around 20 per cent were students at school. Since the majority of the soldiers were involved in agricultural activities, one could expect that joining of a household member into the armed forces would have affected the labour supply of the household. The relationship is straightforward, even if one can expect the existence of seasonal unemployment in rural Ethiopia. It should be clear that there are also peak seasons when labour is relatively scarce. Hence, households were asked whether the leaving of the member affected the work activities of the family or forced the family to hire labour. Most of them (two-thirds) reported that the departure of the family member affected them through a more intensive use of family labour or hiring of extra labour (see Table 6.7). On the other hand, about 36 per cent reported that the recruitment of the member into the armed forces did not affect the family in one way or the other. This might be due to the fact that some of them were students before joining the army and their contribution to farm work had been insignificant.[16]

*Duration of stay.* Out of the ex-soldiers in the sample, 69 per cent served for 18 or more months in the armed forces. The remainder stayed only for less than 18 months. This is useful information to evaluate the demobilization programme, since one of the criteria for providing assistance was length of time served in the army.

**Table 6.8   Types of assistance and beneficiaries**

| Type of assistance | No. of beneficiaries | Amount | Minimum | Maximum |
| --- | --- | --- | --- | --- |
| Land | 49 (46.2) | 0.7 | 0.00008 | 2 |
| Cash | 25 (23.6) | 350.6 | 28 | 700 |
| In-kind | 35 (33.0) | 108.5 | 7 | 800 |
| Cash and/or in-kind | 47 (44.3) | 267.3 | 15 | 800 |
| Any assistance | 64 (60.4) | | | |

*Notes*: Land is measured in hectares and cash and in-kind assistance in birr. Means are for those receiving assistance. The large maximum value of cash assistance is likely to indicate support to buy an ox or heifer, or assistance in the form of an ox/heifer in the case of in-kind assistance.

### 3.3   Assistance

Those returned from the army were asked whether they received any assistance, namely land, cash or in-kind, from the government or NGOs (see Table 6.8). However, it is not possible to distinguish between resettlement assistance and reintegration assistance as they are not asked to differentiate between the two. Our analysis is based on one of the targeting mechanisms of the Commission, which was later adopted by donor agencies. That is simply by disaggregating demobilized soldiers in our sample using their duration of stay in the army. Remember that those who served less than 18 months received resettlement allowance but were not part of the reintegration programmes.

*Magnitude and coverage.* In our sample of demobilized soldiers, around 60.4 per cent reported that they have received some form of assistance from the government or NGOs.[17] Only 46.2 per cent received land, with an average size of 0.7 hectare per ex-soldier receiving land. In addition, 23.6 per cent and 33.0 per cent obtained cash and in-kind assistance, equal to birr 350 and birr 109 on average, respectively. In order to avoid double counting of those who received both cash and in-kind, we take the sum of the two as they are measured using the same unit. The result signifies that around 44 per cent secured cash and/or in-kind assistance, amounting to birr 267 on average for those receiving support.

This figure of birr 267 is quite consistent with the gross per-capita cost for rural reintegration programmes by the Commission (birr 307) (which includes administration costs). However, most remarkable is the fact that only about 60 per cent obtained any assistance.

**Table 6.9 Duration of stay and assistance**

| Type of assistance | Less than 18 months | 18 months and above | Total |
| --- | --- | --- | --- |
| Land | 12 (42.9) | 31 (45.6) | 43 (44.8) |
| Cash and/or in-kind | 12 (42.9) | 31 (45.6) | 43 (44.8) |
| Any Assistance | 18 (64.3) | 40 (58.8) | 58 (60.4) |
| Total in each group | 28 | 68 | 96 |

*Notes*: Information on duration of stay is available only for 96 ex-soldiers. Numbers in parentheses are percentage values calculated from each group.

Mean cash or in-kind assistance across *all* ex-soldiers is only birr 117. The distribution of the support given is also skewed towards a relatively small number of individuals: the lower half of the distribution of those receiving support in the form of cash or in-kind only received a median value of about birr 50.

*Assistance and duration of service.* As we pointed out earlier, reintegration assistance was given only to those who served for more than 18 months in the army or rebel forces. The others received only resettlement allowance. The following discussion will, therefore, help to evaluate to some extent the targeting mechanisms of the Commission. But we need to be cautious once again, as our sample of ex-soldiers is small compared to the total number of demobilized soldiers.

In our sample only 59 per cent of those who served for more than 18 months received assistance from any source. More specifically, 45 per cent of them obtained land and 45 per cent received cash and/or in-kind assistance (note that some of them received multiple assistance). In other words, about 40 per cent of them were not covered in either of these schemes. On the other hand, though the Commission believed that those who served for less than 18 months had not received reintegration assistance, our sample indicates that more than 60 per cent of them received assistance in the form of land, cash and/or in-kind assistance. This implies that some of them were part of the reintegration programme, which casts doubt on the targeting efficiency of the Commission.

So far we were concerned with the coverage of assistance using the targeting mechanism of the Commission. Here we will try to see the magnitude (amount) of assistance obtained by our sample of demobilized soldiers. In terms of magnitude, those who served for less than 18 months received birr 293.8 while the other group obtained only 259.4 on average in the form of cash and in-kind assistance, indicating that the former received a greater amount than the latter in absolute terms, unlike the targeting mechanism of the Commission. The difference, however, is not statistically significant when we use an *F*-test on the difference of the mean.[18] In the case of land those who served for more than 18 months seem better off in absolute terms, obtaining 0.78 hectares as compared to 0.57 hectares on average. Once again, the difference is not statistically significant with an *F*-statistic of 1.564. In general, demobilized soldiers in our sample are not landless, or at least they belong to a household which has its own land, although the figures indicate that only less than 50 per cent received land on their return home. From this we can speculate that some of the ex-soldiers had access to a plot of land while they were in-service and had not lost it during their absence. It is thus not as claimed by the Commission, at least in our sample, that all of them were helped to have access to land upon their return. In the case of cash and in-kind assistance our results are not entirely consistent with that of the Commission (1994) and Colletta *et al.* (1996b). This is because the Commission claimed that all rural ex-combatants, except those who have not reported for formal demobilization, received a resettlement allowance of birr 137 and a food ration for about 10 months. In addition, those who served for more than 18 months were supposed to have received assistance estimated about birr 306 on average. However, the ex-soldiers in our sample reported that they received assistance which is less than the per-capita cost of the reintegration programme in the form of in-kind assistance. A large percentage did not receive assistance. Whether this implies that they did not report for formal demobilization is hard to assess. Further, the distribution of the assistance is quite skewed to relatively few individuals, and those serving longer did not necessarily obtain more assistance, against stated policy. These points suggest that the targeting efficiency of the programme was far from perfect and the possibility of leakage in programme implementation cannot be easily dismissed.

### 3.4  Some welfare indicators

The reintegration of ex-combatants into civilian life, socially, economically and politically, is the ultimate objective of any demobilization process. If they are not able to reintegrate at least in the long run, the consequence might be destructive. First it might result in a loss in scarce resources, which may then endanger internal peace and security both at micro- and macro-level. Therefore, we will try to evaluate whether the ex-soldiers in our sample reintegrated themselves into civilian life. It is, however, too early for strong conclusions based on the available information as reintegration is a slow process. Besides, we do not have a direct and appropriate yardstick to gauge the success of the reintegration process from different perspectives.

The methodology followed is to compare ex-combatants with their civilian counterparts using some welfare or human development indicators,[19] namely, per-capita consumption expenditures, nutritional status with the help of body mass index (BMI),[20] land holding (which may be considered a most critical factor for the success of rural reintegration) and asset holding using livestock as a proxy, as it is the most important asset in rural areas. A simple comparison, however, will not be meaningful without correcting for differences in the characteristics of ex-soldiers and non-soldiers (i.e. with civilian background) in the sample. In particular, ex-soldiers are all male, they belong to a particular age group and returned to particular villages in the sample. Besides the effects of differences in sex, belonging to a particular age group may result in being at different points of the life cycle, and therefore differences in earnings and assets. Similarly, if ex-soldiers live proportionately more in poorer villages than the rest of the sample, then mean welfare indicators may suggest that ex-soldiers are worse off. But this has little to do with the demobilization, but rather with the effects of living in a poor community. Accordingly, we calculated weights to be used in the calculation of descriptive statistics for the non-soldiers group to reflect the distribution of the ex-soldiers group using age, sex and survey site as selection criteria. Since no females are included in the sample of ex-soldiers, they were excluded for the calculations in the non-soldiers sample. To provide weights correcting for the difference in the age distribution, the sampling weight (one over the number of observations, since the sample is random) is multiplied by the ratio of the frequency of a particular age in the soldiers distribution divided by the frequency of this age in the non-soldiers distribution. If a particular age is more frequent in the soldiers distribution then the descriptive statistics on the non-soldiers sample will be corrected for this higher weight.[21]

Furthermore, the comparison between ex-soldiers and civilians is conducted at two different levels. First, we compare the welfare or

**Table 6.10 Comparing welfare indicators**

|  | Civilian background | | Ex-soldiers | Testing the difference in the mean (F-statistic) | |
|---|---|---|---|---|---|
|  | All sites | Selected sites |  | Ex-soldiers with non-soldiers from all sites | Ex-soldiers with non-soldiers from all selected sites |
| Consumption expenditures | 85.87 | 83.88 | 86.09 | 0.00 | 0.21 |
| BMI | 19.85 | 20.32 | 20.18 | 1.84 | 0.69 |
| Land in hectares | 0.31 | 0.48 | 0.42 | 8.29 | 3.11 |
| Value of livestock (birr) | 319.65 | 460.31 | 285.86 | 1.32 | 37.07 |

human development level of ex-soldiers with those of male non-soldiers from all sites. The second and more appropriate one is the comparison with non-soldiers from the four villages from which most of the ex-soldiers come. The age-corrected weights were recalculated using data on the four villages only (see Table 6.10).

*Consumption expenditures.* In survey data, especially from rural areas, income is always underreported. As a result we use consumption expenditures as a proxy for income in order to measure and compare the standard of living of ex-soldiers and their civilian counterparts. The results indicate that the per-capita consumption expenditures of ex-soldiers was birr 86.1 per month. This figure is slightly higher than the age-weighted average per-capita consumption expenditures of civilians from all sites (birr 85.9) and selected sites (birr 83.9) in absolute terms, albeit the differences are not statistically significant. Note that these mean levels of consumption per capita per month are quite low – about US$16 per month per capita, and imply considerable poverty.[22] Ex-soldiers appear to be sharing the poverty of most of rural Ethiopia.

*Nutritional status.* As indicated earlier, we are using BMI in order to measure nutritional status. We found a mean of 19.85, 20.18, and 20.32 for all sites, ex-soldiers and selected sites, respectively. There is no difference among the group means statistically. Ex-soldiers are definitely not worse off than other male adults.

*Land.* Land is one of the most important factors of production in rural areas. Hence, for the reintegration process in rural areas to be successful, there is a need to make sure that ex-combatants have access to cultivable land. Its importance is considerable when ex-combatants lack the necessary skill to engage in non-farm activities, and equally when there is lack of off-farm employment opportunities in the rural areas and small towns in the vicinity. From our previous analysis we confirmed that ex-combatants in our sample have access to land or belong to a household which has land. This is likely to have contributed for ex-soldiers to have the same amount of consumption expenditures as their civilian counterparts.

Table 6.10 confirms this finding when comparing the amount of per-capita land holding of ex-soldiers with the other group. The results reveal that ex-soldiers on the average had 0.42 hectares of land, which is more than the average land holding of the non-soldiers from all samples. In this case the hypothesis that the group means are equal is rejected using an ANOVA test statistic with an *F*-statistic of 8.29. This comparison, however, may not be sensible as the majority of ex-soldiers belong to the sites where land is not relatively scarce. Consequently, we compared it with the average land holding of the selected four sites. We found that the per-capita average land holding for the four selected sites was 0.48 hectares, which is slightly greater than the average of ex-soldiers in absolute terms, though not statistically significant. From this one can conclude that there is no pronounced access problem for ex-soldiers in the case of Ethiopia, compared to other male adults. This may have helped them to have similar consumption expenditures and will also help them to be at least in the same position as their civilian counterparts in the future.

*Livestock.* In rural Ethiopia traditional coping mechanisms are crucial during bad years due to the absence of formal insurance and limited credit markets. Livestock is one of the relatively liquid assets in rural Ethiopia. It is easily used by households to smooth their consumption through sale whenever they face a fall in their current output. This implies that those with no livestock will be highly affected during non-idiosyncratic negative shocks. Furthermore, in many areas oxen are crucial in the farming system. Higher levels of livestock are therefore a clear sign of wealth, especially since few alternative assets are available for accumulation in rural Ethiopia.

In this regard, comparison is also more meaningful between ex-soldiers and their civilian counterparts from the four selected sites rather than with the total sample. The reason is that the majority of the ex-soldiers are from the sites with farming systems where the rearing of livestock is relatively important. The results indicate that the total value of livestock owned by ex-soldiers (birr 285.9) is lower than by their civilian counterpart from all sites (birr 319.7) and selected sites (birr 460.3). The difference as compared to the selected sites is statistically significant. This may be due to the fact that, while nurturing of livestock is a long-term phenomenon, ex-combatants spent their time out of their community. Hence, they did not have sufficient time to accumulate wealth in the form of assets such as livestock. This may signify that ex-soldiers are more susceptible to community-wide risks as compared to those with a civilian background. Years of absence from the community are likely to have resulted in an important long-term loss of wealth accumulation, compared to male adults at a similar point in their life cycle.

In general, the above findings as a whole indicate that ex-soldiers are neither better off nor worse off in many respects, except that they are less endowed with livestock, which is very crucial during bad years. Reintegration has apparently taken place with success, although their long-term wealth and vulnerability have been affected by the years of absence. But this reintegration is only relative to the rest of the community: ex-soldiers in our sample are as poor as their civilian counterparts, implying that they are sharing the poverty of the rural poor. Little benefit has been derived from their stay in the army. To the extent that one would have expected that better-educated adults could earn more, it appears that this higher education at present only serves them to get the same welfare as the relatively less educated non-soldiers.

### 3.5 Econometric analysis: explaining the (lack of) welfare differences

So far we have discussed the profile, assistance and some welfare indicators of ex-combatants using mean values. Here we will try to establish behavioural relationships. First we will try to identify individual, household and community variables that will differentiate ex-soldiers from others. Second we will try to estimate earnings function using a sample selection model.

*The characteristics of the ex-soldiers.* Section 3.2 presents some descriptive statistics on the demobilized soldiers. It is useful to go a step further and investigate in a multivariate framework the distinguishing features of this group. To predict that a male adult in the rural household survey is a demobilized soldier we used a logistic regression. This regression technique regresses the logarithm of the odds ratio (a ratio of probabilities) that an individual belongs to a particular group relative to a base group on a series of explanatory variables $X$, assuming the errors ($u$) to be logistically distributed. In our context we consider only two choices: being a demobilized soldier ($S = 1$) or not ($S = 0$) in the sample, so that the model can be written as:

$$\log(\text{Prob}(S = 1)/\text{Prob}(S = 0)) = X'B + u \tag{1}$$

Using $B$ as the vector of estimated parameters, the probability of an individual in the sample being a demobilized soldier can then be shown to be:

$$\text{Prob}(S = 1) = \exp(X'B) \cdot (1 + \exp(X'B))^{-1} \tag{2}$$

and the probability of being a non-demobilized soldier is:

$$\text{Prob}(S = 0) = (1 + \exp(X'B))^{-1} \tag{3}$$

In the interpretation of the results, marginal effects of each variable on the probability of an individual being a demobilized soldier are of interest. In this non-linear model marginal effects are not directly obtained from equation (1). While marginal effects on the probability of being a soldier can be calculated from using (2), we will focus on the marginal effects on the odds ratio per unit change in the explanatory variable. From (1) it can be readily seen that this (multiplicative) marginal effect is equal to $\exp(b)$, in which $b$ is an element of the vector of estimated parameters $B$.

Factors potentially explaining whether someone is a demobilized soldier can be divided into different groups: individual-, household, community- and regional-level characteristics. To be demobilized one had of course to join the army first. Joining the army could happen through two mechanisms: conscription and volunteering. In the data it was impossible to distinguish the two forms. Consequently, the variables chosen will either reflect factors which made it more likely that a person would have been conscripted or factors which may explain volunteering. However, as will become clear, some variables may have an interpretation in both directions. Nevertheless, since most soldiers in the sample were Derg soldiers, conscription is the most likely reason for being a soldier.[23]

Specifically, individual characteristics included are age and age squared (to allow for non-linear effects), marital status in 1989 and educational level. Household characteristics included are ethnicity – some ethnic groups may have been more targeted for conscription than others –

**Table 6.11**  **Factors determining being ex-soldier (dependent variable: log odds ratio being ex-soldier over non-soldier)**

| Explanatory variable | Parameter estimate (b) | Standard error | Significance level | Marginal effect (exp(b)) |
|---|---|---|---|---|
| Age | 0.257 | 0.065 | 0.000 | 1.293 |
| Age squared | –0.003 | 0.001 | 0.000 | 0.997 |
| Primary school (1 if completed and highest grade) | 1.419 | 0.312 | 0.000 | 4.131 |
| Junior school (1 if completed and highest grade) | 0.284 | 0.400 | 0.478 | 1.328 |
| High school or more (1 if completed) | –3.834 | 7.169 | 0.593 | 0.022 |
| Marital status 1989 (married = 1) | –0.395 | 5.265 | 0.136 | 0.674 |
| Household size 1989 (number) | –0.073 | 0.030 | 0.016 | 0930 |
| Amhara (1 if head is Amhara) | 0.410 | 0.485 | 0.398 | 1.507 |
| Oromo (1 if head is Oromo) | –0.169 | 0.554 | 0.760 | 0.844 |
| Southern (1 if head is one from Southern Peoples) | –1.470 | 0.585 | 0.012 | 0.230 |
| Tigrie (1 if head is Tigrie) | 0.430 | 0.576 | 0.455 | 1.538 |
| All-weather road? (1 if such road exists in village) | 0.180 | 0.415 | 0.665 | 1.197 |
| Distance to town (in km to nearest town) | –0.044 | 0.031 | 0.150 | 0.957 |
| Arsi (1 if village is in Arsi region) | 1.729 | 0.527 | 0.001 | 5.636 |
| Shewa (1 if village is in Shewa region) | 0.816 | 0.318 | 0.010 | 2.261 |
| Sidamo (1 if village is in Sidamo) | 2.620 | 0.552 | 0.000 | 13.738 |
| Constant | –7.277 | 1.239 | 0.000 | |

Chi-squared joint significance = 91.34.
Number of observations = 1936.
Number of demobilized soldiers = 106.

and household size. Community-level variables included are whether an all-weather road is available and the distance from the nearest town. Finally, we include some regional dummies to capture broader effects of regions – in some regions recruitment may have been more effectively organized.

The results are given in Table 6.11. The joint significance of the overall model is high, while several variables have significant results which are straightforward to interpret. The results suggest an increasing probability of being a soldier with respect to age, although it is non-linear. The probability of being a soldier relative to not being one is increasing until the age of about 39, after which it is decreasing (i.e. the log odds ratio reaches a maximum until that age). While completing junior or high school is irrelevant for the relative probabilities, the completion of primary school has a very large effect. The results show that the odds ratio for those who have completed primary school is more than four times as high as those for the rest. This confirms again the relatively high level of education of the demobilized soldiers. One reason may be that an individual needed to have at least some level of education to be allowed to enrol – literacy was supposedly a requirement. An alternative explanation may have been that those who had completed primary education and were not able to continue junior or high schools may have chosen to enlist in the army. Completion of primary education might have changed their attitude negatively towards agricultural activities, and joining the army may have been an alternative. It also may have been the case that the army used schools as a simple means to identify young males to join the army.

Marital status and household size in 1989 were used to proxy conditions in the household to which the soldier belonged around the time of recruitment. It appears that married men were less likely to enlist or be conscripted into the armed forces. Also, belonging to larger households – suggesting more dependants – decreases the chances of being an ex-soldier. Ethnicity does not appear to have been an important basis for recruiting or enlisting, with only some evidence of less recruitment in Southern ethnic groups.

Finally, of the community-level variables, the distance to the nearest town was significant at a 15 per cent level. A 1 kilometre increase in the distance from the nearest town reduces the odds ratio of being an ex-soldier by 5 per cent. The possible explanations are: (i) if there is a nearby town to the respective sites then male adults would have been more easily susceptible to conscription into the armed forces, say, during market days; and (ii) it could be easy for higher officials to enforce peasant associations to meet their quota as conscription to the national service was (especially at the end of the military regime) based on a quota system due to the lack of volunteers. Some of the regional dummies are also significant: particular regions appear to have been supplying relatively more soldiers. However, it is not clear whether this pattern is the consequence of a small number of villages in our particular sample, or whether it is a genuine regional difference. In any case, the evidence points to a very diverse pattern of the intensity of recruitment in different villages and the extent to which recruitment policy was implemented: as was mentioned before, in some villages there were no ex-soldiers at all, while in a small number we found the majority of them.

*Explaining welfare differences.* One of the main findings of the previous section was that very little evidence could be found for any differences in welfare between demobilized soldiers (and their families) and the rest of the population. This is despite the fact that, as the logistic regression showed again, there are important differences in age or education between ex-soldiers and other male adults. In this section we will explore whether we can identify any factors which may account for this. For example, it could be that the higher education pays for the ex-soldiers to earn some additional money, but they may lose some earnings from lower returns to land or from off-farm activities, e.g. due to fewer years of experience. To investigate this problem we will use the best proxy we have for household income levels, i.e. the estimated consumption per capita, and explore which factors determine these levels. The issue is then to see which factors have a different coefficient for ex-soldiers and non-soldiers.

A reduced-form model of income levels, proxied by consumption per capita, is constructed using different asset variables, individual, household- and community-level characteristics. In particular, we expect that higher income is linked to higher asset holdings in the form of land per capita, the value of oxen and bulls per capita and other assets (mainly other livestock). We also included household-level characteristics describing the available labour supply: the number of male adults, the number of female adults, the number of male and female children between 5 and 15 years of age (since children may contribute to income-generating for the household), the age of the head, the education of the head of household and the average educational level of the other male adults. The latter are measured by whether the head has (at least) completed primary education or not, and by the proportion of male adults who have completed primary education. We also included the distance to the nearest town and whether there is an all-weather road passing through the village. The latter are included since infrastructural links with the rest of the economy may be very important in explaining welfare differences: they are crucial public goods which could serve as inputs in economic activity. For example, roads give access to markets and therefore reduce transactions costs for sales and purchases, while they also reduce the costs for using public services such as health care.

Coefficients on these variables could be seen as a return to the particular form of human and physical capital, including public goods. To test differential returns to capital for ex-soldiers compared to non-soldiers, one could run two regressions, one for ex-soldiers and one for non-soldiers' households. To allow for a direct test we will use a nested version by including a set of inter-action terms for households with at least one ex-soldier and see whether they are significantly different from zero. We include one extra variable: whether the ex-soldier in the household has com-pleted education, to check whether the returns to education are at all different for ex-soldiers.

Finally, we may have an econometric problem, related to sample selection. The problem is referred to as a 'treatment' or 'programme effects' model problem. Essentially, if we run a regression to ex-plain welfare differences between two groups, and we do this by including a dummy (and interaction terms) for those taking part in the programme, we may create an endogeneity problem if par-ticipation in the programme is a choice variable. An endogeneity problem arises if the unobserved factors explaining participation in the programme are correlated with the unobserved factors ex-plaining welfare differences. The endogeneity creates non-consistent estimates. In our problem the 'programme' is whether an individual is an ex-soldier. Most soldiers may be conscripted but some may have volunteered; also, selection and conscription of soldiers may have been on some (for the researcher) unobservable characteristics, which have an influence on welfare differences – examples are physical and mental strength, commitment, discipline, etc.

To solve this problem we use a two-step procedure suggested by Heckman and Hotz. We calculate the probability of a house-hold of having at least one soldier using the logit model discussed above, and include it in the model. The way it is calculated is by assuming that recruitment of one member is independent of any other member of the household. For a household with three male members of the relevant age group the probability of at least one member being a soldier is the sum of having exactly one member, plus the probability of having two members, plus the probability of having three members. Let the probability of person $i$ being a soldier be $p_i$, with $i = 1, 2, 3$; this can easily be calculated from (1). The probability of having exactly one member is equal to

$$p_1 \cdot (1-p_2) \cdot (1-p_3) + (1-p_1) \cdot p_2 \cdot (1-p_3) + (1-p_1) \cdot (1-p_2) \cdot p_3.$$

Similarly, the probability of having exactly three soldiers in the household is equal to $p_1 \cdot p_2 \cdot p_3$. From these types of terms the probability of having at least one member as a soldier can be cal-culated for all families of all sizes.

**Table 6.12  Factors determining welfare levels (dependent variable: consumption per capita)**

| Explanatory variable | Parameter estimate | Standard error | Significance level |
|---|---|---|---|
| Constant | 88.960 | 9.379 | 0.000 |
| Land per capita (ha) | 20.572 | 6.088 | 0.001 |
| Oxen and bulls value per capita (birr) | 0.042 | 0.015 | 0.005 |
| Other assets value per capita (birr) | −0.003 | 0.007 | 0.711 |
| Male adults | 1.589 | 2.398 | 0.508 |
| Female adults | −2.138 | 2.015 | 0.289 |
| Male children between 5 and 15 years | −6.938 | 2.144 | 0.001 |
| Female children between 5 and 15 years | −6.671 | 2.259 | 0.003 |
| Age head | −0.635 | 0.182 | 0.000 |
| Primary school (1 if head completed) | 6.338 | 9.203 | 0.491 |
| Percentage male adults primary school completed | 17.854 | 8.934 | 0.046 |
| All-weather road? (1 if such road exists in village) | 40.823 | 5.053 | 0.000 |
| Distance to town (in km to nearest town) | 0.492 | 0.504 | 0.329 |
| Ex-soldier (dummy = 1 if ex-soldier) | −3.690 | 16.876 | 0.827 |
| Ex-soldier × Land per capita (ha) | 27.278 | 26.553 | 0.304 |
| Ex-Soldier × Oxen and bulls value per capita (birr) | 0.010 | 0.088 | 0.910 |
| Ex-soldier × Other assets value per capita (birr) | 0.002 | 0.050 | 0.664 |
| Ex-soldier × Male adults | 5.339 | 12.103 | 0.659 |
| Ex-soldier × Female adults | −11.106 | 12.197 | 0.363 |
| Ex-soldier × Male children between 5 and 15 years | −20.688 | 13.044 | 0.114 |
| Ex-soldier × Female children between 5 and 15 years | 1.842 | 9.205 | 0.841 |
| Ex-soldier × Age head | 0.575 | 0.860 | 0.504 |
| Ex-soldier × Primary school (1 if head completed) | −7.380 | 27.462 | 0.788 |
| Ex-soldier × Percentage male adults primary school completed | 34.023 | 57.059 | 0.551 |
| Ex-soldier × All-weather road | −36.260 | 22.817 | 0.112 |
| Ex-soldier × Distance to town (in km to nearest town) | −0.960 | 2.264 | 0.672 |
| Dummy whether ex-soldier in household has completed primary education | −18.274 | 58.682 | 0.756 |
| Probability of at least one soldier in household | −19.072 | 32.666 | 0.559 |

Adjusted $R^2$ = 0.153.
$F$-joint significance = 8.977 (prob. = 0.000).
Number of observations = 1194.

The regression results are presented in Table 6.12. First, looking at the terms for the entire sample, we notice expected signs on most coefficients, especially on the significant ones. More land and oxen has a clear and strong positive effect on welfare, while old heads of the household affect the earning capacity. The educational level of the male adults in the household is very important while there is also a very large effect on the presence of all-weather roads. In short, stocks of physical capital in terms of land, livestock and public goods and human capital in the form of education are very important for explaining welfare levels, as expected. Looking at the effects of being in a household with an ex-soldier, we first notice that the predicted probability of having a soldier in the household is insignificant – endogeneity is not likely to be an important problem. Further, we notice that almost all other effects are insignificant. The highest significance (11 per cent) is obtained by the variable related to the presence of an all-weather road. It is not clear what importance can be attached to this effect: it suggests that families with ex-soldiers cannot benefit as much from the presence of roads to earn income than others. This is remarkable, since ex-soldiers, by virtue of having travelled and having been in touch with more urban culture, could be expected to be better at some off-farm or trading activities. Clearly, this is not the case – on the contrary.

Still, the fact that the families of ex-soldiers cannot be distinguished from non-soldier families in this behavioural model suggests that the returns to their endowments are the same as those of non-soldier families. In other words, they are integrated in the local economy in the same way. This puts another interpretation on the findings related to their higher educational levels. They have indeed a positive contribution to their incomes from their relatively higher educational levels, but in Section 3.3 we also found that their livestock levels are lower. The lack of differences in their welfare levels is due to higher educational levels compensating lower livestock levels, so that in the end their earnings are similar to other families.

Recall also, however, that the lower asset levels in the form of livestock are most likely explained by having had fewer years of accumulation, due to missed income earnings for their families during their time as soldiers. If they had been using the returns to education for all these years, and given that their families did not have obviously less land, they could have been considerably richer now via the accumulation of high return assets. In fact, despite higher education, they are only just as well off as the non-soldiers. Their time spent in the army was – as ever – just a waste of time.

## 4  Conclusions

In 1991–92 Ethiopia undertook a demobilization of about half a million combatants. In this chapter we looked at the impact on the individuals concerned, their families, society at large and the economy. At the macro-level the picture is one of reasonable success. The whole operation occurred against the backdrop of important economic change, which resulted in a tight budgetary and labour-market situation. Nevertheless, the demobilization appears to have occurred relatively smoothly. Financially, a substantial part was financed by the government, later with additional support from several donors.

The effects of the demobilization on society were seemingly kept at minimal level. Security measures and a weapons-collection policy appears to have resulted in only sporadic and limited increases in insecurity in some areas. The effect of the reduction of the army on government finances has been relatively unimportant, especially compared to other shifts in the budgetary position, mainly due to a large reduction in government revenue during the period. Urban labour markets may well have had difficulty absorbing the urban ex-soldiers, since demobilization occurred during a period of general retrenchment in public-sector employment. In rural areas, potentially, vulnerability may have been high, although alternative local community safety nets may have been present. Overall, however, it appears that the actual impact of demobilization on society at large in Ethiopia has been relatively neutral, or at least limited: the economic, security or welfare consequences do not appear to have been very large.

This macro-picture has been supplemented by some micro-level analysis, using primary data. Some of the findings on the overall success of the demobilization programme appear not to be in line with the findings from the micro-data. Contrary to official policy, only two-thirds received assistance in terms of cash or in-kind help. Targeting does not appear to have been very effective and the amounts of support are very different across individuals. Nevertheless, the findings suggest that overall reintegration was a relative success. Both in terms of welfare levels and the factors determining welfare levels, ex-soldiers seem to be difficult to distinguish from the non-soldiers. However, ex-soldiers appear to have been much more educated than similar age groups in the sample and in the country as a whole. This finding is not confined to our sample. While education tends to imply quite substantial earnings in rural areas, for ex-soldiers these earnings are only sufficient to compensate them for lower asset levels in the form of livestock, probably due to having missed several years of potential accumulation during their time in the army. This micro-level evidence gives more meaning to the relatively successful picture of the demobilization programme and the relatively limited impact of the demobilization on society: ex-soldiers appear to have become quite quickly reintegrated in the rural areas, but integration means the sharing of the deep poverty of rural Ethiopia.

## Notes

1 For a further analysis of some selected microeconomic issues of demobilization in Ethiopia, see Dercon and Daniel (1998).

2 The fundamental cause of the 1974 revolution was the land-tenure system that encouraged absentee landlordism and the lack of political determination on the part of the imperial government to undertake profound political and economic changes. Different movements in the urban areas – of students, teachers, taxi drivers and the army – made a significant contribution to the downfall of the imperial regime, though the urban movement finally turned into a military dictatorship. In addition, the famine in Wollo and Tigray contributed to the final demise of the imperial government.

3 No overview report has been released. The reported data are based on regional reports, except Somali Region for which no data have been collected.

4 We are not able to compare with the same age group due to lack of disaggregated information from the 1994 census. One may object to a direct comparison between the educational level of ex-soldiers and the rest of the (male) adult population, since the age distribution of the ex-soldiers is quite different from the rest of the population. In Section 3, we will deal with this problem further. However, the educational levels of ex-soldiers are sufficiently high not to affect our conclusion: about half the male adults of the same age groups as ex-soldiers in the survey did not attend school, while this was less than a quarter for the ex-soldiers in the sample.

5 The Commission simply classified the process of demobilization into two broad phases: rehabilitation and reintegration.

6 Colletta *et al.* (1996b) used the word 'reinsertion' in lieu of 'resettlement' to differentiate the transition from military to civilian life from the physical movement from camp to community. Kingma (Chapter 2) argues in favour of 'resettlement'. Here we prefer to use the term 'resettlement'.

7 We do not have clear information as to whether the officers received the same type of assistance as the ordinary ex-soldiers. However, Colletta *et al.* (1996b) indicated that the urban settlers included the 'military elite' of the Derg; most likely the word 'elite' refers to the officers.

8 Note that the 6000 Derg ex-soldiers integrated into the ENDF and those who resumed their formal education at various levels are not part of the urban settlers. The figure, therefore, overestimates the number of ex-combatants who received assistance as a percentage of the total urban target group.

9 For the basis of comparison and method of measurement, see Colletta *et al.* (1996b).

10  Free health services are not special only to ex-combatants and their families. Others can also get these services if they certify from their respective 'kebeles' that they belong to the lowest income group. In addition, school fees are very low in Ethiopia.

11  Recall that there is indeed a low level of education of the ex-soldiers in an absolute sense, but not relative to the rest of the population in Ethiopia.

12  Using the former regional divisions, the villages are in Tigray, Wollo, Gojjam, Shoa, Sidamo, Gama Gofa and Hararghe.

13  The survey is also a panel survey, i.e. information is collected on the same variables over time, but this feature is not used in the present study.

14  The sample consisted of about 9000 individuals; 124 ex-soldiers is about 1.4 per cent of the sample. This is very close to the total number of demobilized soldiers as a proportion of the total population (about 1 per cent of the population).

15  Note therefore that the data on marital status all relate to the situation in 1994; not to the situation at the time of their recruitment into the armed forces.

16  These survey questions were asked in 1994, but referred to the situation at the time of recruitment. After their return, most (about 75 per cent) ended up being farmers or family farm workers.

17  There might be ex-soldiers who obtained more than one form of assistance.

18  The *F*-statistic is equal to 0.140.

19  See Chapter 3 for a discussion of possible indicators. We are forced to use a small number of indicators by the constraints imposed by data availability.

20  The Body Mass Index is weight in kilograms divided by height in metres. For adults above the age of 18 this index can be used as a measure for malnutrition. Values below 18.5 are generally considered evidence of some malnutrition, while values below 16.5 are rather dangerous. In the ERHS about 25 per cent of males and females are found to be malnourished with BMI below 18.5 (Dercon and Krishnan, 1997).

21  Since all soldiers are within the age group 15–60, all observations on individuals above this age are excluded.

22  For comparison, the World Bank (1990) suggests that US$1 per day per capita is needed to be considered non-poor. Using this definition about 80 per cent of the rural population would be poor. Dercon and Krishnan (1996) calculated a (substantially lower) specific poverty line for the sample used in the paper, adjusted to local diets and prices, and still found poverty levels of about 30–40 per cent of the sample.

23  During the late 1980s the fear of conscription was very high. In an urban survey of youth between 15 and 30 years of age, conducted in 1990, many households appear to have refused to mention that there were any men of this age group in the household. The result was a sample in which only 35 per cent was male. In the census of 1994 this figure was well above 45 per cent.

# 7

# 'Reducing Costs through an Expensive Exercise': the Impact of Demobilization in Mozambique

*Iraê Baptista Lundin, Martinho Chachiua, António Gaspar, Habiba Guebuza and Guilherme Mbilana*

## 1 Introduction

Within a few years of its independence – achieved in June 1975 as a result of 11 years of armed struggle lead by the Mozambican Liberation Front (Frelimo) – Mozambique experienced a new armed conflict. The new confrontation lasted for more than a decade and ended on 4 October 1992 with the signing of the General Peace Agreement (GPA) in Rome between the two parties to the conflict, the Government and the Mozambican National Resistance (Renamo). The reasons for the latter conflict are still to be fully understood. There is no consensus yet which explains it or draws conclusions, and politics in the country are still polarized.

Although impossible to measure, the destruction of the war has been enormous in terms of the loss of lives and devastation of infrastructure. These consequences will surely reverberate for more than a generation in people's hearts and souls, and in the price of physical infrastructure that has to be reconstructed at high costs. One of the most difficult recovery processes in Mozambique is dealing with the 'human instruments of war' – the combatants. Contrary to weapon systems, which can be collected and stored in armouries before being destroyed, soldiers have to be demobilized and – most importantly – reintegrated into the normal socioeconomic environment of their community. Reintegration of demobilized combatants into productive civilian life is difficult, not only because of the complex psychological and social transformations involved, but also because of the high material costs. It is an all-encompassing process, covering all aspects of life: satisfaction of material as well as psychological demands; meeting rational as well as spiritual needs; and providing goods and services as well as strengthening the infrastructural basis.

Interestingly, the driving force for demobilization and reintegration is assumed to be the need to reduce military expenditure in order to be able to reallocate funds to productive and social sectors. The paradox is that Mozambique is trying to reduce costs through a very expensive undertaking. The GPA was a result of the realization that the war could no longer be sustained by either the warring parties or society at large. The solution was to stop fighting and bring about a new political set-up where conflicts could be dealt with in a peaceful manner. Multi-party elections were held in 1994. Since then no significant political violence has been reported, despite clear political disagreements still existing between the Government and opposition. In spite of the apparent post-conflict political success, the war legacy of more than 90 000 former combatants requiring reintegration has since become a challenge to both the political leadership and society at large.

Demobilization and reintegration processes are not new to Mozambique. Between 1975 and 1978 they were carried out twice. First, demobilization took place in the enthusiastic spirit of independence from Portugal. Some freedom fighters[1] were removed from the armed forces, the People's Mozambican Liberation Army (FPLM). It was a time of the creation of the new army by injecting 'new blood' into that military institution. The government of the day 'did not have a clear and consistent plan and criteria' for demobilized people (Zacarias, 1993). The First Battalion stationed in Machava (Maputo province) was for example demobilized as a result of a mutiny in December 1975. Combatants had complained about their salaries; as a response the Government decided to include them in the demobilization.

The third demobilization, in 1994, was implemented in a completely different context and with different objectives. It was the result of negotiations and had strong international support for the demobilization and reintegration programmes. In the period shortly after the signing of the GPA it was widely expected that demobilization would free resources which could be diverted towards development and the social sectors. This was expressed by the use of the term 'peace dividend'. However, years after the official end of the demobilization, society is still struggling with the reintegration. This chapter attempts to assess whether there has been any 'peace dividend' resulting from the demobilization process in Mozambique. It does so first of all by looking at military expenditure during the war as well as the costs of the demobilization exercise. But, clearly, the benefits of peace could be much broader and deeper than that.

This chapter continues with sections on methodology and the nature of the conflict in Mozambique. The section on military expenditure during the war and the process of demobilization attempts to understand whether there has been any financial 'peace dividend' from the demobilization exercise. The section on human development outlines the circumstances that demobilized combatants found after demobilization, including the efforts made by the Government and international agencies to accelerate reintegration. It deals with the conditions in the communities of destination and settlement, in terms of job opportunities, land for agriculture or self-employment and human solidarity. The section on security deals with the effects of the demobilization and disarmament on crime and political instability in the country and the region. Our general conclusion is that the impact of demobilization, through the reintegration process and development of communities, is peace. The major 'dividend' achieved in Mozambique, is peace itself.

## 2 Methodology

This chapter is based on (1) information gathered from existing reports and studies on the demobilization; (2) information collected in the field, in open dialogue with ex-combatants[2] in various different urban and rural areas of the country,[3] and (3) a comparison of data and perceptions of different institutions and individuals who have been directly or indirectly involved in the demobilization and reintegration processes. The United Nations Development Programme (UNDP) has prepared a comprehensive report[4] on the reintegration programmes for demobilized combatants in Mozambique (UNDP, 1997b), accounting for programmes, expenditures and outcomes. The report describes the programmes, including the role of the international community. In order not to duplicate, we make use of previous studies, but aim to be more analytical than descriptive as regards the impact of demobilization.

Our own data collection in the field was done following a specially prepared guide. Interviewees covered a wide range of ages, gender, and social groups, as well as places of origin and (re)-settlement. We covered not only ex-combatants, but also many of their spouses and other community members. The 'listen-and-hear method' was used to capture the feelings of ex-combatants, since they were the ones who stand to benefit from the programmes. Their perceptions were important for understanding the difficulties in the reintegration process still experienced by some. Moreover they had a critical role in the process of maintaining and consolidating peace. Observation of daily rural and urban life have also contributed to this research: observing survival strategies at work, often through informal activities. Exchange of information with people working on similar issues and an open dialogue with ex-combatants and individuals involved in demobilization and reintegration support enriched our insights.

## 3    The context of the armed conflict in Mozambique

Portuguese colonies had a double dependency: from Portugal and from the centres of power that Portugal itself was dependent upon. During the wars of liberation in former Portuguese colonies, most Western nations either avoided an open position in the international fora or took the side of Portugal. The domain of anti-colonial struggle was therefore placed in the hands of the so-called Eastern European block. Some members of the elite who led the liberation struggle shared the opinions presented by the Eastern European States, about freedom for all, power to the people and, above all, solidarity. This was important for the elite as well as for the common people feeling oppressed by colonialism. Either because the elite really believed in the socialist ideology, or because they perceived its domain as the only way to achieve independence; they embraced the ideology and acted accordingly. Many of the elite had been educated by colonial or mission schools, and came in contact with the basics of the paradigm of Western thought through those ideological channels. Feeling oppressed, they joined a struggle to 'liberate the minds and the land'. In addition, aid for the struggle was part of a package, also comprising scholarships for individuals from colonized regions. This led to the formation of a group of elite with a model of the political universe in their heads copied from the model they became familiar with through their close association with Europe. Therefore the elite who liberated African colonies were formally educated by the colonial power and Protestant Churches, and their numbers were then enlarged by people trained by the socialist states. Thus the political elite had to make a compromise in taking sides after independence, and adopted the political system and the economic model which was to move the country towards socialism. Whether this was intentional or just a pretence is not important in this analysis. On the eve of independence a political environment was prepared for new states: the model was to be socialism, and the pattern for development a centrally planned economy.

In addition there are geopolitics. Mozambique is situated in a region that in 1975 was the bastion of apartheid. At that time Rhodesia and South Africa not only had governments led by a white minority, but they also had well-functioning market economies. In contrast, at independence Mozambique presented to the world a government controlled by a black majority, and introduced a model of development which was intended to lead to socialism in all aspects of social life. This did not bode well for a good 'regional chemistry'. Moreover the Mozambican economic model led to social exclusion within the country: the model may have been solid in theory, but in practice it excluded some social groups from the process of national reconstruction. For example, the socialist model excluded religions and religious people, the emerging bourgeoisie, and people who did not share socialist ideas and ideals. The expression of local culture was also questioned or prohibited. Many people and cultural practices were thus left outside the sphere of political and economic power. This provided a fertile social base for destabilization: those who felt marginalized in Mozambique became easy tools for destabilization – and actually promoted it in the end. Political conditions were created within and outside the region, and unrest was financed from the outside.

Eventually two sides emerged, aiming at different goals. First, the Government trying to develop the country: it implemented a development programme with the help of Eastern European, Scandinavian and a few other Western countries, such as the Netherlands. In addition, it received support from solidarity groups with a handful of people committed to the cause of socialism, all cooperating with personal expertise. Secondly, there was a movement that became known as Renamo, taking active measures to destroy the implementation of the Government programme. Renamo received assistance from the outside channelled via Rhodesia (before it became Zimbabwe) and apartheid South Africa. Those two sides became adversaries in an armed conflict in the late 1970s, a few years after independence.

The actual motives of each side may had been different from the above interpretation. Renamo for example justified its war as a struggle for democracy. We are simply reporting what we have seen on both sides, observing the reality during the war. The nature of the conflict, its genesis and development explains the structure of the programmes of demobilization, implemented with substantial outside intervention, under the 'umbrella' of the United Nations (UN). It may also explain decisions taken outside the sphere of power of Mozambique, such as why the UN was given the task of implementing programmes in the post-conflict period, the general elections, and 'political pressures and delays in programme planning for demobilization and reintegration' (UNDP, 1997b, pp. 6–8).

## 4   Military expenditure during the war and the cost of demobilization

### 4.1   Military expenditure and the costs of conflict

Following independence in 1975, the Frelimo Government intended to modernize and professionalize its forces – transforming them from a guerrilla group to a regular army. The lack of resources, however, forced President Samora Machel to keep a tight budget, which may have prevented large military spending during the first two years. 'The austerity measures that Machel imposed on the army were harsh and caused much dissatisfaction' (Berman, 1996, p. 12). Military spending witnessed a considerable increase with the Rhodesian raids into Mozambique as a response to the 1976 trade embargo of Rhodesia and Frelimo's support of ZANLA (Zimbabwean African National Liberation Army). The Government was forced to increase the army from the 1975 level of 10 000 men to 21 000 within three years. Defence became one of the top budget items (*Africa Contemporary Record*, 1978–9, p. C331), starting a long-term trend which different sources seem to confirm.

Berman (1996) estimates that in the second half of the 1980s military expenditure consistently used up between 40 and 50 per cent of the Government budget, excluding the Soviet assistance. Official figures show, however, that defence expenditure has consistently been between 20 and 30 per cent of the budget. Throughout the 1980s military expenditures were higher than those on health and education (see Table 7.1). They decreased their share after 1994. (Nominal increases are less relevant due to high inflation.) Despite the apparent lack of agreement on the figures, it is clear that de-

**Table 7.1 Military, health and education expenditure, 1985–97 (meticais, billion)**

| Year | Total government expenditure | Defence expenditure | Defence expenditure as a percentage of total | Education and health* | Education and health as a percentage of total |
|------|------|------|------|------|------|
| 1985 | 39.6 | 11.0 | 27.7 | 8.7 | 21.9 |
| 1986 | 51.6 | 12.4 | 24.0 | 9.8 | 18.9 |
| 1987 | 161.0 | 41.7 | 25.9 | 23.7 | 14.5 |
| 1988 | 288.5 | 58.2 | 20.1 | 41.5 | 14.8 |
| 1989 | 473.0 | 102.4 | 21.6 | 64.4 | 13.6 |
| 1990 | 692.8 | 136.0 | 19.6 | 96.1 | 13.8 |
| 1991 | 958.3 | 178.0 | 17.8 | n/a | n/a |
| 1992 | 1451.6 | 259.3 | 18.5 | 314.9 | 21.6 |
| 1993 | 2270.1 | 416.8 | 18.3 | 460.1 | n/a |
| 1994 | 4097.4 | 762.0 | 18.5 | 931.0 | 22.7 |
| 1995 | 5162.0 | 522.0 | 10.1 | 1148.0 | 22.2 |
| 1996[†] | 4724.0 | 712.0 | 15.0 | n/a | n/a |
| 1997[†] | 5027.0 | 718.0 | 14.2 | n/a | n/a |

*Source*: Banco de Moçambique, 1995, Table V.B.

* Education and health includes salaries, goods and services.
[†] Data obtained from Presidência da República, 1996, p. 38.
n/a = Not available.

fence has been a heavy burden for the Government. But it should also be noted that Government spending on health and education in the early 1990s was significantly higher than in the late 1980s.

The conventional concept of defence expenditure is state-centric in nature. It assumes that the security and defence demands of a state are met through official resources from the Government budget. This concept fails, among other things, to include large proportions of social resources outside the state budget that are drawn on in a situation of a civil war. For instance, during the Liberation War (1964–74), Frelimo had liberated areas where it organized not only social institutions, such as education and health, but also a commercial and transportation network. This implied that peasants of a region could produce more than what they and the guerrillas needed for subsistence. The surplus was exported or exchanged for other goods with Tanzania, the seat of the military camps. Through these means, weapons were probably acquired (Abrahamsson and Nilsson, 1994, p. 182). These are similar to the kind of military costs that Renamo bore during the armed conflict. It is widely known

**Table 7.2   Monthly wages for officers according to rank in 1991[6]**

| Rank | Wage (US$) |
|------|-----------|
| Sergeant | 46.06 |
| Lieutenant | 81.28 |
| Captain | 108.00 |
| Major | 178.00 |
| Colonel | 287.20 |
| Brigadier | 298.03 |
| Major-General | 327.13 |
| General | 352.22 |

*Source*: Despacho Presidencial No. 06/91, 23 May 1991, fixing the salary of military personnel according to rank within the FAM.

that Renamo sold ivory and other natural resources to pay for weapon deliveries. In addition, Renamo fed itself by taking food from the population – on a voluntary basis or by force.

The war was thus financed by society at large. Indeed, in a situation for instance in which a sergeant received less than US$50 per month (see Table 7.2) in the Government army and literally nothing in the Renamo forces, soldiers had to find other sources to meet their daily needs. Some popular accounts report that, apart from some goods which could be freely offered, soldiers took goods from the population by force.[5] These resources were used to sustain the military and the war but they are usually not accounted for in any analysis. A comprehensive assessment of the costs of the military effort in Mozambique should therefore add an estimated 40–50 per cent to the official military expenditures in order to account for resources taken directly from the society at large and for Renamo resources autonomously generated.

In assessing the impact of postwar demobilization one should also consider the general effects of the war. Society is the subject and object of the armed conflict. Hence, it is difficult to distinguish the costs of carrying out the war and its effects; and, of course, the pressure to end the conflict comes from both sides of the equation. In other words, even if hypothetically military expenditure has never constituted a serious burden for the state, the need for conflict resolution and hence demobilization could stem from the side-effects of the armed conflict.

As far as direct economic effects are concerned, estimates indicate that the armed conflict cost about 20 billion meticais, and indirectly the GDP was only half of what it would have been without the war (Hanlon, 1997). In the social sector 60 per cent of the existing 5886 primary schools were closed as a result of armed conflict. Only 500 health centres could provide services in 1985. More than 3000 small shops in the rural area were closed (Ratilal, 1990). Between 1985 and 1987 the number of inhabitants per health unit rose from 9753 to 12 980 (Ratilal, 1990). In terms of the human burden, hundreds of thousands of Mozambicans died as a result of the armed conflict; by 1989 about 4.6 million rural dwellers had been displaced; about a million had fled the country; and 250 000 children had been orphaned or separated from their parents (United Nations, 1995, p. 12). Roads, bridges and other physical infrastructure were destroyed, and production was dramatically reduced.

The whole society was involved in the war in one way or another, suffering its effects (death, scarcity, destruction, etc.). Minds were constantly focused on its reality – facing whatever was about to happen. In total, about 4.5 million people were either internally displaced or became refugees in neighbouring countries. At times all people suffered and felt like soldiers because of the political climate instilled by the war. The international community working on demobilization often had difficulty assessing the magnitude and the complexity of the process; what is actually going on is a social reintegration of the whole society.

Clearly, the costs of the armed conflict were much higher than military expenditure suggested, and most of them seemed to be outside Government control. Of course, with this broader concept the picture becomes more realistic, but a definite figure cannot be established: for most of the costs there are no data, and other costs are immeasurable.

## 4.2 Demobilization and reintegration support

The cease-fire in October 1992 was to be followed by a programme of separation of forces, assembly of all combatants in special areas, disarmament, demobilization and the creation of a smaller unified army. Forty-nine assembly areas and 199 non-assembled troop locations were agreed. In order to assist the demobilized combatants in re-establishing themselves into civilian life, and to avoid security problems during their (re)socialization, several support efforts were planned, ranging from financial packages to special training and information on employment opportunities. Those to be demobilized received severance payment, food and assistance with transportation to a place of their choice. Along with this, their

**Table 7.3 Number of demobilized and distribution of subsidies, by province**

| Province | Demobilized total | Renamo | Total money paid from the RSS and the Government (meticais, million) |
|---|---|---|---|
| Cabo Delgado | 6 772 | 313 | 22 438 |
| Gaza | 4 808 | 333 | 16 923 |
| Inhambane | 6 571 | 905 | 22 297 |
| Manica | 9 034 | 2 651 | 38 830 |
| Maputo | 3 901 | 313 | 16 138 |
| Nampula | 12 053 | 3 043 | 40 456 |
| Niassa | 8 357 | 1 182 | 28 089 |
| Sofala | 12 767 | 5 505 | 56 473 |
| Tete | 5 479 | 1 109 | 19 780 |
| Zambezia | 15 444 | 6 417 | 50 222 |
| Maputo City | 7 399 | 199 | 37 094 |
| No information | 60 | 9 | 269 |
| *Total* | 92 645 | 21 979 | 348 477 |

*Source*: UNDP (1997b).

weapons were collected. Each soldier was considered to be demobilized as soon as he or she reached the place of settlement.

The details of the demobilization were defined by the GPA and the Commission for Reintegration (CORE). The civilian component of the demobilization was under the responsibility of the Technical Unit of the UN Operation in Mozambique (UNOMOZ). The International Organization for Migration (IOM) transported them and their dependants to their destination. The programmes were supposed to start after the signing of the GPA. However, due to political differences, delays occurred. The Special Representative of the UN Secretary-General, Mr Aldo Ajello, arrived in Maputo in October 1992 with the first team of military observers but UN forces only arrived in 1993, and demobilization did not start until late 1993.

The exact numbers of demobilized combatants differ slightly depending on the reporting agencies. The figures provided by UNDP are believed to be the most accurate, since they are based on the donor's monitoring system, including the last payment made to the demobilized combatants in January–March 1997 (see Table 7.3). In total, about 92 890 combatants were demobilized,[7] of which 70 910 were Government soldiers and 21 980 Renamo fighters. Of the demobilized combatants 1380 (1.5 per cent) were women. The demobilized had a total of 215 000 dependants. Although there are no official figures of the percentages of ex-combatants who (re)settled in urban or rural areas, it is clear that the great majority resettled in rural areas, particularly of the ex-Renamo fighters.

The demobilization was placed in the hands of the Commission for Reintegration (CORE). As stipulated by the GPA, CORE was supposed to approve a package of programmes, including the Reintegration Support Scheme (RSS), to which several donors contributed. The local UNDP office was to implement the programme, with the Mozambican bank, Banco Popular do Desenvolvimento (BPD) making the payments to the ex-combatants in the districts. The major international organizations involved in the process of demobilization and reintegration of ex-combatants were: the European Union, GTZ, IOM, UNDP,[8] USAID (US Agency for International Development), and the World Bank. Involved in this operation were also a great number of governmental (bilateral cooperation) and non-governmental organizations. The major donors of these projects were Switzerland, the Netherlands, Sweden, Denmark, Italy, Finland, Norway, Spain, Portugal, Germany, the United States and the World Bank.

The Government of Mozambique, through the Ministry of Labour, was to take over project execution after the departure of UNOMOZ. Later, the Ministry of the Coordination of Social Welfare also become involved. More recently a National Commission for Social Reinsertion, attached to the office of the Prime Minister, has been created to take care of all people affected by the armed conflict.

A targeted approach was initially not preferred by the Government. It felt that demobilized combatants were only one of several groups of people in need. Nevertheless, due to some pressure from the international community, several major projects predominantly for reintegration of ex-combatants were initiated. Through the RSS, demobilized soldiers received subsidies for a fixed period of 24 months. Six months was to be the responsibility of the Government and 18 months of the international community. Payment began four months after demobilization. According to the donor community the economy was too weak to absorb so many ex-combatants in such a short period, but this scheme was important to the first period of the demobilized person's civilian life because it provided a sense of security and gave an opportunity to contribute to the household

**Table 7.4  Distribution of RSS salaries (in meticais) by rank**

| Rank | Monthly salary | Total number of recipients by rank | Percentage of total RSS recipients |
|---|---|---|---|
| Common soldier | 75 000 | 47 681 | 51.3 |
| 1st Lieutenant | 229 320 | 12 833 | 13.8 |
| 1st Sergeant | 149 940 | 10 367 | 11.2 |
| 2nd Sergeant | 114 660 | 9 330 | 10.0 |
| Captain | 352 800 | 3 982 | 4.3 |
| 3rd Sergeant | 88 200 | 3 177 | 3.4 |
| Lieutenant | 264 600 | 3 002 | 3.2 |
| 2nd Lieutenant | 176 400 | 1 073 | 1.2 |
| Major | 582 120 | 966 | 1.0 |
| Squadron Commander | 294 000 | 154 | 0.2 |
| Lieutenant Colonel | 687 960 | 148 | 0.2 |
| Company Commander | 485 100 | 67 | 0.1 |
| Colonel | 934 920 | 67 | 0.1 |
| Major-General | 1 058 400 | 18 | 0.0 |
| Brigadier | 970 200 | 13 | 0.0 |
| Lieutenant General | 1 146 600 | 7 | 0.0 |
| General | 2 000 000 | 2 | 0.0 |
| Colonel General | 2 541 100 | 1 | 0.0 |
| Total | | 92 888 | 100.0 |

*Source*: UNDP (1997b) p. 18.

income, thus making them part of the family. Monthly payments were equivalent to the basic pay[9] received by each soldier at the time of demobilization, for all but the lowest rank (see Table 7.4). The common soldier (47 681 individuals) received 75 000 meticais[10] per month.

From January to March 1997, UNDP supposedly made final RSS payments, namely a lump sum of 600 000 meticais (about US$52), to all ex-combatants regardless of their rank. This payment was made possible by an unexpected surplus in RSS funds, due to savings and the devaluation of the meticais. However, according to *Diário De Moçambique* (15 February 1997), there was 'a last payment almost with no candidates to receive it'. The problem was that about 1800 demobilized soldiers had lost their demobilization identity card, which prevented them from receiving money at the BPD branches. The money was indeed to be paid to every demobilized person, but it is still an open question how many ex-combatants actually received the last payment in 1997 (*Diário De Moçambique*, 10 June 1997; *NOTÍCIAS*, 11 June 1997).

**Table 7.5  Geographic distribution of Information and Referral Services (IRS) coverage**

| Province of resettlement | Total number of demobilized soldiers | Percentage of total | Number of demobilized soldiers using the IRS | Percentage of demobilized soldiers visiting IRS | Percentage of visits by province |
|---|---|---|---|---|---|
| Cabo Delgado | 6 772 | 7.29 | 549 | 8.1 | 2.2 |
| Gaza | 4 808 | 5.18 | 1 525 | 31.7 | 6.2 |
| Inhambane | 6 571 | 7.07 | 2 219 | 33.8 | 9.1 |
| Manica | 9 034 | 9.73 | 3 030 | 33.5 | 12.4 |
| Maputo | 3 901 | 4.20 | 1 622 | 41.6 | 6.6 |
| Nampula | 12 053 | 12.98 | 1 569 | 13.0 | 6.4 |
| Niassa | 8 357 | 9.25 | 1 290 | 15.4 | 5.3 |
| Sofala | 12 767 | 13.75 | 5 416 | 42.4 | 22.1 |
| Tete | 5 479 | 5.90 | 1 844 | 33.7 | 7.5 |
| Zambezia | 15 444 | 16.63 | 3 670 | 23.4 | 15.0 |
| Maputo City | 7 399 | 7.97 | 1 829 | 24.7 | 7.5 |
| No information | 60 | 0.05 | 2 | 3.3 | 0.0 |
| *Total* | 92 881 | 100.00 | 24 502 | 26.4 | 100.0 |

*Source*: IOM, UNDP/RSS from UNDP (1997b) p. 31.

Several other major programmes were developed to support integration, either by offering new marketable skills, or through direct funding. The Occupational Skills Development (OSD) project was implemented by the International Labour Organization (ILO) and UNDP to provide vocational and entrepreneurial training. Self-employment was the main aim of the programme, because few (formal sector) jobs were available. The project also provided tool-kits to ex-combatants and other people in need. Its approach was somewhat slower in starting up and had a smaller number of beneficiaries.[11] The Provincial Fund (PF) was a decentralized mechanism to finance local initiatives (employment, training, education, business start-ups). It was supposed to offer a 'quick-impact model' to facilitate the social inclusion of the demobilized in their communities and provide economic stability. OSD and PF were supposed to make a considered social impact, but were not as comprehensive as initially planned. The Open Reintegration Fund (ORF), with the primary purpose of creating jobs, emphasized different aspects of economic and social integration. The Information and Referral Service (IRS) aimed to be a link between demobilized soldiers and the programmes, by directing them to employment and training opportunities and promoting realistic expectations. As shown in Table 7.5, only a quarter of the demobilized benefited from the IRS. The IRS and PF

**Table 7.6   Direct financial cost of demobilization and reintegration support**

| Targeted projects and programmes | Cost (US$ thousand) |
|---|---|
| Government severance payment, transport and other benefits* | 26 045 |
| Reintegration Support Scheme (RSS) | 35 500 |
| Information and Referral Service (IRS) | 7 865 |
| Occupational Skills Development (OSD)† | 14 888 |
| Provincial Fund (PF) | 11 340 |
| Sub-total | 94 913 |
| Pensions for Demobilized Combatants‡ | 5 800 |
| *Total* | 100 713 |

*Source*: UNDP (1997b) p. 10.

* Including reintegration services in the assembly areas and transport home.
† Including tool kits and food-for-home ration.
‡ Figure refers to pensions given to demobilized combatants in 1996 (see Conselho de Ministros, 1996).

mechanisms, which supported each other, worked well when funds were available, but criticism of the PF was common regarding the limited funds available.

### 4.3   Costs of demobilization and reintegration support

The first bill of demobilization was US$26 million, which was paid by the Government as six months' severance salary worth US$22.5 million and the remainder by the international community for three months' food, a kit of production tools and seeds (Brito and Mussanhane, 1997). These costs were incurred before the soldiers were taken to the places of settlement. The total bill for the Reintegration Support Scheme (RSS) was about US$35.5 million (Brito and Mussanhane, 1997). The Occupational Skills Development project cost around US$14.9 million to train some 7700 demobilized combatants of which only 5 per cent are believed to have been employed as a direct result of the training obtained (Brito and Mussanhane, 1997, p. 6). The PF seems to have had a budget of US$11.3 million.[12] The IRS had some US$7.9 million to assist the demobilized to obtain information concerning job opportunities and legal matters in their new civil status (IOM, 1996b).

The overall costs of demobilization and reintegration support are estimated at around US$95 million (Coelho and Vines, 1996, p. 51) – slightly more than US$1000 per demobilized soldier. However, according to the Minister of Finance, an additional US$5.8 million budget burden resulted from pensions granted to demobilized combatants in 1996. Indeed, the effect of the pensions payment has been dramatic. In 1996 alone a total of 9856 pensions were granted. Of this figure, 91 per cent were to demobilized combatants. That contributed to the high proportion of 7 per cent of the government budget allocated to social assistance in general (Conselho de Ministros, 1996, pp. 2–3). It is striking that, despite this figure for pensions, a UNDP analysis found that, in 1996, 80 per cent of those eligible had not yet received their first pension (UNDP/RSS, 1996, p. 1). This suggests that the figure of US$5.8 million may rise dramatically, as more eligible ex-combatants start receiving their pensions. Therefore, it is clear that the actual costs of demobilization and reintegration can only be established after several years have passed; the Government will be paying reintegration costs for an unforeseeable future.

According to UNDP (1997b, p. v), the Government provided 11 per cent of the funds (US$10.4 million). The figure reported by the War-Torn Societies Project is US$22.5 million (Brito and Mussanhane, 1997, p. 20) demobilization support (six months subsidies to ex-combatants) from the Government, using sources from UNDP, IOM, GTZ, the Ministry of Labour and CORE. Altogether the international community provided US$80.6 million.

The picture of the demobilization burden becomes more complicated when one recognizes that the costs above are but a portion of the resources that the state and society at large are spending in order to cope with the demobilization question. This is confirmed by the findings of a study prepared by Creative Associates International Inc. (CAII) for the IOM, which shows that 68 per cent of the demobilized combatants tend to look to family, friends and traditional authorities for solution of their problems (CAII, 1996b, p. 5).

## 4.4  Reintegration

The primary objectives of the reintegration support programmes were to guarantee a minimum cash income, encourage the demobilized to stay in the district he or she chose, and 'keep them quiet' – contributing to the 'pacification'. From that perspective the programmes have been successful. From an economic perspective, however, they have been much less effective. About 71 per cent of all the demobilized were still unemployed in 1997 (UNDP/RSS, 1996). Also, in more general terms, it was found that, despite the internationally supported efforts, postwar reconstruction had not reached the remote rural areas where the majority of the people lived (Hanlon, 1997). As shown above, the ex-combatants were actually only a small proportion of the total group of people who needed to resettle. The economy does not seem to be capable of generating sufficient jobs. On the contrary, the structural adjustment programme is causing lay-offs. Thus family, friends and communities continue to provide for the subsistence of the demobilized. As an indirect effect the state will continue to bear political, economic, social and security costs resulting from increased unemployment.

In the process to 'transform' ex-combatants to civilians, the official reintegration programme did in principle take the poverty in the communities into account and provided goods and money to facilitate return. However, our field work shows little economic impact of that effort. Communities received people who had been absent for years (combatants, refugees and displaced people) with little outside help. The cash the ex-combatants received every two months, for two years, was an infusion that implied a revolution in several rural districts; however, it did not visibly solve family problems[13] or generate development. According to UNDP (1997b) the ex-combatants spent most of the cash subsidy in the district where they resided – mostly on basic utilities, housing, agricultural inputs, animals, and supporting small business. The opportunity to construct something bigger and lasting was lost because of fragmented planning or lack of will to think about development. The cash could have been better used for broader development programmes in areas where ex-combatants settled. Unfortunately, the 'mentality of emergency' was too strong and lasted too long.[14]

The cash infusion of US$32.4 million for two years into rural areas which had hardly seen money for more than a decade was a blessing for many. Half of the ex-combatants who were common soldiers received a monthly payment which, by 1996, was higher than the minimum wage. Part of the reason why this did not make a significant impact in terms of economic development was that the RSS payments were in bimonthly instalments, which made savings difficult. When asked whether they would prefer to receive the money as a lump sum, 62 per cent of the demobilized answered 'yes' (UNDP, 1996). The majority (59 per cent) said they would have used it to start a business or a project; 22 per cent indicated that it would facilitate setting up a new life and the start of the reintegration; 7 per cent would have bought material for the *machamba*[15] and/or animals. Smaller groups answered that it would have been safer and easier to build a house or to buy larger consumer goods. Another disadvantage of the phased payment was that the ex-combatants had to travel to the nearest bank to receive the money. Only 68 of the 128 districts in the country had a BPD agency. Therefore, 17 per cent of the demobilized had to travel outside their district to cash coupons (UNDP, 1997b, p. 22). These trips were costly, and owners of transport facilities took advantage of the situation. In addition, in the cities and larger villages, other possibilities existed: a considerable part of the money landed up in places of amusement.

Some of the support programmes used intermediaries (businesses) to create employment for ex-combatants. However, this produced problems in several cases. The identification of intermediaries constituted a major bottleneck in programme implementation, not only because of the intermediaries' capacity, but also because of their location and willingness to become involved with demobilized soldiers (USAID, 1995). They were often more interested in obtaining a project than providing implementation capacity. The problem of intermediaries using money paid by projects and not employing demobilized combatants, or discriminating against them in the place of work, was common and still reported in the press (Ângelo, 1997). A demobilized person in Cabo Delgado said '[Intermediaries] receive the money and improve their own business; [they] don't care about us.'

The reintegration support was pieced together rather than developed as a coherent programme from the outset (USAID, 1995, p. 62). On the part of some donors there was a reluctance to involve local sectors and the Government in the programmes (USAID, 1995, p. 7). Some decided to give financial support only to programmes implemented by international organizations or NGOs (UNDP, 1997b, p. 29). Poor coordination between local and international organizations or NGOs, and also among sectors in government, aborted good opportunities to contribute to sustainable development in rural areas and support the real reintegration of ex-combatants in their communities. The Government was aware of the problems, but many of its agencies were engaged in making a political peace.

We conclude that significant assistance came from the communities themselves, with little to offer in terms of finance and programmes, but with a commitment to survive and provide a better life for relatives or former strangers. 'We gave our daughters in marriage to ex-soldiers, so they could settle here with us and help to feed our children. They are our sons now, and are doing good so far.'[16] Seventy-one per cent of the ex-combatants never contacted the Provincial Fund or the GTZ's Fund (UNDP/RSS, 1996). Interestingly, UNDP's report (1997b) does not mention the role of the communities, but figures regarding the involvement of the demobilized in the programmes of the PF and the ORF clearly imply that somebody else was providing the support.

## 5 Human development: from military to civilian life

### 5.1 Conversion

In 1995, after the first general election that voted in the first multi-party parliament, the Government presented a plan of governance with a development strategy to consolidate democracy. The plan was unanimously approved by the new parliament. The policy objective was economic growth plus social development to attain poverty reduction. Other goals were to strengthen the judicial system, build an effective small army, improve security, and strengthen governance. The strategy was to restore productive activities, develop human resources, deliver basic health services with budgetary priorities aiming to increase the expenditures on health and education by 44 per cent in real terms. In order to make this possible, military expenditures were to fall by 36.7 per cent in real terms in 1995 to 2.4 per cent of GDP (Government of Mozambique, 1995). Conversion from the military to the civilian was also to take place at the more directly physical level. The Minister of Defence talked about transforming military buildings into rural education units because the new army would not be as large as before (*NOTÍCIAS*, 17 June 1997). He also talked about an appeal he had received from sectors of the civil society to use old military facilities for schools of higher education in provinces such as Niassa.

It should be noted that reconstruction had two sides: (1) rebuilding the physical infrastructures, and (2) restoring the social fabric of the society. The development process depended as much on social healing as on physical reconstruction. With the end of the war the military identity of the demobilized was to disappear – a problematic process because, for many, a military identity was the only one they had. Many combatants from both sides had been recruited through unorthodox procedures. Renamo used to kidnap people,

**Table 7.7 Demobilized[18] soldiers, by origin, place of military service and resettlement**

| Province | Born | Residence pre-army | Location of military unit | Registration | Resettlement |
|---|---|---|---|---|---|
| C. Delgado | 9.1 | 8.0 | 5.4 | 5.8 | 7.3 |
| Gaza | 6.7 | 5.4 | 5.5 | 5.1 | 5.2 |
| Inhambane | 10.2 | 8.8 | 5.3 | 5.4 | 7.1 |
| Manica | 8.0 | 8.4 | 7.9 | 7.9 | 9.7 |
| Maputo | 1.8 | 1.9 | 7.2 | 8.9 | 4.2 |
| Nampula | 13.7 | 14.6 | 9.7 | 9.8 | 13.0 |
| Niassa | 9.8 | 10.8 | 9.3 | 9.6 | 9.3 |
| Sofala | 12.1 | 13.3 | 18.2 | 17.2 | 13.8 |
| Tete | 6.9 | 6.1 | 8.2 | 7.1 | 5.9 |
| Zambezia | 10.1 | 19.6 | 14.4 | 15.1 | 16.6 |
| Maputo City | 1.7 | 3.2 | 9.1 | 8.1 | 8.0 |
| *Total* | 100.0 | 100.0 | 100.0 | 100.0 | 100.0 |

*Source*: UNDP (1997b) p. 12.

forcing them to fight through coercive methods. They were made to kill relatives and destroy villages where they used to live. With this behaviour, people became alienated from their social environment, far from families and communities. The method used by Renamo to make people transform their villages into 'desecrated castles' force people into the guerrilla army. Even after demobilization many would not return home, but settled elsewhere.[17] This may explain the differences between place of origin, service and resettlement reflected in Table 7.7.

In spite of the law for Compulsory Military Service, the Government at times did not do any better than Renamo. On many occasions special patrols used to be sent to specific places to 'recruit' people by force, picking up even those who had already served. The operation 'take out the shirt', forcing people to follow special units to centres of military training, was used for instance near the city of Beira in the early 1980s. The recruitment process was not uniform and the period of two years for military service, stipulated by law, was not respected. Many served more than ten years. The majority of those demobilized have grown up to become adults with 'death and destruction' as the highest goal (*NOTÍCIAS*, 28 April 1997, p. 3). Thus, most ex-combatants did not really have much experience of civilian life.

## 5.2  Rural areas

Reintegration in rural areas has been shown to offer more stability than in urban areas. Subsistence in rural areas is based on agriculture. Every family has the right to cultivate a plot of land, a right for the collective not for individuals. There are rules regulating the right of strangers to settlement and the use of land. Usually through marriage, but also with the introduction of a 'godfather' who answers for acts or attitudes of the newcomer, ex-combatants were able to settle and cultivate in rural communities. To open the communities and offer an opportunity to strangers to settle is part of a local system that by tradition strengthens the local capacity for social reproduction. These local traditions have indeed provided a very important base for settlement or resettlement, especially in rural areas.

The traditional work in rural areas – agriculture, hunting and fishing – does not require skills other than those that could be learned by observing. According to Coelho and Vines (1996) agricultural activities were probably seen as a 'secure ground' by those who did not know what other opportunities there would be. Many demobilized combatants started cultivating small plots (or put some of their relatives to cultivate), while searching for other opportunities. Since many had a family, the responsibility to ensure subsistence was considerable.

From what can be observed, there are no major inequalities between the host community and the ex-combatants. Similarities in the way of life and concerns about survival help to decrease the possibility of economic conflicts. Because land is community-controlled, access to land should no longer be an issue once the person has become a member of the community. In general, however, conflict concerning land is in fact a major issue in Mozambique at present, especially between refugees, displaced people and those who had stayed behind. Most of these conflicts have yet to be solved.[19]

## 5.3  Urban areas

In urban areas the situation is different. At present Mozambique is going through a transition, with economic, political and cultural changes. Following the rules of market economies, a process of privatization is on the way. Productive units end up in private hands. However, many new owners do not have enough capital or economic skills to care properly for the business. One of the first measures taken is often to lay off labour. Thus the economic situation is difficult, and the urban environment makes economic reintegration of ex-combatants even more difficult. Opportunities for reintegration through formal employment are virtually nonexistent. Apart from private security companies created after the peace accord,[20] self-employment and the informal sector generally form the only possible way. Still, these solutions often do not provide for all the needs of urban people, especially housing and food.

To overcome this difficult situation urban people have generally adopted survival strategies, in which social networks based on kinship play a major role. Although these strategies are similar to those in the rural environment, the situation in urban areas is however different, since there is no land to live off. They provide for a social network of individual protection – social or symbolic capital that opens doors. The initial capital embedded in kinship is good, but not enough. Therefore, people may 'take away'[21] what is needed from their workplace in order to survive, take care of the family and other members of the social network. They take bribes and misuse official resources to care for themselves and their kin. Often jobs and opportunities are given to relatives or close friends, but full employment is usually not possible (Baptista Lundin, forthcoming).

Data from fieldwork show that the majority of the demobilized fit into these networks. However, there is also a small group of ex-combatants settling in urban or peri-urban areas as a social group with a clear social identity of its own. They hardly ever search for integration in a social network based on kinship, disqualifying themselves for possible support. This group may be partly responsible for violence in urban areas and on inter-provincial roads, which tends to scare people with fresh memories from the war.[22]

## 5.4   Skills and education

As shown in Table 7.8, the level of schooling of the ex-combatants is very low. Table 7.9 shows that Renamo's ex-combatants had even lower levels of schooling than the Government's. In general, due to low levels of schooling, it has been difficult for ex-combatants to integrate themselves into productive life in urban areas. To become a security guard often seemed the only solution available for the majority. It has been estimated that about 5000 ex-combatants have become employed in the private security business (Brito and Mussanhane, 1997, p. 9).

Lack of formal training does not however mean that the ex-soldiers do not posses specific skills which are of use in times of peace.

**Table 7.8   Educational background of the ex-combatants**

| Schooling[23] | Number of demobilized soldiers | Percentage of total | Adjusted percentage |
|---|---|---|---|
| None | 26 434 | 28.26 | 31.79 |
| Primary – 4th Grade | 16 863 | 18.16 | 21.56 |
| Primary – no specification | 8 528 | 9.17 | 10.89 |
| 6th Grade | 12 057 | 12.98 | 15.41 |
| 7th Grade | 4 921 | 5.30 | 6.29 |
| 8th Grade | 3 087 | 3.32 | 3.95 |
| 9th Grade | 3 689 | 3.97 | 4.72 |
| 10th Grade | 534 | 0.57 | 0.68 |
| 11th Grade | 1 536 | 1.65 | 1.96 |
| 12th Grade | 127 | 0.14 | 0.16 |
| Superior[24] | 271 | 0.29 | 0.35 |
| Other | 185 | 0.20 | 0.24 |
| No information | 14 659 | 15.78 | |
| *Total* | 92 881 | 100.00 | 100.00 |

*Source*: UNDP (1997b) p. 13.

Members of ADENIMO (Association of Disabled Demobilized Soldiers) have complained that they would be better used in the process of demining. They argued that work to identify mined places in the absence of reliable maps could suit them well. After all, they said, they were the ones who planted those 'deadly toys' and were familiar with the concept behind the planting of mines during the war. Driving is also a skill providing opportunities. Drivers make quite a good living at present because transportation is profitable in rural as well as urban areas. In peri-urban areas the demobilized and their families combine petty trade with farming in order to survive. In rural areas farming is still the main occupation. Nurses, medical doctors, engineers and others with clear professions are almost all settled in the cities and are almost totally integrated in civilian life.

Much has been said about the lack of skills of the ex-combatants, maintaining that their skills are not of use in a situation of peace. This has created a stigma, a general feeling in society that any ex-soldier has little or no training. Even after training in one of the various programmes, it is difficult to have society accept the changed reality. Any former soldier is still seen as a potential security guard, nothing more.

The above picture indicates that literacy and good schooling may

**Table 7.9  Educational level of ex-Renamo fighters, compared with total number of soldiers demobilized**

| Schooling | Total group of ex-combatants (%) | Renamo (%) |
|---|---|---|
| None | 34 | 41 |
| Primary | 32 | 18 |
| 7th–9th Grade | 30 | 5 |

*Source*: UNDP (1997b) pp. 44–5.

make a difference with regard to economic and social reintegration. Training was indeed important for the demobilized, particularly for those recruited very young who had no civilian experience. However, it did not achieve the expected results in terms of the impact on the life of ex-combatants because the implementers did not take some important practical aspects into account. For instance, places of training offered the same type of course for a number of demobilized in the same or nearby areas and thus the beneficiaries could not use the acquired skills and actually worsened an already difficult market situation by offering more of the same skills. A limited number of trainees per region, focusing on different marketable skills, could have been a solution but this would probably be too expensive because of the required transportation and housing.

### 5.5  Child soldiers

Demobilization implied special problems for the so-called 'child soldiers', or ex-child soldiers. At recruitment 28 per cent of the demobilized had been younger than 18 (UNDP, 1997b, p. 14). Some combatants had been recruited at only eight years of age. Many reached adult life during the war. They were demobilized with little special institutional follow-up. For the group of child soldiers still under age, UNICEF started a programme with the then Secretariat of Social Welfare, the Mozambican Red Cross, Save the Children Fund and the International Committee of Red Cross to care for them because they were not recognized as soldiers and could therefore not formally be demobilized. A databank was established and the children were placed in special transitory centres. Posters with a photo and information on the child were displayed around the country asking for help to identify parents or other relatives. In less than six months eight hundred families had been identified.

When leaving the centres the children received a kit with clothes for themselves, *capulanas*[25] for the women in the family, and food for two months. Save the Children Fund followed up and monitored the development of their life inside the communities. However, this applied only to children who had been identified. Many children just left the army when the pressure to fight was no longer there, and very little is known about what happened to them after the war.

### 5.6   Disabled demobilized combatants

The number of demobilized who were handicapped is estimated at about 6000 (UNDP, 1997b). There is little special information about them. The database of the programme did not account for the handicapped as a special group to track. It is quite clear, however, that they faced special difficulties. There were no traditional taboos against being handicapped but if they were unproductive they might constitute a burden for their families or communities. Three-quarters of those interviewed by CAII perceived disability as a major impediment to reintegration (1996b, pp. 15–16). During a seminar on 'Disabled Demobilized Female Soldiers' in Maputo in August 1997, three problems were identified, common to both men and women: pension, prostheses and employment. Many disabled persons who had been demobilized had no pensions and those who settled in rural areas or provincial districts had difficulty contacting provincial authorities to help them solve problems. Lack of a prostheses made movement difficult. Local production did not meet the requirement, particularly because the number of mutilated registered was on the increase. Given the difficult employment situation the disabled often turned to begging or selling stolen goods. Demobilized female combatants who were disabled face difficulties in rural areas, especially those with no husband to share responsibilities for the house, cultivation and children.

From a humanitarian point of view disabled ex-combatants should receive special care and are entitled to special pensions. According to law a soldier is eligible for a disability compensation pension, if he or she is 'demobilized due to permanent, partial or total disability, as a result of a direct accident suffered while in military operations, or due to other types of accidents directly related to duties' (Decree 3/88, Art. 17, 25 July 1988). After the GPA new legislation established the right of compensation for all disabled combatants from both armies, demobilized under the process directed by UNOMOZ (Decree 20/94, 20 June 1994). The disabled ex-combatants also had access to the general reintegration support programmes:

38 per cent of the total disabled demobilized combatants benefited from IRS (more than the 26 per cent of the total number of demobilized persons benefiting from the programme); 10 per cent benefited from the PF and 2 per cent from the ORF (Open Reintegration Fund) (of the total persons demobilized 28 per cent benefited from one of the two programmes). In the vocational training programme, 8 per cent of the total were disabled.

The level of dissatisfaction among the disabled ex-combatants was high in spite of the reintegration support and the entitlement to pensions. Their main complaint was that they did not receive the promised assistance from the state, such as health care and housing (Brito and Mussanhane, 1997, p. 9). Between 1992 and 1994 there were several demonstrations by this group; for example they established road blocks to draw attention to their specific needs and problems. Such action was performed by a group of disabled demobilized, living without the support of their families, in former demobilization centres. By July 1997 the group had quietened down in spite of internal disputes within ADENIMO. The authority of its secretary was questioned and a new one had already taken over by mid-1997 (*Diário De Moçambique*, 30 May 1997; *MÉDIAFAX*, 2–3 June 1997).

## 5.7 Reintegration in the communities

In general the demobilized seek help not from the military institutions, but from within the local community itself. Family, friends and traditional leaders are called upon to help resolve conflicts and personal problems. The ex-combatants then, step-by-step, shift their focus from military to civilian behaviour. This is not to suggest that they have all broken their political ties; some do retain affiliations to political organizations.

A visible form of reintegration can be illustrated by looking at local social–cultural and sport organizations. The most popular organizations are religious and soccer associations. Once accepted as part of the community, and benefiting from the same civilian rights and laws, it is unlikely that a fellow would embark on violence against what can be called 'common good'. The relationship between the demobilized and the communities is usually one of constructive working together. In most cases this also applies to the relationship with the civilian authorities. In rural areas the demobilized receive their pensions from the local government offices. Conflict Resolution Teams have already been created by government officials, comprising the Ministries of Labour, Defence, and Planning and Finance. Among other things these teams are intended to act as flexible mechanisms aimed at resolving existing and potential crisis situations related to the demobilized. From the community's point of view, little resentment or hostility exists, which is partly due to some visible benefits provided by programmes such as micro-projects and the RSS subsidies.

In the provinces of Tete and Manica, fact-finding reports concluded that the demobilized were received as 'sons returning home'. This implies that the Ghandian norms of non-violence, which stress the need of living together with those you struggle against and of doing constructive work for their good, can be applied and, among other things, create a reconciliatory atmosphere.

Testimonies from the demobilized help us to evaluate the influence of local traditional mechanisms on the social reintegration of ex-combatants. A 25-year-old ex-soldier in Madal Nicoadala is reported as saying: 'When I came home after the war, my father took me to the house of a traditional doctor. That was done because in my area there is a tradition saying that "When someone leaves the military life, ... coming home, ... in the first place, ... before eating anything, ... your father has to take you to the house of a traditional doctor to treat your head, so it may stop going round as it used to do when in the army". That means a ceremony has to be performed, in order to slow down the rhythm [of] the heart as it used to beat when in the bush, in order to become normal again' (*NOTÍCIAS*, 28 April 1997, p. 3).

Such ritualized processes of reintegration in community life are performed with the help of a healer, even if it is private. The ritual includes three specific aspects. First is the treatment of the ex-soldier: a symbolic act where he or she reacquires a civilian identity and puts aside the military identity of 'a killing machine'. This creates the social collective perception that 'now he is a person again'.[26] This ceremony includes a 'cleaning' in the real sense, involving a steam bath and water with herbs. It is the reconciliation of the demobilized with him- or herself. The second aspect is the announcement made to the dead relatives that the 'lost' son is back home. This is followed by a ceremony to thank the spirits for their protection during the war which made the safe return possible. This is the reconciliation with the collective – the community. The last part of the ritual is the reconciliation with the spirits of the people killed by the ex-soldier – the 'encounter' with his or her victims. In this last part, forgiveness is asked for the wrong-doing committed during the conflict. A payment is made of money or goods asked for by the dead (through the mouth of the traditional doctor).[27] In some regions a collective meal is served to show the joy of reunion with family members in the community.

---

**Box 7.1  The importance of rituals**

The importance of the ritual for reconciliation can be illustrated by the example of a case in the district of Inhassoro in the province of Inhambane. In the province, a group of ex-combatants settled after independence, far from their area of origin. During the last conflict a commander had killed a traditional doctor. As the story is reported, no ritual was performed after the war, until one member of the group died, and then another, and another. A traditional doctor was consulted and attributed the death to the fact that there had been 'no reconciliation' and 'no healing'. Many had already died when the case became public. When finally a ceremony was performed, the 'spirit' asked for a child born from a family of an ex-combatant. In principle that child was supposed to be killed, but after intervention of the elders in a dialogue with the 'voice of the dead', the spirit accepted that the child be given to and raised by a relative. The spirit asked also for an amount of money and a baby goat to be sacrificed.[28]

---

Ceremonies are important in many situations in life, but to clean and be cleaned after killing – especially after an armed conflict – is crucial to uphold social order in communities where people live close together and are dependent on each other for survival. Often they are all relatives. In the period of independence such local rituals were often considered 'obscure' and were not carried out. However, this often led to a dilemma because people connected failure, bad luck, disgrace, misery, hazard or misfortune to the non-fulfilment of such cultural obligations. The psychological character of those rituals, and the cultural property it has to alleviate hard feelings, acquire a vital importance in community life creating social harmony.

Another important factor for social reintegration of the demobilized is marriage, especially in rural areas. A married man, or a man with a woman at his side, is viewed as respectable, particularly if children reinforce the relationship. Any mistrust in his actions disappears when he presents himself to the community as a 'family man' because it is presumed that no-one thinks of weapons or war. A man with a family is regarded as a full citizen, able to love and respect others, capable of giving advice, mediating and resolving situations of conflict.

## 6   Security

### 6.1   Demobilization as a security concern

Following the GPA it was clear that the cease-fire did not necessarily mean the end of the conflict in Mozambique. Termination of war must be understood in its complexity as 'one stage in the conflict process' (Massoud, 1996). An effective settlement depends on a variety of factors, such as (1) the interests and goals of the parties in the conflict, (2) the expectations and fears of combatants to be demobilized or to join the new army, and (3) the morale of those to be reintegrated, implying that they want 'no more war'. Possibilities of escalation and renewed hostilities remained.[29] This was evident by late 1992 and early 1993, and justified the deployment of close to 7500 UNOMOZ military personnel for the peace-keeping operation in the country. The size of the military operation was a request from the UN representative in Mozambique. Its acceptance can be explained by the influence of the 'Angola-syndrome' on the UN Security Council and the failure of other previous UN peace-keeping missions. Some argued that, from a strategic point of view, the force was too big and had too little flexibility (Brito *et al.*, 1995).

UNOMOZ recognized officially that 'demobilization was the most difficult and dangerous phase of pacification' (United Nations, 1995, p. 38) and a challenge for the UN's mandate in Mozambique. The process occurred not only under pressure of time, but also under pressure from soldiers: pressure of time stemmed from the deadline for the General Elections in October 1994, while the pressure from ex-combatants was due to a kind of 'war fatigue'.

Security problems had already developed during demobilization. One of them was caused by both sides and concerned the selection of assembly areas – 29 for Government troops and 20 for Renamo's. Timing and conditions of the assembly areas were the main problems. The majority of the assembled combatants were forced to remain in these locations much longer than they had expected, causing dissatisfaction. The soldiers' aspirations were not taken into consideration either by the Government or by the Renamo leadership. As a result the assembled combatants used the only method they knew: violence. Innocent people suffered through hostage-taking, blocked roads, seizing of vehicles, being threatened at gunpoint, through destroyed shops and houses, and through having their lives put at risk. The violent protests resulted in 317 incidents, of which 30 per cent were by Government troops, 21 per cent by Renamo forces, and 41 per cent from both sides (Gaspar, 1995). Among mutineers and innocent people, 28 were killed and 84 wounded and large material damage was reported (Gaspar, 1995; Welsh-Honwana, 1994; United Nations, 1995).

## 6.2   Formation of the FADM

According to the GPA, demobilization was supposed to be carried out simultaneously with the formation of the new army, the Armed Defence Force of Mozambique (FADM). However, it was difficult to find enough people to join the FADM. Whereas the GPA stipulated that the new forces required 30 000 men, with equal numbers coming from the Government and Renamo, only about one-third of this number volunteered for service. At the time of the General Elections in 1994, there were only 11 579 men, most of them officers rather than soldiers. By mid-1998 the figure was still only about 11 800.

To UNOMOZ it was clear that it was necessary that the General Elections could take place as scheduled – with the technical and human resources available (Gaspar, 1995). To many observers it was also clear that elections were the priority; remaining issues left over by UNOMOZ, such as the formation of the new army, could be dealt with by the new Government. However, the lack of trust and the slow deployment of UNOMOZ contingents led to a slow cantonment of the troops. The parties tried to gain strategic advantages. In this regard Renamo was frequently accused of the so-called 'dilatory manoeuvre' during the cantonment and demobilization processes, in order to gain the time needed to transform itself from a military movement to a political party. The Government, on the other hand, had an interest in speeding up the process to minimize the cost of keeping troops in assembly areas.

Following the elections, two acts have been voted by parliament, related to defence and security matters: the Law on Defence and the Policy on Defence and Security. On the basis of these documents it will be possible to reorganize the defence sector which had been prevented during the pacification process. The law concerning the recruitment of young people to military service – the Conscript Act – had however not been voted on by late 1997, constituting an obstacle to the renewal of military personnel. The new civil–military relations are still weak. However, the Minister of Defence – himself a civilian – has invited civil society to discuss new defence and security policies in the country, which is a significant innovation. So far, the FADM has been quiet. No incidents have been reported involving military personnel, a major improvement over the past, in particular the early phases of the demobilization.

### 6.3  Reintegration and security

Demobilization as such was carried out within a relatively short period of time, still in a climate of political and social instability. There was a constant threat that the peace process would be disrupted. The reintegration process was much less tense. According to some observers the demobilization of forces from both sides had eliminated the risk of escalation of conflict. However, a fear did exist that 'men of war' could emerge (Abrahamsson and Nilsson, 1994, p. 23), such as for example in Somalia. The exclusion of the child soldiers and of those demobilized from Renamo's army from eligibility to receive pensions is still one of the 'hot points' of disagreement between the Mozambican Association for Demobilized Soldiers (AMODEG) and the Mozambican authorities, and a potential source of violent conflict.

Given the socioeconomic profile of the demobilized, their reintegration was initially expected to be difficult and to lead to security problems. Half of the ex-soldiers had spent over ten years in the army, two-thirds lacked schooling or had only rudimentary education, and one-third had interrupted their studies at the time of recruitment (IOM, 1997a). However, there have been few incidents directly related to reintegration. Indications are that skills acquired in the military life are gradually becoming irrelevant. Community structures (family, traditional authorities, community organizations) have been (re)emerging or have been reinforced and are playing a considerable role in the resolution of conflicts, dissuasion from violence, in solving problems and disagreements and in providing social support (CAII, 1996b).

By and large, relations among civilians and ex-combatants have remained friendly, both in rural and urban areas. Although there have been criminal actions involving demobilized soldiers, it cannot be said that they are specifically disposed to crime or violence, at least not more than any other citizens facing social or economic difficulties. The negative image created at the beginning of the process with riots in the assembly areas has been transformed into mostly positive attitudes. However, it should be noted that accurate information on the identity of criminals is seldom available.

It was also feared that, once the money given under the reintegration schemes was finished, the ex-combatants would embark in large numbers on illegal activities, such as smuggling of small arms, selling weapons that had escaped state control, abuse of vulnerable individuals,[30] and attacking roads or pillaging goods in areas distant from urban centres. So far these worries have not proven justified. Since for most beneficiaries the subsidy was not the only source for survival, it is unlikely that the end of this payment would deeply affect their lives. Possibilities to turn to criminal activities still exist when there is no legal way of maintaining a certain standard of living. However, that is not a general trend. A study carried out in September 1996, using a so-called 'high-risk' sample,[31] reported that 'no evidence could be found in any visited areas, to link [the] demobilized to crime' (CAII, 1996b, p. 24).

Surveys made in rural and urban areas indicated that most of the demobilized did not consider violence as a valid option for resolving differences (IOM, 1997b). AMODEG's President – although often angry over the difficult situation of the members of the organization – emphasized the need for a constructive dialogue: 'We demobilized soldiers are very angry, because of the unsatisfactory fulfilment regarding our expectations. . . . Nevertheless, . . . we should search for solutions to the problem by means of a constructive dialogue. . . . We should be the major protagonists of peace, reconciliation, and maintenance of confidence among the Mozambican Family' (*TEMPO*, 17 November 1996). He feared that if they chose violence, their concerns would be misunderstood and misinterpreted.[32]

The possibility of erupting tension or unrest is nevertheless still there. Tensions could be a result of the so-called 'unfinished business', such as the delay of payment of pensions to eligible ex-combatants. There are already isolated cases of incidents. In January 1996, for instance, a group of men attacked a private bus, stealing money, food and luggage from the passengers, some of whom were wounded. Problems could also be expected from Renamo's former middle- and high-ranking ex-officers. With the end of the war very few of their expectations were met. At present it is said that it was the Mozambican people who won the war rather than the former fighters.

It is hard to distinguish the impact of demobilization on the security situation from more general changes in security as a result of the broader processes of democratization, economic liberalization and the required institutional strengthening. Several people in higher spheres of power fear the loss of privileges. Some look for easy and immediate economic gains in order to face political changes with (short-term) economic security, for example through corruption or trafficking in drugs or arms. Strengthening the police force to deal with internal security is therefore extremely urgent. In 1996 a former Director of the Criminal Investigation Police publicly aired the opinion that there was a risk of the police becoming dominated by criminals. He said that, given the vulnerability of the police force, the traffic of drugs and military equipment was already taking over the police force (*TEMPO*, 17 November 1996). It should be noted, however, that in Mozambique 'white-collar crime' is well organized and carried out by 'invisible' people, well placed in sociopolitical and economic spheres. It is thus highly unlikely that demobilized combatants play a significant role; but they could of course be manipulated to join these criminal groups, even if they only serve as cheap labour.

### 6.4 Disarmament and uncontrolled weapons

Demobilization in Mozambique also involved a disarmament component. Under the GPA the Cease-fire Commission was to collect weapons from the FAM and Renamo soldiers. A survey in December 1995 indicated that UNOMOZ had collected many weapons including a large amount of unexploded ordnance (UXO) (6 097 727 pieces of ammunition; 3677 grenades; 351 kg of mortar bombs) and 225 717 mines (Gaspar, 1995). At the same time 24 124 unspecified weapons and 1 263 424 pieces of ammunition and mortar bombs were collected and destroyed (Gaspar, 1995). The weapons collected under the UNOMOZ mandate were but a modest part of the total in Mozambique. No accurate numbers of uncontrolled arms in circulation exist. Like the landmines, it has been estimated that there are millions of uncontrolled small arms and light weapons in Mozambique, such as the Soviet-made AK-47s. These large numbers of weapons never were, or are no longer, in government control, partially because UNOMOZ gave too little attention to the issue. UNOMOZ was strongly criticized for not accomplishing the verifi-

**Table 7.10  Weapons collected from caches throughout the country, in 1996 (in units)**

| Province | Heavy weapons | Light weapons | Landmines | UXO[33] |
|---|---|---|---|---|
| Zambezia | 154 | 124 | | 412 |
| Maputo | 38 | 31 | 251 | 5 251 |
| Gaza | 5 | 314 | non-specified | non-specified |
| Inhambane | 5 | 360 | – | 450 |
| Manica | – | 427 | 734 | 46 906 |
| Sofala | – | 801 | 1279 | 70 110 |
| Tete | – | 150 | 130 | non-specified |
| Nampula | – | 22 | 101 | non-specified |
| Niassa | – | 23 | – | – |
| Cabo Delgado[34] | – | – | – | – |
| *Total* | 202 | 2252 | 2495 | 123 129 |

*Source*: General Command of Police, Statistical Data on Cache Weapons, 1997.

cation of arms depots and caches. UNOMOZ later admitted this by saying that this task was not fully carried out. According to Ajello the arms were not the danger at that time, because he was sure that the war was the result of a political decision. He argued that weapons were the instrument of war and not its cause (Ajello, 1996). Clearly the problems were not only due to UNOMOZ's failure because, during the long period of war (1964–92), weapons were easy to obtain. The warring parties were using lethal material without efficient mechanisms of control.

The mere presence of so many weapons now contributes to violence throughout the country. Their proliferation has become a concern for the people as well as the Government. But it is clear that under the new understanding of the concept of security (see Chapter 2), the threat is more one to human security than to the survival the state. Following up UNOMOZ's efforts, the Mozambican police seized and destroyed hundreds of caches of different types of military equipment throughout the country (see Table 7.10). People were generally well aware of the harm the weapons could cause when in improper hands. In several cases communities themselves indicated the existence of the caches.

The police also carried out a modest appeal to the population to hand over the guns they had in their possession; but the impact of this appeal was as modest as the appeal itself. The authorities have not tried to use incentive schemes to get people to hand in their guns. Given that the side-effects of the armed conflict are still present, some conditions for these schemes to be successful, such as an effective police force or alternative economic opportunities, have not yet been met. A buy-back programme has however been tried by the Christian Council of Mozambique, entitled 'Turning swords into ploughshares'. It is believed to have made a modest contribution to reducing the number of weapons used in crime in Southern Mozambique, as well as encouraging community members to report weapon hideaways (*NOTÍCIAS*, 25 April 1997, p. 7). The Council is expanding its activities to the North and Central regions.

It has been widely reported that many small and heavy weapons have been smuggled from Mozambique to South Africa where the crime rate is one of the highest in the world. Smuggling weapons has become a profitable trade both in Mozambique and South Africa, where organized crime syndicates are operating in other types of crime also, such as vehicle robbery and the drug trade. Under the Regional Cooperation Agreement of Police Forces, Mozambique is taking advantage of South African skills and facilities in combating crime. Both police forces have been engaged in dismantling weapon caches in Mozambique. In August 1997 it was reported that more that ten caches of different types of military armaments had been discovered in the provinces of Gaza, Maputo, Manica, Sofala and Zambezia. The police indicated that 324 arms, 103 landmines and 30 547 UXO (ammunition, anti-personnel landmines and defensive grenades) had been collected (*MEDIAFAX*, 8 August 1997). Since this is such a profitable trade it is fairly unlikely that it is mainly conducted by demobilized soldiers and officers.

In general, the dangers caused by the link between demobilization, lack of employment and the availability of weapons have been somewhat exaggerated in Mozambique. The information available does not show that the common citizen is likely to revert to crime when these weapons are available. The argument that the demobilized soldier from Angola and Mozambique 'has increasingly turned to banditry and other nefarious criminal activities' (Solomon and Cilliers, 1996), due to the easy availability of small arms and ammunition, must still be questioned.

Landmines pose a special security issue. The indiscriminate and irresponsible use of anti-personnel landmines over the past 15 years has created enormous physical and psychological suffering for many people. The number of landmines in the country is estimated at half-a-million to four million. The accurate number of landmines is probably not as important as the location of the minefields themselves which, in most cases, are not marked, resulting in the death of thousands of civilians and unaccounted injuries. The National Coordinator of the Campaign Against Landmines indicated in 1997 that landmines are victimizing 10 persons per week in Mozambique (*NOTICIAS*, 27 August 1997).

During the war, Renamo was accused of mining places such as cultivated fields, access paths, and areas near schools, hospitals, cattle-dips, water wells and factories. Moreover, the Government used mines for what they called a defensive strategy. They were laid to protect economic and strategic targets such as electricity pylons, bridges and pipelines. Mines planted by both sides are at present still killing civilians. In spite of the atmosphere of peace there is still appalling devastation. Mines also affect socioeconomic development in the country by disrupting agriculture and preventing the social and economic reintegration of vulnerable people. At the time of demobilization, mines were a serious danger to the transportation of passengers and goods, to farmers and to the large numbers of refugees returning from neighbouring countries, to displaced people and demobilized combatants returning to their places of origin.

The process of demining was one of the crucial actions to be taken immediately after the signing of the peace accord, in order not only to reinforce peace but also to reduce the side-effects of the war. The National Clearance Programme was created in early 1993 but the process of demining has suffered considerable delays. After the departure of UNOMOZ, demining was taken over by the Mozambican authorities and executed by the Mozambican Mine-clearance Organization (MOZMO), which is at the moment responsible for the demining process in the country. The Government also created a National Commission to deal with mine clearance. It functions at the national level to provide policy orientation and operational standards throughout the country. It undertakes its task with assistance of international NGOs, which operate with Mozambican personnel. The large numbers of people for this operation were recruited among the demobilized combatants.

## 7  Conclusions

Following the GPA in 1992, Mozambique went through several major transition processes. The entire demobilization process, the support programmes and the involvement of the international community are now coming to an end, but the country as a whole is still in a broad process of reconstruction and peace-building – at many levels, and with ups and downs. The complexity of the interrelated measures and processes makes an assessment of the impact of demobilization difficult. We also noted that accurate quantitative data are almost impossible to establish.

Looking at the 'peace dividend' in a narrow sense, at first glance it seems as if the Government has gained a considerable financial benefit. The official defence and security share of the government budget has decreased from the armed conflict levels of 40–50 per cent in the late 1980s to 15 per cent in 1996 and 17 per cent in 1997, representing 3.6 per cent and 3.5 per cent of GDP. It has been estimated that, due to the reduced number of soldiers in the new army, there was a real reduction of defence spending of 37 per cent in 1995 (Armiño, 1997, p. 56). However, the costs of reintegration support, including the increase in the pensions' burden of some 7 per cent of the Government budget in 1996, considerably reduced this figure. The financial dividend is further reduced when the costs of demobilization and reintegration of about US$95 million are considered, even when 85 per cent was externally funded. The recorded costs of the demobilization represent some 11 per cent of the 1996 and 1997 Government budget together.

The conclusion is therefore that the Government has not yet had any financial dividend from the demobilization process. Above all, the picture does not take into account the resources that society, namely relatives, friends and the local community, are expending as a result of the lack of means of livelihood of their demobilized fellows. The pillage and plundering has ceased and people can produce in peace in the rural areas, and travel relatively safely on the roads. Even so, at the level of resources, there has thus far been no substantial 'peace dividend', either for the Government or for the economy as a whole.

There has been a considerable gap between the aspirations and the actual accomplishment thus far. However, partially due to the demobilization and reintegration support, peace *is* being maintained, and that is an extremely important achievement. Indeed, the 'peace dividend' could be much more than merely the identifiable shifts of resources away from the military. As has been noted frequently in Mozambique, even if the costs of demobilization and reintegration are high, the 'peace dividend' is in fact the *peace* itself – providing an environment for productive and financial dividend-generating activities.

A significant impact caused by the demobilization has been due to the cash payment. After many years of non-monetary economy, money has given a new impetus to social life, especially in the rural areas. It has succeeded in 'keeping the demobilized quiet' and made their settlement possible in a crucial time of tension and unrest. But the money did not contribute significantly as a development stimulus; also the last sum paid in February–March 1997 did not have the expected development impact. The majority of ex-combatants had in fact already found ways to survive, mostly in agriculture. The payment was welcome but, as for the real impact, it was too little too late.[35] The inflow of money during the UNOMOZ exercise did have a considerable effect at the macro-level by speeding up inflation.

The central conclusion with regard to the reintegration process is that it has been much more successful in rural areas than in cities and towns, and that social integration has been easier than economic integration. The fact that the level of reintegration in rural areas is much higher is paradoxical since the support programmes mostly operated in cities and the capitals of provinces. Clear signs of rural reintegration are for example that (1) in rural areas it is already difficult to identify ex-combatants; (2) most community members do not view a person as a demobilized soldier, but as a neighbour; (3) even if community members know that a person is a demobilized soldier, they often do not know in which army he or she served (except in military areas) (CAII, 1996b).

Those not yet reintegrated are usually persons still living a military type of life in barracks, or those who did not know where their families were, or who started up a new family and were not willing to live in ex-communal villages. However, the rural demobilized still face serious problems regarding employment, markets to sell agricultural products, money to buy tools, and access to school and health facilities. Most of them are *forced* to rely on agriculture. In their own perception that is the reason for seeing themselves as not yet fully reintegrated.

As mentioned above, social reintegration has proved to be easier than economic reintegration, largely due to the following factors:
• limited employment opportunities;
• financial support was not enough to start a sustainable livelihood;
• lack of planning of the cash payments, including little advice to the beneficiaries on how to use the money;
• the family and community played the major role in the

reintegration (once living with a family, the demobilized person had more chances of improving his/her livelihood than otherwise);
- information about the programmes and funds did not reach many of the demobilized;
- the educational level of the demobilized was on average low; and
- access to some places was difficult due to bad roads and minefields.

The ex-combatants relied largely on the family, community, and the first RSS payment, particularly in rural areas. Initially, much of the attention had been on the responsibility of the Government and international organizations, but faced with the realities in the rural areas, both the demobilized and community members came to understand their own role. They are increasingly helping themselves.

The international community has made an enormous contribution. The country as a whole has benefited from humanitarian aid, rehabilitation of infrastructures and ready cash. Most sectors, communities and individuals have received a share. Less bureaucracy, better coordination among implementing agencies and the Government, and better knowledge of the country would however have avoided delays. Increased decentralization and a greater utilization of local knowledge would most likely have helped to solve local problems.

Ex-combatants are a vulnerable group for which society should care by providing them with the means to reintegrate themselves. However, they should not be regarded as a social group of their own for too long; the sooner they are seen to be members of the community, the better for themselves and society. After they have been settled, programmes should no longer discriminate, and support should be given to communities. Specific programmes still in force may actually raise tensions instead of decreasing them. The case of disabled ex-combatants should be viewed differently, because they are the most vulnerable group. However, they should be cared for as disabled people, not disabled ex-combatants.

The issue of weapon control and disarmament – including demining – still requires to be seriously addressed. Failure to properly disarm the combatants upon demobilization has led to a very large number of uncontrolled small arms in Mozambique. Weapons at large still put the security of everyone in danger. Mined roads and fields have affected the settlement and resettlement of the demobilized, refugees and displaced people. This again puts agricultural production and food security – and ultimately development – at risk.

# Notes

1  It is very important to note that, in the context of Mozambique, the term 'ex-combatants' actually refers to the veterans of the liberation war. However, in this study – for the purpose of consistency (see Chapter 2) – the term will also be used for those demobilized after the GPA in 1992.

2  See note 1.

3  Field interviews were carried out in 1995, 1996 and 1997, in Cabo Delgado, Niassa, Nampula, Zambezia, Tete, Manica, Inhambane and Maputo City. The last period in the field was in order to assess the impact of the lump sum paid to all ex-combatants by UNDP in January–March 1997.

4  The report was drafted by Ms Sam Barnes.

5  Some civilians interviewed confirmed that they had been victims of theft by the soldiers of Renamo as well as Frelimo.

6  Converted from meticais to dollars on the basis of the 1991 average exchange rate.

7  However, tables presented by UNDP differ in numbers of total demobilized (compare Table 7.3).

8  UNDP coordinated the RSS fully financed by nine donors: Switzerland, the Netherlands, Sweden, Denmark, Norway, Italy, Finland, Spain and Portugal.

9  The subsidies officers used to receive as a bonus were not taken into account.

10  Approximately US$10 in January 1995.

11  The distribution of kits to demobilized soldiers without training had greatly overestimated the numbers in the targeted group. Only 610 (9 per cent of the objective) were distributed to this category (UNDP, 1997b, p. 41).

12  Based on Brito and Mussanhane (1997) and GTZ (1996).

13  A Report of the War-Torn Societies Project (Brito and Mussanhane, 1997, p. 10) reports intense discussions between ex-combatants and their families, when they returned home without goods to distribute, which, according to tradition, everyone is supposed to do after a period of absence.

14  According to Aldo Ajello, the operation in Mozambique was a confrontation between two cultures: the 'culture of peace-keeping' and the 'culture of development' (1995, pp. 14–21). He defended the first approach. In retrospect, actions to implement the 'culture of peace-keeping' were encouraged and implemented successfully, and peace was indeed the final objective. The international community at large was not convinced that some development could have come together with peace.

15  A cultivated plot of land.

16  Traditional chiefs from matrilineal areas, with matrilocal rule of residence, during a workshop in Cuamba, Niassa, commenting on how they participated in the process of reconciliation. This is a transcription from a workshop held by the project 'Decentralization and Traditional Authority' by the Ministry of State Administration in 1996.

17  Some ex-combatants who settled in Zambezia and were interviewed by us talked about a 'clause' preventing them returning to their place of origin.

18 This does not include a group of 16 000 soldiers demobilized before the UNOMOZ operation.

19 Also economic reforms have opened up land to urban people and foreigners, which is a source of conflict with rural communities. The law approved in July 1997 states that the land belongs to the state and the communities have a word about their own rights. But the question is: Who is supposed to control the state at local and central levels and decide about the use of land?

20 Twenty-four private security companies functioning in urban environments, mainly in Maputo (22) and Beira, with branches in other provincial capitals (*MEDIAFAX*, 11 August 1997).

21 Others may call it robbery or corruption.

22 A study apparently carried out by MONAMO, and mentioned by Máximo Dias in a seminar held by the War-Torn Societies Project in April 1997, identified a group of former military commanders engaged in criminal activities in the City of Maputo.

23 Grades 1–5 = primary level; Grades 6–9 = secondary level; Grades 10–12 = middle level.

24 'Superior level' here refers mainly to military training for officers. However, some received skills that could easily be transformed to the civilian sphere and were useful to the development of a civilian society, such as mechanical engineering, becoming a pilot and telecommunications.

25 A peace of cloth married women wrap around the waist that functions as a skirt.

26 Words of an elderly man after a ceremony in which we were present on the outskirts of the city of Dondo in the province of Sofala in 1992.

27 From the same interview as the previous note, as well as from interviews with demobilized and members of communities in Cabo Delgado, Zambézia, Nampula, Tete, Manica and Inhambane.

28 Reported by Radio Moçambique (*Jornal da Manhã*, 28 May 1997). The group was due to get help from the provincial government to move back to its region of origin because members of the group were still dying.

29 Renamo violated the cease-fire after Day-E, taking over Memba and Angoche (Nampula), Maganja da Costa and Lugela (Zambezia), Salamanga (Maputo), Dondo and Savana (Sofala) and Chapa (Cabo Delgado). However, Renamo was forced to leave these places without major negative impact for the implementation of the peace agreement. At this time the UNOMOZ forces were not yet deployed.

30 For example, ex-combatants in need, those dependent upon drugs (drugs were used during the war and now form a problem among youth) or those who used to be under the orders of special commander units.

31 Many demobilized (re)settled in groups in areas of high political tension.

32 AMODEG has adopted measures to educate its members on the values of a culture of peace.

33 Grenades, ammunition, and lethal material.

34 In Cabo Delgado no caches of weapons were found. Probably the work of UNOMOZ was efficient where it began its work.

35 Interviews in the provinces of Tete, Manica and Inhambane in March 1997.

# Part III
# Conclusions

# 8
# The Impact of Demobilization

*Kees Kingma*

## 1 Comparing the case studies

This concluding chapter starts with comparing the findings of the demobilization case studies on Eritrea, Ethiopia and Mozambique (Chapters 5–7) and the demobilization in Uganda described more briefly in Chapter 4. It will subsequently look more specifically at the reintegration processes and the assistance provided. In Sections 4 and 5 it will discuss the development and security impact of demobilization. Lastly, it will reflect on the implications of the findings of this study. How should demobilizations be anticipated, and linked to other peace-building processes? And where could resources best be allocated to optimize their impact for sustainable peace and human development?

Although all four demobilizations occurred after the termination of a long violent conflict, the contexts and approaches were very different. Summing up the main characteristics, we see that Eritrea carried out the largest demobilization relative to its population (almost 2 per cent of the population) with little external funding. The environment was characterized by the need to establish new institutions, and state-formation in general. The demobilization in Ethiopia was by far the largest in absolute numbers, but with the least preparation and reintegration support. The exercise in Mozambique was politically the most complex, and largely managed by outsiders. It attained the most significant demilitarization. The demobilization in Uganda was the smallest in terms of the number of people demobilized, as well as compared to the population (about 0.2 per cent of the population). It received the largest external funding per ex-combatant and took place in the best economic environment.

As was found earlier for a broader set of demobilization cases, decisions to demobilize are always based on specific military, political and socioeconomic circumstances; but a decision to demobilize is usually based on one or more of the following six factors (BICC, 1996, p. 153):

(1) multilateral, bilateral or national peace accord or disarmament agreement
(2) defeat of one of the fighting parties
(3) perceived improvement in the security situation
(4) shortage of adequate funding
(5) perceived economic and development impact of conversion
(6) changing military technologies and/or strategies.

The demobilizations analysed here confirm this pattern; also the other cases of demobilization indicated in Chapter 4, such as at independence in Namibia and Zimbabwe, and following the peace agreements in Djibouti and Liberia, are due to one or more of the above factors – predominantly factor number 1.

In three of the four countries that we specifically look at, the government army was defeated and had to be demobilized (Table 8.1). We saw that in Ethiopia the defeat of the Derg army led to its total demobilization. Regarding Eritrea, the defeated army was demobilized in Ethiopia, but the victorious Eritrean People's Liberation Front (EPLF) also went through a demobilization, following independence. In the case of Mozambique the demobilization was part of a broad peace settlement in which the two fighting parties agreed to stop fighting, demobilize, and create a much smaller new national army, consisting of volunteers from both sides. In Uganda, armed conflicts had virtually disappeared several years before the demobilization was initiated, and a considerable number of soldiers of other rebel groups and of the army of the previous regime had already been absorbed in the new National Resistance Army (NRA). Compared to the other three, Uganda was exceptional in opting for first unifying the armed forces and only then demobilizing.

In all of the four countries factors 3 and 4 played a central role in the decision to demobilize. National security threats had changed and could be addressed with a smaller army. In each of the countries, all with per-capita incomes below US$600 and with limited capability to mobilize domestic resources, public funding was limited and needs for development spending high. Decision-makers believed that demobilization would free up resources for growth and development (factor 5).

In the case of Uganda it could be added that the government perceived the demobilization exercise also as a way to strengthen the remaining armed forces. The government's objectives of the demobilization were threefold: budgetary, social and military (Mondo, 1994). This would lead to a 'peace dividend' by significantly reducing military expenditures – and the reallocation of those resources to productive and social priority sectors. The social goal was to resettle ex-soldiers and their families in their home district and reintegrate them peacefully, productively and sustainably. The military objective was to retain a leaner, better-trained and motivated armed force. But seen in the light of Uganda's relationship with the international aid donors, it is clear that pressure from the group of large donors pushed the decision. On the other hand, Uganda made clever use of its good relations with the donors. One could even argue that the donors have assisted in modernizing its armed forces, by providing alternatives for many soldiers that were in any case not up to the quality required for a modernized force.

The way the war was terminated influenced the type of demobilization required, or opted for. In Mozambique, because the war was ended through negotiations and a peace agreement, there were two armies to be demobilized. This was one of the reasons why in Mozambique a sizeable and independent outside force was required to help conduct the demobilization. Eritrea and Uganda had to deal with one army. Ethiopia was somewhat exceptional. By far the largest group came from the defeated government army; but, since the Oromo Liberation Front (OLF) broke out of the postwar governing coalition, regrouped its forces and fought its former allies for some time, it was dealt with in a separate (much smaller) demobilization. In each of the four cases there was a relatively clear and agreed framework for demobilization. These institutional and policy frameworks established, among others, the logistical details of the demobilization, the specifics of the disarmament process, the conditions and management of the reintegration support and the overall coordination. The Rome Peace Accord created such a framework in Mozambique, including an agreement on the role of the UN Operations in Mozambique (UNOMOZ). This made it possible to overcome sensitive disputes between the formerly warring parties at critical moments in the demobilization process (United Nations, 1995). In Eritrea the framework was provided by the new government itself, which looked after its own fighters very carefully. In Uganda the government created with considerable donor support a separate

**Table 8.1 Overview of demobilization and reintegration support in four countries[1]**

| | Eritrea | Ethiopia | Mozambique | Uganda |
|---|---|---|---|---|
| Why demobilization? (main reason) | Liberation and recognized independence reduced requirement | Defeated army replaced by victorious forces | Peace agreement | Economic and military reasons |
| How did the war end? | Defeat/victory | Defeat/victory | Peace agreement | Defeat/victory |
| When demobilization? | Immediately after independence, 1993–7 | Immediately after the war: Derg, 1991; OLF, 1992–94 | After the war, as soon as UN force was in place 1994 | Six years after the end of the major war 1992–95 |
| How many armies? | 1 (EPLF) | 2 (Derg forces plus OLF) | 2 (Government forces and Renamo) | 1 (NRA) |
| Number demobilized | 54 000 | 509 200 (of which 22 200 OLF) | 92 890 (of which 21 980 Renamo) | 36 350 |
| Size of the armed forces in 1996 | 43 000 | 120 000 | 11 000 | 50 000 |
| Disarmament | At the barracks | Only partially controlled | In the camps by the UN (limited) | At the barracks |

| Demobilization/ Resettlement support | First phase: US$200–1000[2] per ex-fighter, plus six months food; second phase: about US$1830[3] per ex-fighter, plus one year food | US$66 transition allowance per ex-soldier (one time); plus food assistance to a maximum of 12 months (urban settlers received additional monthly stipend of US$24)[4] | 24 monthly payments per ex-combatant, plus food and transport; payments according to last salary in army; for common soldier about US$10 per month.[5] | Average value of demobilization and resettlement packages (cash plus in-kind) was about US$833 over six months |
|---|---|---|---|---|
| Reintegration support | Wide range of support activities organized by the government (Mitias) | About 70 per cent of all ex-combatants benefited from the different programmes | Wide range of mainly donor-supported reintegration programmes | Wide range of reintegration programmes |
| Costs of demobilization and reintegration | US$100 million plus large unfulfilled promises | US$195.5 million | US$95 million plus pensions | US$44.8 million |
| Cost per ex-combatant | US$1852 | US$384 | US$1022 | US$1232 |
| External financing | US$10 million (10%) | US$127.9 million (65%)[6] | US$80.6 million (85%) | US$39.9 million (89%) |

government agency, the Uganda Veterans Assistance Board (UVAB), to deal with the demobilization as well as with some of the initial support for reintegration. The Ethiopian 'Commission for the Rehabilitation of Members of Former Army and Disabled War Veterans' was established relatively shortly before the formal demobilization and had little time to prepare. It was nevertheless able to manage the largest demobilization quite efficiently.

The variation in the character of the wars (length, intensity and location) and their termination led to differences in the environment in which ex-combatants returned, and their expectations. The liberation forces in Eritrea had generally better relations with the population than the armed forces in Ethiopia and Mozambique. Particularly in the areas that had already been liberated for some time by the EPLF, these already received considerable support from the population. This showed also after demobilization, when the population perceived the ex-fighters as the liberators of the country. It should be noted, however, that in Mozambique, given the generally bad relations of Renamo and government forces with the general population in rural areas, they were unexpectedly well received. Some quite amazing stories of reconciliation feature in the chapter on Mozambique. In Uganda the reception differed between regions. The government made efforts to improve the willingness among the population to help the former soldiers reintegrate. Despite the different character and record of the NRA (currently called the Uganda People's Defence Force – UPDF), the history of Uganda in past decades has caused some fear of and disrespect for soldiers. To help overcome some of these perceptions, the UVAB conducted seminars to sensitize soldiers and communities in certain areas (Kazoora, 1998).

In addition, there were differences in expectations on the part of the ex-combatants. The ex-fighters in Eritrea usually did not want to rely on hand-outs or other support. They had won a liberation war of three decades. They perceived the establishment and development of their country also as their responsibility. They were in general very committed and disciplined, and they generally trusted their leadership and had patience when required. This showed clearly the heritage of the philosophy and atmosphere in the EPLF during the 'struggle'. The demobilized fighters in Eritrea were in this regard quite different from the soldiers demobilized in Ethiopia, who had basically failed in their careers as soldiers.

## 2 Reintegration

As we have seen, the countries showed considerable differences in terms of the circumstances and demobilization approach. Also the economic and political environments and the actual behaviour of the ex-combatants were generally different. Nevertheless, some general patterns appear. First of all, most of the ex-combatants found their way back to rural areas. In Mozambique and Uganda there are no estimates of the percentages of ex-combatants who (re)settled in urban or rural areas. It is however clear that the great majority of the demobilized in these countries resettled in rural areas and now participates in farming activities. In Ethiopia somewhat more than half of the ex-soldiers initially opted for resettlement in rural areas over urban areas. It is however not known how many might have changed their mind, and eventually stayed in urban areas. It is also not recorded where those that passed through the special programme for disabled ex-soldiers ended up. Eritrea is the exception. Although 80 per cent of the fighters had a rural background, the study shows that about two-third of the demobilized fighters had settled in and around towns. It is interesting to note that in Eritrea the tendency to live in the somewhat larger towns was strong among the female ex-fighters.

Given the weak economies of the countries in which the demobilizations took place, reintegration appears to have succeeded relatively well, especially in rural areas. In urban areas reintegration is much more difficult, largely because of less community support. Findings indicate that the ex-combatants in rural areas are often hard to distinguish from neighbours that do not have a military background. In Mozambique this was found through direct observation and interviews in several provinces. We should note however that very often family, friends and communities still provide for the subsistence of the demobilized. In Ethiopia data collected in a rural household budget survey showed that in terms of welfare levels – and factors determining welfare levels – ex-soldiers were difficult to distinguish from the non-soldiers. Being reintegrated does not, however, necessarily mean that they are doing well. The research in Ethiopia actually shows that the ex-soldiers are generally poor, but not significantly worse off than comparable civilians in the same location. 'Ex-soldiers appear to be sharing the poverty of most of rural Ethiopia' (Chapter 6). In Ethiopia the most significant difference between the ex-combatants and their comparable civilian counterparts in rural areas is that the returning combatants tend to own less livestock, which makes them more vulnerable to external shocks, such as droughts. The studies clearly show that one of the key factors for successful (social) reintegration was the acceptance and support by the community. This is shown most clearly in the study in Mozambique, but also in Eritrea and Ethiopia we can conclude that community and family support to the ex-combatants has been of importance. In Ethiopia the ex-combatants in rural areas benefited from the traditional labour-sharing agreement. In Eritrea it showed that support from the extended family was often a critical factor for success in setting up a business.

Reintegration obviously did not only depend on outside support. One should acknowledge the efforts of the ex-combatants themselves – and their direct families. No matter what type of support, they had to build up a new livelihood. Field-level research shows indeed that reintegration consists of thousands of *micro-stories*, with individual and group efforts – and with setbacks and successes. The returning ex-combatants in many cases also made very useful contributions to the community. Many of them had useful experiences in other parts of the country. In Eritrea the fighters actually started building the postwar society in the liberated areas before they took Asmara. The trust of the people and the good relationships can be considered as part of the important social capital.

A key factor in the reintegration has shown to be the general economic environment. The economic reintegration appeared to be slower in societies where it is already difficult to start an economic activity or find employment. The demobilization in Uganda shows the positive side of that coin: reintegration took place in an environment of considerable economic growth. The economy and society had already gone through the first phases of the postwar rehabilitation and reform. A consistent economic stabilization and adjustment policy and beneficial external circumstances, such as the price of coffee, had already started to pay off. When the demobilization was initiated the country had had a high economic growth rate for several years. This clearly facilitated the economic reintegration of the ex-combatants. Finding employment was still very difficult, but at least their communities – in most regions – were able to give them support more easily than in economically suppressed situations.

Not only are actual opportunities in the economy relevant, but also the knowledge about them. Ex-combatants – as new participants in the market – did not always have sufficient information about their options. In Mozambique most combatants had been away from home for many years. The experience in Uganda revealed that, for veterans who have been in the army and away from home for a long time, it was difficult to assess what they would be able to do and to identify what they would require for that purpose. It was useful for soldiers to be able to visit their homes before they were actually demobilized (Kingma and Sayers, 1995).

Land is also an important factor for successful reintegration in most countries. Although the evidence in Ethiopia did not show that ex-combatants had less land at their disposal than their civilian colleagues, the availability and accessibility of agricultural land was generally perceived as a critical factor for reintegration in rural areas. In Uganda, District Veterans Advisory Committees were formed to facilitate and mediate, among others in cases of difficulties in getting access to arable land (Kazoora, 1998). One of the constraints for the resettlement of ex-combatants is caused by landmines and unexploded ordnance (UXO). Large areas are therefore not yet available. In Mozambique, for example, it will take decades and a massive human and financial effort to clear the mines and allow all potential agricultural land to be used. As was mentioned above, the majority of ex-combatants found their way to rural areas; but not all went to the areas from where they had joined the armed forces. In Eritrea, men sometimes went to new areas because of land availability. Both men and women settled in special agricultural settlement schemes. A considerable group of female ex-fighters in Eritrea preferred to go to towns in order to find a job and/or escape the control of their family – and the associated traditional social norms. In Mozambique many of the ex-Renamo fighters resettled in other regions than the ones from where they joined the force, since they could not return to their own communities because of the atrocities they had been forced to commit there.

In the process of reintegration some other factors, such as rituals and gifts, also played a facilitating role. This is shown particularly in the case of Mozambique; but there are indications that similar things took place in the other countries, such as Uganda. In Mozambique some ex-combatants spent a good part of their initial demobilization money on gifts to village elders. That played an important contribution to being accepted in the village, becoming part of the 'social security' and sometimes being allowed to marry one of the young women in the village. The latter also had important economic implications, because in some regions land is passed on through the female line. Most ex-combatants had to undergo cleansing rituals in order to be accepted. These rituals have an important impact on acceptance by the community, as well as on the state of mind of the ex-combatants themselves.

For several reasons the reintegration takes time. After leaving the military, ex-combatants are going though a learning and adjustment process. Soldiers and guerrilla fighters are trained in top-down management, which is often different from the appropriate approaches for entrepreneurship in the civilian sector. They also lost a predictable environment with a certain social status – positive or negative. So they are forced to rethink their ambitions and capabilities. They had to find out what was possible – whether the sometimes over-ambitious plans they had while still in the army made sense after they arrived (back) in the village, town or city. In addition, large numbers of the demobilized suffer from psychosocial problems due to post-traumatic stress disorder. One of the practical problems occurring in some cases was that they were sometimes not accustomed to using (large sums of) money. In Eritrea the fighters of the EPLF did not use any cash during the struggle. Some of the ex-MK fighters in South Africa also had initial difficulties in getting used to a cash economy (Motumi and McKenzie, 1998, p. 196).

## 3　Reintegration assistance

In all four countries the demobilized combatants received a package at the time they were released – in cash and/or in kind. In Mozambique and Uganda that was followed by continuing cash payments in the district of settlement. There were also in-kind contributions at the time of resettlement, ranging from health services to food and roofing sheets. In Uganda the cash amount was the same for each ex-combatant, regardless of rank in the military. In Mozambique monthly payments were equivalent to the basic pay received by each soldier at the time of demobilization, for all but the lowest rank.[7] In Ethiopia the ex-combatants who settled in urban areas received more per-capita support than those in the rural areas. Beyond the demobilization and resettlement, several types of reintegration support have been provided such as agricultural implements, credit schemes, training and counselling (see Box 2.2). Temporary employment has for example been provided in the rehabilitation of infrastructure, demining or in emergency operations.

In the countries implementing demobilization and reintegration programmes, economic conditions and public finance were such that the activities could not be funded solely by national resources. Indeed, all exercises received some form of donor support from the outside, although the extent differed considerably. Table 8.1 shows that the financing of the demobilization and reintegration support efforts was for example largely domestic in Eritrea (10 per cent externally funded) and largely foreign in Mozambique and Uganda (85 and 89 per cent externally funded). Ethiopia finds itself in-between, with 65 per cent foreign funding. In Eritrea and Ethiopia the external funding per ex-combatant was relatively low: US$185 and US$251, respectively, while the external contributions per de-mobilized soldier in Mozambique and Uganda were relatively high: US$869 and US$1096, respectively. Since Eritrea did not receive much foreign funding for its demobilization and reintegration support, it has taken a large loan from the state-owned Commercial Bank. This is still a major debt to be paid. The Eritrean Government also still owes its ex-fighters much of the money promised.

Given scarce resources in all of the cases, policy-makers faced a dilemma of how to balance between targeted support to ex-combatants and support for other war-affected or generally disadvantaged groups. Some have argued that it is unfair that ex-combatants receive special support. In countries such as Mozambique they were the ones that 'created all the havoc' and made development and life impossible for others, while many other groups of people also suffered and needed to re-establish their livelihoods. Support programmes have indeed tried to strike a balance between dealing with the specific needs of ex-combatants and not creating discontent among the rest of their often poor communities and other war-affected groups – which could also jeopardize true reintegration.[8] The study in Mozambique (Chapter 7) found that it is hard to find any general development spin-off from the targeted support. A consensus appears to have developed in the development assistance community that special efforts for ex-combatants are necessary during the demobil-ization and resettlement, but that support in the reintegration phase should be as much as possible community-based and part of general postwar rehabilitation efforts. One could thus increase the 'absorp-tion capacity' of communities.

In the light of the above dilemma, and the fact that each de-mobilization is different, the studies presented in this volume seem to confirm an earlier argument (Kingma, 1998; BICC, 1998) that reintegration of ex-combatants might require support for the following reasons:

(1) Demobilized soldiers and fighters require support from a humanitarian point of view. Upon demobilization they are out of a job and usually away from their home. Thus, they require at least the provision of basic needs for some time and physical resettlement.

(2) In some cases it can be argued that the demobilized combatants have sacrificed several years of their life to liberate their country and to improve the development perspectives for their compatriots (e.g. the EPLF in Eritrea). In other cases some of the demobilized might have been recruited under pressure (e.g. Derg army in Ethiopia and Renamo in Mozambique). In those cases support could be justified as a compensation for forgone education or other investment.

(3) A third reason why it makes sense to support ex-combatants is because of their potential contribution to the general development in their community, and the country as a whole. Their skills and other capabilities might bring new economic activities and employment opportunities (see Chapter 3).

(4) Lastly, but in some cases most importantly: lack of attention for the risks involved in demobilization could jeopardize sustainable peace-building and human development. Without support, demobilized soldiers and guerrilla fighters might have great difficulties re-establishing themselves in civilian life, and frustrated ex-combatants may threaten the peace and development process by becoming involved in criminal activities or violent political opposition.

## 4   Development impact

This study aims at an assessment of the impact of demobilization. The case studies have shown that it is extremely difficult – if not impossible – to provide an actual quantification of the impact. The reasons are related to the complexity of the economic and social processes in the years following the termination of a violent conflict on the one hand, and on the other hand the lack of comprehensive and reliable data. Our ambition to make a broad assessment of one of the many postwar processes in particular (demobilization) – and to include secondary effects – makes us rely on less quantifiable indicators. It also follows that it is hard to compare between the country cases. We will thus also continue to critically ask ourselves whether we can distinguish between the impact of the demobilization as such and that of other policies and processes.

In this broader assessment of postwar development, it should first of all be noted that the wars themselves clearly had a very negative development impact. In all countries they obstructed significant development. During the wars – to varying degrees – transport was difficult, risks high, markets unpredictable and capital hard to obtain. Many small businesses suffered or disappeared. In the case of Uganda, however, there was little large-scale violence in the six or seven years preceding demobilization. There, as a result, the economic impact of the termination of the war was smaller at the time of – and right after – the demobilization.

### 4.1  Narrow peace dividend

Looking at the cuts in military spending over the relevant periods (the narrow 'peace dividend'), we see that generally substantial savings were made in the defence budget. However, only in Mozambique can we observe simultaneously significant increases in social spending. In Ethiopia we see that the peace did not produce a rapid peace dividend in the narrow sense. Military expenditure as a percentage of GDP did decline significantly from an average of 9.5 per cent in the final five years of the war to an average of 2.6 per cent in the first five years of peace. However, only very minor increases took place in government expenditure on health and education as a percentage of GDP (see Table 6.2). This was mainly due to a collapse of the revenue-collection system and heavy domestic borrowing in the last few years of the war. In Uganda, defence spending showed an overall decline over the period 1988/89–1993/94 in terms of its share in government expenditure (from 35.5 to 26.1 per cent) and in terms of its share of GDP (from 2.0 to 1.7 per cent). Over the same period, however, combined government expenditure on health and education rose only marginally in terms of its share in government expenditure or its share of GDP (Colletta *et al.*, 1996b, pp. 327–8).

In Mozambique – with considerable uncertainty about the reliability of the data – the official defence and security share of the government budget has decreased from the armed conflict levels of 40–50 per cent in the late 1980s to about 16 per cent in 1996–97, representing 3.5 per cent of GDP. Combined health and education expenditures increased from about 14 per cent of government expenditure in the late 1980s to a little over 20 per cent in 1994–95. In Eritrea, clearly, such a financial assessment is impossible to make, since during the war it did not exist and therefore did not have an official economy, or monetary defence spending. It did not even have cuts in the wage bill as a result of the demobilization, since during the war fighters were not paid any money. During demobilization, military personnel costs actually increased. In addition, even by 1998 no figures are known about how much the Eritrean army spends on its personnel or armament.

Although the countries had different kinds of financial debt, in all four countries the debt burden affected the government's possibility to increase social spending during the post-demobilization period. It is also quite possible that what appeared to be savings on military budgets never materialized as a contribution to a financial peace dividend, if after demobilization the same service was actually provided by another government agency. These instances have not been specifically identified in the studies, but it is quite likely for example that public health services in Uganda had to make additional efforts to treat demobilized soldiers, since many of them were sick when released from the army. This applies of course also for the 'costs burden' carried by their communities.

## 4.2  Broader peace dividend

A clear relationship between demobilization and declining military expenditure on the one hand and economic growth and development on the other is hard to find and quantify. However, high military expenditure before the demobilization clearly drew resources away from productive investment and had high opportunity costs. In addition, savings were considerably broader than only on military expenditure, because not only financial resources were used to support the war. In Mozambique, for example, much of the war was actually financed by society at large. Many of the combatants used to live off the people in rural areas, some even by stealing and plundering. So large parts of the rural population benefited directly from the demobilization. Since Renamo also used other natural resources to 'fund' its war, these non-monetary Mozambican resources also became available for human development after the war.

There was also a positive impact on the production side, although that is hard to tribute to the demobilization as such. It was more a result of the entire peace process that opportunities for production

**Table 8.2  Demobilization and reintegration costs**

|  | *Total demobilization and reintegration costs per ex-combatant (US$)* | *GDP per capita in 1993 (US$)* |
|---|---|---|
| Eritrea | 1852 | n.a. |
| Ethiopia | 383 | 153 |
| Mozambique | 1022 | 133 |
| Uganda | 1232 | 511 |

and trade in the formal and informal sector reappeared. Virtually all the authors of the case studies actually go as far as concluding that one should see the peace itself as the actual 'peace dividend.' No matter how we look at the peace dividend, we should recognize the costs of the demobilization exercises. Table 8.1 shows that in the four countries together about US$435 million was spent on the demobilization and reintegration of about 692 000 ex-combatants. As shown in Table 8.2, the cost per demobilized combatant were particularly high in Eritrea; but also in Mozambique and Uganda, compared to the per-capita income, large amounts of money were spent per ex-combatant, to get them out of the armed forces and to facilitate their reintegration into society.

The studies show that even the financial costs of the demobilization can be assessed only after several years. The policies on pensions for ex-combatants are sometimes not clearly defined, and due to change. In Mozambique the number of ex-combatants eligible to draw a government pension could still increase. In Eritrea the government was only able to pay initial severance payments. The promises that were made of paying each fighter US$30 per month of service might amount to an additional US$100 million – about one-fourth of the total government budget. The government also still has a debt with the state-owned Commercial Bank of about US$65 million.

Just like the savings on demobilization, the costs of reintegration are also not entirely financial and coming out of public finance. Often the communities and families had to initially absorb costs to help their family and community members – and sometimes newcomers – to start setting up a livelihood.

### 4.3  Employment

In all the African countries that recently implemented demobilization, levels of urban and rural un- and under-employment were already high before the ex-combatants entered the labour market.

In rural settings, however, the economy and society were usually more capable of absorbing extra labour. In previous sections we have seen that most of the ex-combatants returned to rural areas and are thus somehow coping in or around the agricultural sector. It is difficult to establish – or even define – what the actual unemployment rate is among ex-combatants. In Mozambique for example the ex-combatants in rural areas are generally coping; but still, nationally, the monitoring system shows that about 71 per cent of the demobilized combatants were still unemployed in 1997. In Eritrea in 1997, 24 per cent of the surveyed sample (28 per cent of the women and 21 per cent of the men) defined themselves as 'without a job'; 12 per cent had found employment; 11 per cent were participating in training schemes; and 53 per cent were self-employed. Some reasons why in Eritrea unemployment was higher among women were the lack of facilities to care for children during the day and a bias of not perceiving women as adequately skilled for certain jobs – even after training.

In Eritrea the number of combatants demobilized was the largest relative to the size of its population (1.7 per cent). In Ethiopia, Mozambique and Uganda these shares were 0.9, 0.6 and 0.2 per cent of the population, respectively. The ex-fighters in Eritrea were thus a relatively large share of the active labour force, with the largest potential to find the limitations of the labour market. But the total effort of society to reintegrate the ex-fighters was most likely stronger there than in the other countries. In some cases ex-fighters have even been given preference by Eritrean employers, as well as by foreign aid agencies.

In all countries the opportunities for formal employment were very limited, especially in the context of economic reforms and SAPs. Job opportunities in the formal sector were generally declining. Among the exceptions in the private sector were the ex-combatants hired by security companies in urban areas, particularly in Mozambique and Uganda. In all reintegration support efforts, finding or generating employment was a central focus, be it through training, credit, or direct advisory services (e.g. in Mozambique). Usually these programmes focused on self-employment, with some exceptions. In Ethiopia, for example, the government made specific efforts to absorb part of the demobilized into the public sector. Almost 40 000 of them found employment in the Ministry of Agriculture and State Farms. More than 15 000 were assisted in resuming their former jobs in the public or private sector. Eritrea brought many of the ex-fighters into the (new) public sector. The government actually saved costs in the short to medium term by delaying their demobilization. During that period they worked as civil servants, but only received pocket money. By contrast, in Uganda it had been agreed between the government and the major donors that none of the demobilized soldiers would be rehired into the public sector, with exceptions made only for qualified teachers.

### 4.4 Specific groups

Some groups were especially affected by the demobilization. Among them are the female ex-combatants, the spouses of ex-combatants, disabled ex-combatants and demobilized (ex-)child soldiers. The proportion of women in the armed forces that were demobilized was relatively low in Mozambique (1.5 per cent) and in Ethiopia and Uganda (3–5 per cent); however, it was as high as one-third in Eritrea. These female ex-combatants, as well as other women in war-affected communities, had usually acquired new roles during wars, and after the war were often expected by men to return to their traditional roles. This has created considerable tensions. A high divorce rate has for example been observed between ex-fighters in Eritrea. In the sample of the survey conducted in Eritrea, 27 per cent of the female ex-fighters were divorced or separated; 4 per cent were widows. These women very often had to raise children by themselves. Lack of child-care facilities was one of the impediments for economic reintegration of female ex-fighters in Eritrea. In Uganda, wives of returning soldiers, who came from other regions, were frequently not accepted by his family and their community. This led to enormous stress, economic hardship and often separation. With the exception of Eritrea, reintegration programmes have generally taken little consideration of the special needs of female ex-combatants and spouses of ex-combatants.

Special additional support is also needed for former child soldiers. Many of them had become adults by the time of demobilization. But special protection, care and assistance programmes were still necessary, especially for girl soldiers whose existence is often denied and who faced multiple problems after demobilization. Relocation to areas of origin was often more difficult for young ex-combatants. The problems of the ex-child soldiers could in some cases – e.g. Mozambique – still be some sort of time-bomb in society. The experiences of child soldiers have a profound impact on their social and emotional development. Their environment during the war inhibited the development of social values. At demobilization they often lacked parental care and access to school, and many of them, particularly the ex-Renamo fighters, are seriously traumatized by the brutal experiences they have undergone and the violent acts committed. They thus might still contribute to the risk that violence – at different levels – will repeat itself over the years.

Several demobilization programmes, such as those in Ethiopia and Mozambique, did not, however, contain special provisions for former child soldiers. After the NRA victory in 1986, on the other hand, Uganda 'demobilized' child soldiers from active duty but kept them in special primary schools, from which they could later join civil secondary schools and technical institutes. Counselling has been provided to those with behavioural problems. However, children with considerable adjustment problems were sent back for military training.

A large proportion of the demobilized combatants in Africa had a disability, one way or another. Many of them were also in poor health. Incidence of HIV/AIDS has been shown to be high among the demobilized in several countries, such as Uganda and Ethiopia. In all the countries concerned there were special arrangements for health care and special support to the disabled. However, they were still among the groups that had the most difficulties to reintegrate.

### 4.5  Human resources

Chapter 3 provides a detailed framework and perspective for the development and utilization of human resources in the context of demobilization. It argues that effective utilization, as well as the development of human capacities, play an important role in achieving short-, medium- and long-term objectives of demobilization, such as economic and social integration, political stability, social cohesion, and economic and human development. It also observes that planning of policies and design of projects need to be based on data on existing skills, qualifications and experience of the ex-combatants.

Initial findings presented in Chapter 3 and the subsequent case studies show that, due to time pressure, lack of funds and expertise, there has generally been a neglect of data collection on expectations and plans of combatants, and of analysis of skills, training needs and labour and goods markets. Little attention was paid to the content of the skills of the ex-combatants, and the potential of utilizing and developing those after demobilization. Human resource management programmes to support reintegration and human development have therefore been weak or absent.

Overall, the studies show that the educational and skills levels of the ex-combatants were low. This particularly affected the economic reintegration opportunities in urban areas. In Mozambique the education of the average ex-Renamo fighter was even poorer than that of the average ex-soldier. It should however be noted that, despite the low levels, in Eritrea and Ethiopia the average educational level of ex-combatants was still higher than that of other civilians. Indeed, despite little education, the ex-combatants did possess some additional skills. However, although ex-soldiers in Ethiopia appear to be generally more educated than the rest of population, they do not appear to have acquired a large number of useful business skills for successful self-employment. The Ethiopia study found that, although education generally tends to imply quite substantial earnings in rural areas, for ex-soldiers these earnings were only sufficient to compensate them for lower asset (livestock) levels. It should be noted that, in addition to low education and skill levels, the combatants released were in some cases, such as Uganda, the ones with more health problems than others. In Uganda many ex-soldiers died soon after they had been released from the NRA – about one-third due to AIDS (Colletta *et al.*, 1996b).

In all armed forces at least some additional training took place. In the EPLF in Eritrea, considerable training and education occurred during the 'struggle' – in all likelihood more than in the other armed forces. The overwhelming majority of the female ex-fighters were educated in the 'field'. Eritrea also had a scheme after the war through which it provided training to fighters, while preparing for demobilization. Fighters, predominantly based in ministries, could convert and complement their skills obtained in the 'field' for use in civilian life. The study in Ethiopia found that only a few acquired saleable skills in the armed forces which could be used in civilian life. For a small group of about 5 per cent of the Ethiopian soldiers who intended to settle in the urban areas the government issued skill certificates. These reflected some of the marketable skills in the armed force, mainly in terms of technical, electrical, driving and construction skills.

After demobilization, in all four countries training schemes were key components of most of the reintegration support efforts. Various types of training, including on-the-job training, vocational training and special scholarships, were provided. Some efforts were made to stimulate utilization of skills, through counselling and facilitation of access to previous jobs. In Eritrea about 17 per cent of the de-mobilized fighters have benefited from on-the-job training, and 11 per cent of the ex-fighters interviewed were at that time (early 1997) still undergoing some kind of training. Despite their training in the 'field', a lot of catching-up still needed to be done.

Training as such was not always sufficient to find a job. In Mozambique it was found that the special training schemes for ex-combatants were not catering very well for the market. Some were too concentrated in certain locations. In Mozambique it was also found that, even after training, it is difficult to have society accept the ex-combatants as skilled workers, because a stigma re-mains that ex-combatants have few skills. 'Any former soldier is still seen as a potential security guard, nothing more' (Chapter 7). The relatively low prestige of non-formal education and training is in most places affecting economic reintegration. In Eritrea particu-larly female ex-combatants faced difficulties in finding a job – even after training.

## 5  Security impact

The most important aspect of the peace dividend in the postwar situations studied was probably that people feel more at ease. Threats to lives and livelihoods have decreased with the end of war. Con-fidence of people in a more secure future is one of the basic conditions for investment and other entrepreneurial economic activities. Theor-etically, security and demobilization can reinforce each other. Improved security and security perceptions create an environment for additional demobilization, which in turn contributes – in a process of peace-building – to shifting resources towards human development and human security. Demobilization could in such a way contribute to addressing the root causes of conflict. But the other side of the coin is that security problems – real or perceived – might also reverse the process of demobilization.

The question addressed here is to what extent the security situation has changed as a result of demobilization. As indicated in Chapter 2, this could be asked with regard to several concepts of security: e.g. national, military, common, environmental and human security. The most relevant central concept seems to be the latter. In a way, demobilization exercises are a reflection of the shift of emphasis in security thinking from national to human security.

Measuring the security impact is complicated. With regard to the concept of national security, for example, much of it is based on security perceptions. Regarding human security some more useful and measurable indicators exist. Most of those have been presented in the previous section, since the concept overlaps considerably with that of human development.

## 5.1 National security

As noted earlier, demobilization is usually initiated as a result of an improved security situation. In terms of the national and military security impact of demobilization, it is first of all the continuation of the initial improvement which is critical to monitor; and to what extent did the demobilization strengthen the new security situation? Has it decreased tensions in the region? The answers seem to be mixed, and the questions are to an extent still open.

In the first few years after the demobilizations, in all four countries the answers would have been predominantly positive. In the case of Mozambique it is even generally agreed that the demobilization, together with the external support through UNOMOZ and its follow-up, was a critical factor in making the peace hold. At the time the demobilizations were initiated, the governments had changed their perception of the security threats facing their countries. After the demobilization it was found, for example in Eritrea, that the strength of the downsized new army, consisting of the best soldiers of the EPLF, was according to the study (Chapter 5) sufficient for the new security needs. The demobilizations also showed that the countries were concerned with their own development efforts. By reducing the size of the armed forces and military expenditures, the governments communicated the message that they had no military ambitions and wanted to use their national resources as much as possible for domestic human development. There were indeed efforts to present the demobilization as a confidence-building measure in the region.

It appears, however, that the reduction of the size of the armed forces does not necessarily generate an actual reduction of the military capability. Nor have the countries significantly improved the transparency of their military capability, such as openness about military expenditure. In addition, ex-combatants can easily be remobilized, and this is what happened in 1998 following the border clashes between Eritrea and Ethiopia. Indeed, the study on Eritrea already notes that a high percentage of the demobilized fighters can be considered as reserves. Only in Mozambique can the demobilization clearly be perceived as part of a genuine process of demilitarization. Although this country has on paper decided to reintroduce a conscription system, it appears for the foreseeable future unable to finance an actual call-up.

Recent developments in 1998 – about five years after the demobilization exercises had been initiated – make a positive outcome of the demobilization in conventional security terms more problematic. The fighting between Eritrea and Ethiopia in May–June 1998 took place after the completion of the case studies, but it does provide some additional insights. This outbreak of – for many unexpected – violence is too recent and complex to analyse here. The direct trigger was a dispute about a part of the border between the two countries; but the outbreak, and the subsequent difficulties in finding a diplomatic solution, show that it is hard to argue that the demobilization as such decreased regional tensions. A dramatic process of rearmament and remobilization in both countries followed the outbreak. The threat of a full-scale war between the two countries still exists, and it has been reported that on both sides large numbers of demobilized combatants have been brought back into the national armies. For the current leaders in the two countries, the military option clearly still ranks very high on the list of ways of resolving conflicts. In this light we might conclude that the demobilizations in Eritrea and Ethiopia were more part of a postwar adjustment than of a shift towards sustainable demilitarization and human security.

In Uganda also the security situation has deteriorated over recent years, caused by internal and external factors. Again, as with the conflict in the Horn of Africa, there are too many facets to do justice to the complexity of these security issues; but from the perspective of the demobilization we can note that, first of all, the demobilization was quite clearly also part of a military reform exercise. A modernized army with better equipment, skills, information and higher wages could as such potentially improve national security. However, even with a smaller but modernized army the government could not prevent or non-violently resolve new conflicts, and might turn again to increasing its military spending. Second, the long-term option that the internal conflict in Uganda could be managed and resolved through increased government spending in the disadvantaged regions concerned, has not (yet) materialized.

As a result of the increased military spending in Uganda, a large part of the donor community found itself in a difficult position. They had agreed with the Ugandan government to support the demobilization and reintegration exercise under the condition that it would be a permanent reduction in the level of forces, which would lead to a reduction in the level of military spending. However, around the termination of the official demobilization, political problems and violence in the north of the country increased, and the government believed that the military option was the only way to deal with them. It argued that it could not sit back and see its nationals being 'butchered'. Serious discussions took place between the government and the donors. However, eventually the latter could only accept the government's decision, which implied re-recruiting soldiers and increasing military spending.

More recently – and after the assessment of the development impact of the demobilization – Uganda has increasingly involved itself in the conflict in the Democratic Republic of Congo. It is again hard to analyse how these security issues relate to the demobilization in Uganda; but in any case, to be able to call demobilization in Uganda successful – even if settlements are made with groups in the north – depends on a peace process in the Democratic Republic of Congo, Rwanda as well as in – and with – Sudan.

In Mozambique the situation is more positive at the level of national security. There are certainly problems of violent crime, including linkages with trans-national crime. As will be elaborated below, weaknesses in the disarmament of the combatants have contributed to a large number of uncontrolled weapons in the country and the region, but as part of the total peace process the demobilization has on the whole contributed to open and friendly relations with its neighbours. One of the few risks of erupting tension might be due to discrimination against former Renamo fighters.

Although sometimes limited, the demobilizations all took place simultaneously with improvements in civil–military relations, including a strengthening of civilian control over the military. There are indications that the demobilizations have generally increased the likelihood and ability of groups and individuals to deal with (potential) conflicts non-violently. The Eritrea study (Chapter 5) argues that ex-fighters there had a stabilizing influence on other groups of society. Surveys in rural and urban areas in Mozambique indicated (Chapter 7) that most of the demobilized did not consider violence as a valid option for resolving differences.

An additional threat to regional security after demobilization is caused by ex-combatants trying to apply their skills elsewhere. The use of ex-soldiers as mercenaries in official and private armies is increasing in Africa. Many of these people originate from armies that have recently contracted. Our case studies have not provided evidence in this direction; but it cannot be excluded, given evidence found elsewhere. There are reports that Eritrean elite troops – demobilized or not – are providing 'services' elsewhere in Africa. In Southern Africa there is more firm evidence. The South African firm, 'Executive Outcomes', is known to have provided mercenaries to several African countries and to employ mostly ex-members of the former SADF.

## 5.2   Human security

In addition to the human development indicators, such as social spending and employment trends, presented in Section 4, the crime rate is a relevant indicator for human security. It is however hard to distinguish the impact of demobilization on the security situation from the impact of the broader processes of economic reform and social change. The general weakness of the state, for example in Mozambique, makes it difficult to adequately protect people from the direct and indirect effects of new security threats, such as trafficking of arms and drugs. It takes considerable time and effort to build a police force that has the confidence of the entire population and is able to deal with these issues and possibly internal disputes – taking over that task from the (downsized) military.

In the light of the above observations, none of the studies has shown a significant increase in the crime rate in the countries concerned as a result of combatants being released from their armed forces. In Mozambique a high crime rate is observed – and several incidents happened during the encampment and demobilization process. However, there have been few criminal incidents directly related to reintegration. Although there have been criminal activities involving ex-combatants, it is not shown that the latter are more inclined to crime or violence than other citizens facing similar hardship. In Ethiopia, where many soldiers left the army with their weapons, there were initially incidents of theft and armed robbery; but after a few years these incidents were considered insignificant compared to the numbers of soldiers demobilized and to the crime rate in neighbouring countries.

In terms of the security of the ex-combatants themselves, the initial demobilization packages usually provided a sense of security for a limited period of time. Beyond that they relied, as discussed in Section 2, on their communities and income-generating activities. In some cases the individual security of the ex-combatants related to broader security issues. In northern Uganda, for example, many ex-soldiers ended up in a difficult situation because of the conflict between government troops and the so-called Lord's Resistance Army. The ex-combatants had limited protection by the government, while there were on the other hand few peaceful economic opportunities for reintegration and considerable risks and pressures to be absorbed – by force or incentives – into rebel forces.

The ex-combatants in some ways also provided direct positive contributions to human security by being hired to do demining, for example in Mozambique. In Mozambique (about 5000) and Uganda large groups of ex-soldiers were also hired by private security firms to guard against crime, particularly in urban areas.

## 5.3  Weapons

It has often been argued that demobilization could lead to large numbers of uncontrolled weapons. The availability of small arms and light weapons, such as AK-47s, is said to cause dangers at different levels. This increases the risk that disputes between individuals will be settled with deadly violence, since most ex-combatants have learned little else than using violence to solve problems. These weapons might also fuel banditry; and there is a larger potential threat that political groups could arm themselves and disturb non-violent and democratic political processes.

At the time of demobilization there were indeed two related issues with regard to weapons. First, the (new) governments had large stocks of so-called 'surplus weapons', for which no further need existed. Particularly in Eritrea, Ethiopia and Mozambique large amounts of weapons were just left to decay, and might thus have caused environmental pollution. Probably worse, a number of these weapons have in some way ended up in other conflict areas. Indications exist that weapons from Eritrea, Ethiopia and Uganda have been shipped to the SPLA in Sudan; and large numbers of Ethiopian weapons are reported to have ended up (controlled or uncontrolled) in several neighbouring countries.

Second, besides the 'controlled' surplus weapons, the demobilizing countries also had to deal with the risk of weapons remaining or falling into the hands of ex-combatants and other people. This required proper disarmament of the combatants and protection of armouries. As we have seen, the manner in which the disarmament was implemented differed case-by-case. In both Ethiopia and Mozambique the disarmament was not very well conducted – or controlled. This has resulted in large numbers of uncontrolled weapons, although a subsequent weapons-collection policy in Ethiopia seems to have had a positive impact. In Uganda and Eritrea the demobilization itself hardly caused any problem of uncontrolled weapons. In Uganda the weapons were left behind in the barracks when the soldiers moved to the demobilization centres. In Eritrea all weapons used by the EPLF had been carefully registered during the war, and could thus be controlled by the new army.

Disarming the combatants was complicated, particularly in Mozambique. Many combatants owned more than one weapon; so, if they turned in one, another might have been hidden elsewhere. Large stocks have thus remained unreported. The parties might not have been entirely sure that the peace would hold, or combatants might have speculated on future income. The weapons that were reclaimed by the UN in Mozambique were handed over to the (new) government, but it appeared not to be able to adequately control these weapon stocks. Large numbers have ended up in the black market. It has been estimated that there are millions of small arms and light weapons in Mozambique, and since they are easy to smuggle across borders, the entire region is affected. The study in Mozambique found that although the dangers caused by the link between demobilization, lack of employment and the availability of weapons have generally been exaggerated, the mere presence of so many weapons does contribute to violence throughout the country, and the capacity of the police force is too limited to adequately control the weapons problem.

## 6   Perspectives for demobilization

As shown by the demobilizations reviewed and analysed in this study, it is clear that these exercises were all distinctly different from each other. This cautions us not to search for standard lessons of how a demobilization and the subsequent reintegration support should be organized. The study does however provide a clear sense of how to look at the issues and to frame them in anticipation of having to deal with a demobilization. It also provides some strong arguments for initiating these conversion efforts in such a way that they actually benefit the people, in terms of increasing human development and human security.

As shown in this concluding chapter, the impact of the demobilization is difficult to distinguish from the impact of the associated postwar processes and interventions, such as democratization, economic stabilization, infrastructural rehabilitation and repatriation of refugees. However, the study does show that there are usually no major direct financial benefits from demobilization. The savings are often not as high as expected, while the actual costs of the demobilization and reintegration support have been shown to be very high. The savings on military expenditure have in the first few years not translated into significant increases in government social spending. Moreover, there are some longer-term costs involved in demobilization. However, if the reduction in the number of military personnel is kept at the lower level, financial benefits are also likely to materialize in the long run. Of course, when we consider how the demobilization and reintegration support were financed in most cases, a fiscal peace dividend appears quite quickly, since external donors did provide substantial financial support. The external funding contributed to the speed with which the demobilization could be implemented and in principle freed up resources for use elsewhere.

In terms of security, demobilization has the potential to contribute to peace-building, national security, as well as to human security. In Mozambique, for example, the demobilization was critical in making the peace hold, and directly contributed to the human security through the decline of direct threats to the rural population. In all countries the initial fears that demobilization would lead to a boom in crime have not been confirmed by the research. With better-implemented disarmament of the ex-combatants there would probably have been even less crime. However, in the countries studied, a positive impact in more conventional security terms materialized only to a limited extent. Three of the four countries studied have been involved in armed conflict since the demobilization, largely due to militaristic thinking by their leaders.

The findings of this study thus indicate that demobilization is not a 'magic bullet', which automatically and simultaneously takes care of a large set of development and security challenges. A clear example is the case of Angola (Chapter 4): its recent experience has shown twice that demobilization cannot substitute for political will. Although we can observe that in several other African countries, such as the Democratic Republic of Congo and Sierra Leone, ex-soldiers currently threaten security, reintegration efforts in isolation are not likely to help. 'Politics' has to come first; only then, on the basis of a real political solution of the conflict, will demobilization, resettlement and reintegration support be natural – and often in-evitable – components of postwar rehabilitation and development.

Since demobilization is usually part of broader efforts to support and facilitate rehabilitation, human development and reconcilia-tion, every newly planned demobilization exercise has the best results if it makes decisions on resource allocation on the basis of the trade-offs with other types of development spending. First, one could ask the question: what costs are strictly necessary to prevent the war restarting, or to address other direct security threats? As we have seen, demobilization requirements are often urgent, pressing and politically sensitive, and soldiers pose a potential threat for the entire peace process. So there are usually large potential benefits in support to the demobilization itself, through effective logistics, proper implementation of disarmament, timely and sufficient basic needs – including food and health care – counselling, etc. The sub-sequent reintegration support would then again be considered along with funding broader development efforts. The demobilization might have to be implemented quickly, but reintegration is by nature a slow social, economic and psychological process. An enabling en-vironment might prove more effective than specific targeted support measures, and the reintegration in the longer term – and thus impact of the demobilization – depends also on the process of democrat-ization, including the recovery of a weak (or collapsed) state and the maturing of an independent civil society.

More demobilization exercises are likely to occur in Africa in the decade ahead, either for reasons of improved security, peace settle-ments, or because of economic and financial pressures. These demobilizations are thus also likely to continue to challenge the international development agencies' preparedness to deal with (un-expected) requests for support. Preparedness on the side of the donors is required, especially because they can only be effective by being involved early on in the planning processes. However, just as there are no blueprints for economic policies, there exists no blueprint for demobilization. Appropriate strategies need to be developed in the specific context, on the basis of experiences and lessons from elsewhere. This requires close cooperation with all the people in-volved, including the ex-combatants and their communities. It also asks for a large degree of flexibility and willingness to coordinate at all levels on the side of the donors, even more so than in more traditional development cooperation.

This joint research effort found that the main positive effect of the termination of the armed conflicts was clearly the peace itself – proving the basic condition for development and human security. People feel the confidence required for new initiatives. The studies also found that support by the communities was critical for the success of the reintegration of the ex-combatants. These findings imply that any support to demobilization and reintegration processes is more effective if it falls in line with these processes: focus on the broad peace-building process and creation of an enabling environment in which people themselves are encouraged to take initiatives. Demobilization will in such a manner fully contribute to human development and human security.

## Notes

1 Figures on costs and financing are the best possible estimates on the basis on the figures presented in the chapters of this volume.
2 Based on average exchange rate in 1993.
3 Based on average exchange rate in 1994.
4 US$ figures based on average exchange rate in 1991.
5 Exchange rate January 1995. The amount was fixed in meticais, so the real value declined over time.
6 The difference with the share shown in Table 6.2 is due to the rapid devaluation of the birr in the relevant period. The share of external financing if calculated in birr is thus 56 per cent.
7 The government army was the standard, also for ex-Renamo fighters.
8 Special treatment of ex-combatants may also affect the morale of soldiers remaining in the army. Protests and even mutinies in the new Mozambican army (FADM) were partially caused by high payments to the demobilized (*Africa Confidential*, 14 April 1995).

# Appendix

*Note on sources:* The data in this annex are drawn from the BICC database. The first section in Chapter 4 describes how these data are obtained and checked. As is also emphasised in Chapter 4, these data should be treated with much caution.

**Table A.1 Armed forces in Sub-Saharan Africa (in thousands)**

| | 1981 | 1982 | 1983 | 1984 | 1985 | 1986 | 1987 | 1988 | 1989 | 1990 | 1991 | 1992 | 1993 | 1994 | 1995 | 1996 |
|---|---|---|---|---|---|---|---|---|---|---|---|---|---|---|---|---|
| **Central Africa** | | | | | | | | | | | | | | | | |
| Burundi | 7 | 7 | 7 | 8 | 9 | 10 | 10 | 11 | 11 | 12 | 12 | 7 | 7 | 13 | 15 | 22 |
| Cameroon | 14 | 14 | 15 | 15 | 15 | 15 | 15 | 21 | 21 | 23 | 24 | 24 | 24 | 24 | 24 | 22 |
| Central African Republic | 4 | 5 | 4 | 5 | 5 | 5 | 5 | 5 | 5 | 4 | 4 | 7 | 7 | 5 | 5 | 5 |
| Chad | | | | 16 | 16 | 22 | 30 | 33 | 33 | 50 | 50 | 30 | 30 | 30 | 30 | 30 |
| Congo | 14 | 11 | 11 | 15 | 15 | 13 | 14 | 15 | 15 | 9 | 9 | 10 | 10 | 9 | 9 | 10 |
| DR Congo | 44 | 40 | 42 | 60 | 62 | 53 | 53 | 51 | 51 | 55 | 60 | 55 | 55 | 55 | 55 | 60 |
| Equatorial Guinea | 2 | 2 | 2 | 3 | 3 | 2 | 2 | 1 | 1 | 1 | 1 | 1 | 1 | 1 | 1 | 1 |
| Gabon | 7 | 7 | 7 | 7 | 7 | 9 | 9 | 8 | 10 | 9 | 10 | 7 | 7 | 7 | 7 | 7 |
| Rwanda | 5 | 5 | 5 | 5 | 5 | 5 | 5 | 5 | 6 | 6 | 30 | 30 | 30 | 30 | 40 | 39 |
| Sao Tome & Principe | 2 | 2 | 2 | 2 | 2 | 1 | 1 | 1 | 1 | 1 | 1 | 1 | 1 | 1 | 1 | 1 |

## East Africa

| Country | | | | | | | | | | | | | | | | |
|---|---|---|---|---|---|---|---|---|---|---|---|---|---|---|---|---|
| Comoros | | | | | | | | | | | | | | | | |
| Djibouti | 2 | 3 | 4 | 5 | 4 | 4 | 4 | 4 | 4 | 3 | 8 | 8 | 18 | 18 | 17 | 15 |
| Eritrea | 19 | 19 | 18 | 19 | 19 | 20 | 20 | 20 | 20 | 21 | 95 | 82 | 82 | 58 | 45 | 43 |
| Ethiopia | 240 | 240 | 240 | 240 | 240 | 300 | 300 | 300 | 400 | 450 | 120 | 120 | 120 | 120 | 120 | 120 |
| Kenya | 28 | 28 | 28 | 27 | 26 | 20 | 20 | 20 | 20 | 21 | 24 | 24 | 24 | 24 | 24 | 24 |
| Madagascar | 29 | 28 | 28 | 27 | 26 | 26 | 21 | 21 | 21 | 21 | 21 | 21 | 21 | 21 | 21 | 21 |
| Mauritius | 1 | 1 | 1 | 1 | 1 | 1 | 1 | 1 | 1 | 1 | 1 | 1 | 1 | 1 | 1 | 1 |
| Seychelles | n.a. | n.a. | n.a. | | | | 47 | 47 | 47 | 50 | | | 0 | 0 | 0 | 0 |
| Somalia | 54 | 48 | 43 | 43 | 43 | 50 | 65 | 65 | 65 | 59 | 65 | 82 | 82 | n.a. | n.a. | n.a. |
| Sudan | 87 | 86 | 65 | 65 | 65 | 59 | 65 | 65 | 65 | 59 | 40 | 46 | 46 | 110 | 110 | 109 |
| Tanzania | 43 | 43 | 43 | 43 | 43 | 40 | 40 | 40 | 40 | 40 | 46 | 46 | 46 | 46 | 35 | 35 |
| Uganda | 6 | 10 | 13 | 15 | 15 | 15 | 25 | 35 | 50 | 70 | 90 | 90 | 70 | 50 | 48 | 50 |

## Southern Africa

| Country | | | | | | | | | | | | | | | | |
|---|---|---|---|---|---|---|---|---|---|---|---|---|---|---|---|---|
| Angola | 53 | 54 | 54 | 60 | 66 | 70 | 74 | 107 | 107 | 115 | 150 | 128 | 128 | 100 | 100 | 97 |
| Botswana | 3 | 3 | 3 | 3 | 3 | 4 | 4 | 4 | 6 | 6 | 7 | 6 | 7 | 7 | 7 | 8 |
| Lesotho | 2 | 2 | 2 | 2 | 2 | 2 | 2 | 2 | 2 | 2 | 2 | 2 | 2 | 2 | 2 | 2 |
| Malawi | 6 | 6 | 6 | 6 | 6 | 7 | 7 | 7 | 7 | 8 | 8 | 10 | 10 | 10 | 8 | 10 |
| Mozambique | 30 | 30 | 32 | 34 | 35 | 65 | 65 | 65 | 65 | 65 | 65 | 50 | 50 | 10 | 12 | 11 |
| Namibia | | | | | | n.a. | 65 | 65 | 65 | 8 | 8 | 8 | 8 | 8 | 8 | 8 |
| South Africa | 78 | 78 | 77 | 97 | 95 | 90 | 102 | 100 | 100 | 85 | 80 | 72 | 84 | 72 | 120 | 107 |
| Swaziland | 2 | 2 | 3 | 3 | 3 | 3 | 3 | 4 | 3 | 3 | 3 | 3 | 3 | 3 | 3 | 3 |
| Zambia | 17 | 16 | 16 | 16 | 16 | 17 | 17 | 17 | 17 | 16 | 16 | 16 | 18 | 16 | 18 | 18 |
| Zimbabwe | 74 | 50 | 46 | 46 | 46 | 45 | 45 | 45 | 51 | 45 | 45 | 48 | 47 | 48 | 45 | 43 |

continued on p. 246

**Table A.1** *continued*

| | 1981 | 1982 | 1983 | 1984 | 1985 | 1986 | 1987 | 1988 | 1989 | 1990 | 1991 | 1992 | 1993 | 1994 | 1995 | 1996 |
|---|---|---|---|---|---|---|---|---|---|---|---|---|---|---|---|---|
| **West Africa** | | | | | | | | | | | | | | | | |
| Benin | 6 | 6 | 6 | 6 | 6 | 4 | 4 | 5 | 5 | 6 | 7 | 6 | 6 | 7 | 7 | 6 |
| Burkina Faso | 8 | 9 | 9 | 9 | 9 | 9 | 9 | 8 | 8 | 10 | 10 | 9 | 9 | 7 | 10 | 9 |
| Cape Verde | 4 | 4 | 4 | 6 | 6 | 4 | 4 | 3 | 3 | 1 | 1 | 1 | 1 | 1 | 1 | 1 |
| Gambia, The | 1 | 1 | 1 | 1 | 1 | 1 | 1 | 1 | 2 | 2 | 2 | 1 | 1 | 1 | 1 | 1 |
| Ghana | 9 | 9 | 8 | 15 | 15 | 9 | 11 | 16 | 16 | 9 | 9 | 7 | 7 | 7 | 7 | 7 |
| Guinea | 28 | 28 | 28 | 28 | 28 | 24 | 24 | 15 | 15 | 15 | 15 | 15 | 15 | 15 | 12 | 10 |
| Guinea Bissau | 12 | 9 | 9 | 11 | 11 | 11 | 11 | 10 | 10 | 12 | 12 | 11 | 11 | 11 | 9 | 9 |
| Ivory Coast | 7 | 7 | 8 | 8 | 8 | 8 | 8 | 8 | 8 | 15 | 15 | 15 | 15 | 15 | 15 | 14 |
| Liberia | 5 | 5 | 5 | 6 | 6 | 6 | 6 | 7 | 7 | 8 | 5 | 2 | 2 | n.a. | n.a. | n.a. |
| Mali | 8 | 8 | 8 | 8 | 8 | 8 | 8 | 8 | 8 | 13 | 13 | 12 | 12 | 12 | 7 | 7 |
| Mauritania | 12 | 16 | 16 | 16 | 16 | 16 | 16 | 14 | 16 | 17 | 17 | 16 | 16 | 16 | 16 | 16 |
| Niger | 6 | 5 | 5 | 5 | 5 | 4 | 5 | 4 | 4 | 5 | 5 | 5 | 5 | 5 | 5 | 5 |
| Nigeria | 144 | 144 | 144 | 144 | 134 | 138 | 138 | 107 | 107 | 94 | 94 | 76 | 76 | 74 | 77 | 77 |
| Senegal | 14 | 18 | 18 | 18 | 18 | 18 | 18 | 14 | 15 | 18 | 18 | 18 | 18 | 14 | 13 | 13 |
| Sierra Leone | 4 | 4 | 6 | 4 | 4 | 4 | 6 | 4 | 4 | 5 | 5 | 6 | 6 | 6 | 6 | 14 |
| Togo | 6 | 6 | 6 | 7 | 7 | 7 | 8 | 6 | 6 | 8 | 8 | 6 | 6 | 7 | 7 | 7 |

**Table A.2  Military expenditure in Sub-Saharan Africa (in millions of US$; prices and exchange rates of 1993)**

|  | 1983 | 1984 | 1985 | 1986 | 1987 | 1988 | 1989 | 1990 | 1991 | 1992 | 1993 | 1994 | 1995 | 1996 |
|---|---|---|---|---|---|---|---|---|---|---|---|---|---|---|
| **Central Africa** |  |  |  |  |  |  |  |  |  |  |  |  |  |  |
| Burundi | 25 | 22 | 22 | 26 | 27 | 27 | 22 | 22 | 23 | 28 | 28 | 52 | 60 | 50 |
| Cameroon | 206 | 209 | 232 | 263 | 253 | 183 | 170 | 176 | 157 | 161 | 181 | 178 | 175 | 175 |
| Central African Republic | 22 | n.a. | n.a. | n.a. | 22 | n.a. | 21 | 22 | 25 | 27 | 32 | 42 | 40 | 35 |
| Chad | 10 | 13 | 19 | 26 | 36 | 49 | 65 | 64 | 62 | 32 | 35 | 32 | 32 | 32 |
| Congo | 71 | n.a. | 80 | 104 | 98 | 90 | 90 | 83 | 138 | 125 | 108 | 42 | 40 | 50 |
| DR Congo | n.a. | 160 | 102 | 203 | n.a. | 268 | n.a. | n.a. | 240 | 207 | 245 | 115 | 117 | n.a. |
| Equatorial Guinea | n.a. | n.a. | n.a. | n.a. | n.a. | n.a. | n.a. | n.a. | n.a. | n.a. | n.a. | 2 | 2 | 2 |
| Gabon | 106 | 97 | 131 | 209 | 176 | 206 | 165 | 155 | 145 | 144 | 155 | 110 | 100 | 120 |
| Rwanda | 33 | n.a. | 26 | n.a. | 32 | 27 | 25 | 26 | 113 | 114 | 119 | 112 | 110 | 100 |
| Sao Tome & Principe | n.a. | n.a. | n.a. | n.a. | n.a. | n.a. | n.a. | n.a. | n.a. | n.a. | n.a. | n.a. | n.a. | n.a. |
| **East Africa** |  |  |  |  |  |  |  |  |  |  |  |  |  |  |
| Comoros | n.a. | n.a. | n.a. | n.a. | n.a. | n.a. | n.a. | n.a. | n.a. | n.a. | n.a. | n.a. | n.a. | n.a. |
| Djibouti | n.a. | n.a. | n.a. | 42 | 46 | 46 | 32 | 36 | 43 | 40 | 28 | 24 | 25 | 25 |
| Eritrea |  |  |  |  |  |  |  |  |  | n.a. | n.a. | n.a. | n.a. | n.a. |
| Ethiopia | 261 | 270 | 520 | 610 | 655 | 900 | 990 | 1030 | 480 | 240 | 230 | 215 | 200 | 200 |
| Kenya | 135 | 125 | 185 | 220 | 280 | 275 | 260 | 275 | 220 | 180 | 165 | 150 | 181 | 160 |
| Madagascar | 51 | 60 | 56 | 56 | 54 | 46 | 43 | 41 | 37 | 35 | 36 | 28 | 25 | 22 |
| Mauritius | 4 | 4 | 4 | 4 | 4 | 5 | 6 | 8 | 10 | 11 | 11 | 11 | 12 | 12 |
| Seychelles |  |  |  |  |  |  |  |  |  | n.a. | n.a. | n.a. | n.a. | n.a. |
| Somalia | 32 | 26 | n.a. | 30 | n.a. | n.a. | 13 | 8 | n.a. | n.a. | n.a. | n.a. | n.a. | n.a. |
| Sudan | 110 | 140 | 132 | 116 | 179 | 223 | 255 | 187 | 488 | 901 | n.a. | n.a. | n.a. | n.a. |
| Tanzania | 59 | 52 | 52 | n.a. | 59 | 67 | 84 | 101 | 100 | 96 | 78 | 67 | 60 | 60 |
| Uganda | 53 | 48 | 92 | 90 | 91 | 81 | 101 | 123 | 121 | 89 | 71 | 65 | 120 | 120 |

continued on p. 248

**Table A.2** *continued*

| | 1983 | 1984 | 1985 | 1986 | 1987 | 1988 | 1989 | 1990 | 1991 | 1992 | 1993 | 1994 | 1995 | 1996 |
|---|---|---|---|---|---|---|---|---|---|---|---|---|---|---|
| **Southern Africa** | | | | | | | | | | | | | | |
| Angola | 467 | n.a. | n.a. | 872 | n.a. | n.a. | n.a. | n.a. | n.a. | n.a. | n.a. | n.a. | n.a. | n.a. |
| Botswana | 40 | 48 | 45 | 64 | 100 | 125 | 130 | 165 | 180 | 180 | 233 | 229 | 215 | 215 |
| Lesotho | n.a. | n.a. | 20 | 22 | 22 | 22 | 29 | 26 | 22 | 30 | 27 | 23 | 23 | 23 |
| Malawi | n.a. | n.a. | 20 | 23 | 20 | 18 | 18 | 15 | 14 | 12 | 15 | 18 | 19 | 20 |
| Mozambique | n.a. | n.a. | 130 | 130 | 135 | 125 | 169 | 152 | 150 | 127 | 132 | 118 | 95 | 90 |
| Namibia | | | | | | | | 46 | 67 | 65 | 60 | 55 | 50 | 70 |
| South Africa | 4 627 | 4 287 | 3 847 | 3 967 | 4 595 | 4 721 | 4 938 | 4 848 | 4 033 | 3 306 | 3 482 | 2 840 | 2 630 | 2 500 |
| Swaziland | 10 | 9 | 9 | 10 | 10 | 10 | 10 | 15 | 13 | 16 | 21 | 16 | 16 | 16 |
| Zambia | n.a. | 183 | 105 | 200 | 185 | 134 | 74 | 81 | 75 | 46 | 56 | 38 | 39 | 40 |
| Zimbabwe | 286 | 302 | 370 | 410 | 420 | 425 | 430 | 435 | 410 | 325 | 250 | 240 | 220 | 240 |
| **West Africa** | | | | | | | | | | | | | | |
| Benin | 39 | 39 | 40 | 40 | 40 | 40 | 38 | 35 | 30 | 26 | 25 | 40 | 25 | 25 |
| Burkina Faso | 50 | 50 | 49 | 70 | 60 | 63 | 70 | 75 | 80 | 65 | 60 | 60 | 60 | 60 |
| Cape Verde | n.a. | n.a. | n.a. | n.a. | n.a. | n.a. | n.a. | n.a. | 4 | 3 | 3 | 3 | 3 | 3 |
| Gambia, The | n.a. | n.a. | n.a. | n.a. | 1 | 2 | 2 | 2 | 3 | 5 | 3 | 6 | 8 | 10 |
| Ghana | 12 | 22 | 38 | 36 | 38 | 20 | 27 | 27 | 40 | 55 | 75 | 60 | 60 | 60 |
| Guinea | 46 | 44 | n.a. | n.a. | n.a. | 29 | 30 | 31 | 32 | 44 | 46 | 49 | 50 | 50 |
| Guinea Bissau | 14 | 7 | 6 | 5 | 5 | 5 | 6 | 6 | 7 | 7 | 8 | 8 | 8 | 8 |
| Ivory Coast | 105 | 113 | 108 | 125 | 167 | 184 | 131 | 137 | 129 | 137 | 120 | 100 | 95 | 90 |
| Liberia | 50 | 40 | 48 | 61 | 65 | 67 | n.a. | n.a. | n.a. | n.a. | n.a. | n.a. | n.a. | n.a. |
| Mali | 46 | 46 | 47 | 49 | 52 | 51 | 54 | n.a. | n.a. | 62 | 58 | 50 | 50 | 40 |
| Mauritania | 48 | n.a. | 50 | 44 | 34 | n.a. | 37 | 35 | 32 | 38 | 37 | 35 | 30 | 30 |
| Niger | 16 | 14 | 17 | 17 | 20 | 21 | 26 | 28 | 30 | 29 | 32 | 30 | 30 | 30 |
| Nigeria | n.a. | n.a. | 950 | 800 | 520 | 640 | 700 | 730 | 690 | 525 | 630 | 770 | 800 | 800 |
| Senegal | 125 | 119 | 126 | 128 | 110 | 108 | 106 | 109 | 107 | 155 | 120 | 90 | 80 | 80 |
| Sierra Leone | 5 | 4 | 4 | 5 | 5 | 7 | 13 | 13 | 24 | 29 | 29 | 59 | 60 | 55 |
| Togo | 28 | 30 | 36 | 41 | 51 | 51 | 52 | 50 | 47 | 44 | 48 | 40 | 40 | 35 |

# Bibliography

Abrahamsson, Hans and Anders Nilsson (1994) *Moçambique em Transição* [Mozambique in transition] (Maputo: Padrigu and CEEI-ISRI).

ADB (African Development Bank) (1995) *African Development Report 1995* (Abidjan).

Africa Leadership Forum (1991) 'The Kampala Document: Towards a Conference on Security, Stability and Development and Cooperation in Africa', jointly with the secretariats of the OAU and ECA (Kampala).

Ajello, Aldo (1996) 'The Role of UNOMOZ in the Pacification Process', in Brazão Mazula (ed.), *Mozambique: Elections, Democracy and Development* (Maputo: Inter-Africa), pp. 119–23.

Alemayehu Haile (1996) 'Rehabilitation and Reintegration of Disabled Ex-combatants in Ethiopia' (Addis Ababa: Commission for the Rehabilitation of the Former Members of the Army and Disabled War Veterans).

Anandarup, Ray (1984) *Cost–Benefit Analysis: Issues and Methodologies*, World Bank Publication (Washington, DC: Johns Hopkins University Press).

Ângelo, Teodósio (1997) 'Desmobilizados dizem-se discriminados nas empresas – e falam de despedimentos arbitrários e de remunerações incompatíveis com o seu trabalho' [Demobilized feel discriminated in the place of work – and tell about arbitrary lay-offs and salaries incompatible with the work]', *NOTÍCIAS*, 18 August, p. 3.

Anglin, Douglas (1997) 'Conflicts in Sub-Saharan Africa, July 1996–June 1997', paper for publication in *Les Conflit dans le monde, 1996–1997: Rapport annuel sur les conflits internationaux, sous la direction de Albert Legault et John Sigler* (Québec: Institut québécoise des hautes études internationales).

Armiño, Karlos Peres (1997) *Guia de reabilitación pos-belica: el processo de Mozambique y la contribuicion de la ONG* [Guide to postwar rehabilitation: the Mozambican process and the contribution of the NGO] (Bilbao: Hegoa).

Azam, Jean-Paul (1994) 'How to Pay for the Peace? A Theoretical Framework with Reference to African Countries', in J.-P. Azam *et al.* (eds), 'Some Economic Consequences of the Transitions from War to Peace', Policy Research Working Paper 1392, Policy Research Department, Public Economics Division (Washington, DC: World Bank), pp. 29–38.

Azam, Jean-Paul, David Bevan, Paul Collier, Stefan Dercon, Jan Gunning and Sanjay Pradhan (1994) 'Some Economic Consequences of the Transition from Civil War to Peace', Policy Research Working Paper 1392, Policy Research Department, Public Economics Division (Washington, DC: World Bank).

Ball, Nicole (1988) *Security and Economy in the Third World* (London: Adamantine Press).

—— (1993) *Development Aid for Military Reform: A Pathway to Peace*, ODC Policy Focus No. 6 (Washington, DC: Overseas Development Council).

—— (1997) 'Demobilizing and Reintegrating Soldiers: Lessons from Africa', in Krishna Kumar (ed.), *Rebuilding Societies after Civil War: Critical Roles for International Assistance* (Boulder, CO, and London: Lynne Rienner), pp. 85–105.

—— (1998) 'The International Development Community's Response to Demobilization', in K. Gebrewold (ed.), 'Converting Defence Resources to Human Development'. Proceedings of an International Conference, 9–11 November 1997. Report 12 (Bonn: BICC), pp. 21–7.

—— with Tammy Halevy (1996) *Making Peace Work: The Role of the International Development Community*, ODC Policy Essay no. 18 (Washington, DC: Overseas Development Council).

Banco de Moçambique (1995) *Statistical Bulletin*, no. 11, year 3.

Baptista Lundin, Iraê (forthcoming) 'The Role of Kinship in an Urban Context – a Study of Survival Strategies in an Urban Context in a Situation of Generalised Crisis – the Special Case of the City of Maputo', work in progress (Maputo).

Becker, Gary S. (1975) *Human Capital* (New York: National Bureau of Economic Research).

Bennett, Olivia, Jo Bexley and Kitty Warnock (eds) (1995) *Arms to Fight, Arms to Protect: Women Speak Out About Conflict* (London: Panos).

Benoit, Emile (1973) *Defense and Economic Growth in Developing Countries* (Lexington, MA: Lexington Books).

Benson, Charles (1989) *Taxonomies of Skill Development: A Search for Criteria to Define the Relative Efficiency of Alternative Programs of Occupational Training* (Washington, DC: World Bank, Population and Human Resources Department).

Berdal, Mats R. (1996) 'Disarmament and Demobilization after Civil Wars', Adelphi Paper no. 303 (London: International Institute for Strategic Studies).

Berman, Eric (1996) *Managing Arms in Peace Processes: Mozambique* (Geneva: United Nations Institute for Disarmament Research).

Beyene, Haile (1992) 'Integration Process of Eritrean Ex-fighters: Idea for Project Development', September (Addis Ababa).

BICC (Bonn International Center for Conversion) (1996) *Conversion Survey 1996: Global Disarmament, Demilitarization and Demobilization* (Oxford: Oxford University Press).

—— (1998) *Conversion Survey 1998: Global Disarmament, Defense Industry Consolidation and Conversion* (Oxford: Oxford University Press).

Boomgard, James J. (1989) *A.I.D. Microenterprise Stock-Taking: Synthesis Report* (Washington, DC: US Agency for International Development, Center for Development Information and Evaluation, Bureau for Program and Policy Coordination).

Boutros-Ghali, Boutros (1992) *An Agenda for Peace: Preventive Diplomacy, Peacemaking and Peace-keeping: Report of the Secretary-General* (New York: United Nations).

—— (1994) *An Agenda for Development*, Report of the Secretary-General, A/48/935 (New York: United Nations).

—— (1995) *Supplement to an Agenda for Peace: Position Paper of the Secretary-General on the Occasion of the Fiftieth Anniversary of the United Nations*, A/50/60 (New York: United Nations).

Bowman, Mary J. (1980) 'Education and Economic Growth: an Overview', in T. King (ed.), *Education and Income*, World Bank Staff Working Paper no. 402, pp. 1–71.

Boyce, James K. (1995) 'Adjustment towards Peace: an Introduction', *World Development*, 23 (12): 2067–77.

Brett, Rachel and Margaret McCallin (1996) *Children: The Invisible Soldiers* (Växjö: Rädda Barnen – Swedish Save the Children).

Brito, Miguel de and Eduardo Mussanhane (1997) 'Relatório sobre a integração de desmobilizados', Draft para discussão. Projecto 'War-Torn Societies' [Report on integration of demobilized; draft for discussion; project WTS] (Maputo: UNRISD).

—— et al. (1995) 'Relatório do Seminário "Transição Política em Moçambique"' (Report on the Seminar on 'Political Transition in Mozambique') (Maputo: CEEI-ISRI).

Brömmelhörster, Jörn (ed.) (forthcoming) *Paying the Peace-Dividend* (Bonn: BICC).

Bruchhaus, Eva-Maria (1994) 'Evaluation of Self-help Potential in Fifteen Eritrean Villages' (Asmara).

Brzoska, Michael (1993) 'Disarmament and Development: Positive Measure', *Peace and the Sciences*, XXIV.

—— (1995) 'World Military Expenditures', in K. Hartley and T. Sandler (eds), *Handbook of Defense Economics*, vol. 1 (Amsterdam: Elsevier Science), pp. 46–67.

——, Kees Kingma and Herbert Wulf (1995) *Military Conversion for Social Development: Report on BICC Panel Discussion at the World Summit for Social Development, Copenhagen, 8 March 1995*, Report 5 (Bonn: BICC).

Buchanan-Smith, Margaret and Simon Maxwell (1994) 'Linking Relief and Development: an Introduction and Overview', *IDS Bulletin*, 25(4): 2–16.

Buzan, Barry, Ole Wæver and Jaap de Wilde (1998) *Security: A New Framework for Analysis* (Boulder, CO and London: Lynne Rienner).

CAII (Creative Associates International Inc.) (1994) 'The Assessment of Children and Youth in Renamo Zones: Strategies and Recommendations', prepared for UNICEF, Mozambique (Maputo).

—— (1996a) 'Study of Demobilized Soldiers Facing Difficulties in the Reintegration Process', Final Report. Prepared for the International Organization for Migration (Washington, DC, February).

—— (1996b) 'Study of Demobilized Soldiers Facing Difficulties in the Reintegration Process', Draft Final Report. Prepared for the International Organization of Migration (rural areas, 'high risk areas'). (Washington, DC, September).

—— (1997) 'Assessment of the Demobilization and Disarmament Process in Liberia', Final Report to the US Agency for International Development (Washington, DC).

Campbell, J. P. and R. D. Pritchard (1976) 'Motivation Theory in Industrial and Organizational Psychology', in Marvin D. Dunette (ed.), *Handbook of Industrial and Organizational Psychology* (Chicago, IL: Rand-McNally).

Cawthra, Gavin (1997) *Securing South Africa's Democracy: Defence, Development and Security in Transition* (Basingstoke: Macmillan).

Clapham, Christopher (ed.) (1998) *African Guerrillas* (Oxford: James Currey).

Cock, Jacklyn and Penny McKenzie (eds) (1998) *Defence to Development: Redirecting Military Resources in South Africa* (Cape Town: David Philip).

Coelho, João Paulo and Alex Vines (1994) 'Demobilization and Re-integration of Ex-combatants in Mozambique', Pilot Study (Oxford: Refugees Studies Programme, Queen Elizabeth House, University of Oxford).

—— —— (1996) 'Desmobilização e reintegração de ex-combatentes em Moçambique' [Demobilization and reintegration of ex-combatants in Mozambique], *ARQUIVO*, no. 19, 5–110.

Cohen, S. I. (1994) *Human Resource Development and Utilization* (Aldershot: Avebury).

Colclough, Christopher (1982) 'The Impact of Primary Schooling on Economic Development: a Review of the Evidence', *World Development*, 10(3): 167–85.

Colletta, Nat J., Markus Kostner and Ingo Wiederhofer (1996a) *The Transition from War to Peace in Sub-Saharan Africa*, Directions in Development Series (Washington, DC: World Bank).

—— —— —— (1996b) *Case Studies in War-to-Peace Transition: The Demobilization and Reintegration of Ex-Combatants in Ethiopia, Namibia and Uganda*, World Bank Discussion Paper no. 331, Africa Technical Department Series (Washington, DC: World Bank).

Collier, Paul (1994a) 'Civil War and the Economics of the Peace Dividend', Working Paper Series (Oxford: Centre for the Study of African Economies, University of Oxford).

—— (1994b) 'Demobilisation and Insecurity: a Study in the Economics of the Transition from War to Peace', in J.-P. Azam *et al.* (eds), 'Some Economic Consequences of the Transition from Civil War to Peace', Policy Research Working Paper 1392. Policy Research Department, Public Economics Division (Washingtotn, DC: World Bank), pp. 39–45.

—— (1994c) 'Introduction', in J.-P. Azam *et al.* (eds), 'Some Economic Consequences of the Transition from Civil War to Peace', Policy Research Working Paper 1392. Policy Research Department, Public Economics Division (Washington, DC: World Bank), pp. 1–8.

—— (1994d) 'Demobilisation and Insecurity: a Study in the Economics of the Transition from War to Peace', *Journal of International Development*, 6(3): 343–51.

—— (1996) 'On the Economic Consequences of Civil War' (Oxford: Centre for the Study of African Economies, University of Oxford).

—— and Sanjay Pradhan (1994) 'Economic Aspects of the Ugandan Transition to Peace', in J.-P. Azam *et al.* (eds), 'Some Economic Consequences of the Transition from Civil War to Peace'. Policy Research Working Paper 1392. Policy Research Department, Public Economics Division (Washington, DC: World Bank), pp. 119–33.

Commission for the Rehabilitation of Members of the Former Army and Disabled War Veterans (1994) 'Demobilisation and Socio-economic Reintegration of Ex-combatants: Ethiopian Experience', paper presented at the IRG Workshop on Demobilization in the Horn of Africa, December (Addis Ababa).

Conselho de Ministros (1996) 'Apresentação do Orçamento Geral do Estado de 1997 à Assembléia da República' [Council of Ministers – Presentation of the General State Budget to the Parliament], by Tomáz A. Salomão, Maputo, 16 December.

Crana, Michael (ed.) (1994) *The True Cost of Conflict*, study by Saferworld (London: Earthscan Publications).

CRS (Catholic Relief Services) (1994) 'Questionnaire on the Roles of NGOs in Demobilisation and Reintegration Programs', mimeo (Addis Ababa).

Dasgupta, Partha, Stephen Marglin and Amartya K. Sen (1972) *Guidelines for Project Evaluation* (New York: UNIDO).

Demes, Clovis (1995) 'Report to the International Centre for Human Rights and Democratic Development' (Ottawa).

Dercon, Stefan and Daniel Ayalew (1998) 'Where have all the Soldiers Gone: Demobilisation and Reintegration in Ethiopia', *World Development*, 26(9): 1661–75.

—— and Mekonen Taddesse (1997) 'A Comparison of Rural and Urban Poverty in Ethiopia', mimeo (Oxford: Centre for the Study of African Economies, University of Oxford).

—— and Pramila Krishnan (1996) 'A Consumption-based Measure of Poverty for Rural Ethiopia in 1989–1994', paper presented at the Conference of the Ethiopian Economic Association, Debre Zeit, Ethiopia.

—— —— (1997) 'In Sickness and in Health: Risk-sharing within Households in Rural Ethiopia', mimeo (Oxford: Centre for the Study of African Economies, University of Oxford).

Dolan, Chris and Jessica Schafer (1997) 'The Reintegration of Ex-combatants in Mozambique: Manica and Zambezia Provinces', Final Report to USAID Mozambique (Oxford: Refugees Studies Programme, University of Oxford).

ERRA (Eritrean Relief and Rehabilitation Agency) (1994) 'An Update of the Reintegration Process of Demobilising Eritrean Fighters', no. 2, July.

Eshetu Chole and Makonnen Manyazewal (1992) 'The Macroeconomic Performance of the Ethiopian Economy 1974–90', in Mekonen Taddesse (ed.), *The Ethiopian Economy: Structure and Policy Issues*, Proceedings of the First Annual Conference on the Ethiopian Economy (Addis Ababa).

Fluitman, Fred (ed.) (1989) *Training for Work in the Informal Sector* (Geneva: ILO).

Forsberg, Randall (1992) 'Why Cooperative Security? Why Now?', *Peace and Democracy News*, Winter, pp. 9–13.

Galtung, Johan (1969) 'Violence, Peace and Peace Research', *Journal of Peace Research*, no. 3.

Gaspar, António (1995) 'O Papel da ONUMOZ na Pacificação e Democratização de Moçambique' [The Role of UNOMOZ in the Pacification and Democratisation in Mozambique], paper presented in the Final Seminar on the Political Transition in Mozambique (Maputo: CEEI).

Gebremedhin, Tesfagiorgis (1996) *Beyond Survival: The Economic Challenges of Agriculture and Development in Post-Independence Eritrea* (Lawrenceville: Red Sea Press.)

Gebre-Medhin, Jordan (1989) *Peasant and Nationalism in Eritrea: A Critique of Ethiopian Studies* (Trenton: Red Sea Press).

Gebrewold, Kiflemariam (ed.) (1998) 'Converting Defence Resources to Human Development', Proceedings of an International Conference, 9–11 November 1997, Report 12 (Bonn: BICC).

Getachew Minas (1994) 'A Review of Macroeconomic Imbalances in the Ethiopian Economy in the 1980s and Recent Years', in Mekonen Taddesse and Abdulhamid B. Kello (eds), *The Ethiopian Economy Problems of Adjustment*, Proceedings of the Second Annual Conference on the Ethiopian Economy, Addis Ababa.

Getahun Tafesse (1996) 'Poverty Focus during the Transition Period and Afterward', paper presented at the Economic Association Panel Discussion on Poverty Alleviation in Ethiopia, Fourth General Assembly (Addis Ababa).

Goodale, Gretchen (1989) 'Training for Women in the Informal Sector', in F. Fluitman (ed.), *Training for Work in the Informal Sector* (Geneva: WHO) pp. 47–69.

Government of Eritrea (1994a) 'National Programme for the Reintegration of Demobilised Combatants in Eritrea', Programme Document (draft unpublished), June (Asmara).

—— (1994b) 'Statement to the International Donor Community Meeting', Consultative Group Meeting (Paris), December.

Government of Mozambique (1995) 'The Programme of the Government of Mozambique' (Maputo).

Government of South Africa (1996) 'Defence in a Democracy: White Paper on National Defence for the Republic of South Africa' (Pretoria).

Graham, Mac, Richard Jolly and Chris Smith (eds) (1986) *Disarmament and World Development*, 2nd edn (Oxford: Pergamon Press).

Green, Reginald H. (1993) 'Neo-liberalism and the Political Economy of War: Sub-Saharan Africa as a Case-study of a Vacuum', in C. Colclough and J. Manor (eds), *States or Markets: Neo-Liberalism and the Development Policy Debate*, IDS Development Studies Series (Oxford: Clarendon Press), pp. 238–59.

GTZ (German Agency for Technical Cooperation) (1994) *Internal Handbook of the Reintegration of Ex-servicemen, Returnees and Displaced Persons Program* (Addis Ababa).

Hanlon, Joseph (1997) *Paz Sem Benefício: Como o FMI Bloqueia o Desenvolvimento de Moçambique* [Peace without profit: how the IMF block the development of Mozambique] (Maputo: Imprensa Universitária).

Haq, Mahbub ul. (1995) *Reflections on Human Development* (Oxford: Oxford University Press).

Harbison, Frederick H. (1973) *Human Resources as the Wealth of Nations* (New York, London: Oxford University Press).

Havemann, Robert H. and Barbara L. Wolfe (1984) 'Schooling and Economic Well-Being: the Role of Non-Market Effects', *Journal of Human Resources*, 19(3): 377–407.

Herbst, Jeffrey (1996) 'Responding to State Failure in Africa', *International Security*, 21(3): 120–44.

Hoeven, Rolph van der and Fred van der Kraaij (eds) (1994) *Structural Adjustment and Beyond in Sub-Saharan Africa* (The Hague: Ministry of Foreign Affairs (Netherlands) in association with James Currey and Heinemann).

Hutchful, Eboe (1997) 'Demilitarising the Political Process in Africa: Some Basic Issues', *African Security Review*, 6(2): 3–16.

ILO (International Labour Organisation) (1986) *Vocational Training* (Geneva: ILO).

—— (1995a) 'Reintegration of Demobilised Combatants: Experiences from Four African Countries', prepared for the Expert Meeting on the Design of Guidelines for Training and Employment of Ex-Combatants, Harare, 11–14 July.

—— (1995b) 'The Reintegration of Young Ex-Combatants into Civilian Life', prepared for the Expert Meeting on the Design of Guidelines for Training and Employment of Ex-Combatants, Harare, 11–14 July.

—— (1995c) 'Rehabilitation and Reintegration of Disabled Ex-Combatants', prepared for the Expert Meeting on the Design of Guidelines for Training and Employment of Ex-Combatants, Harare, 11–14 July.

—— (1995d) 'Reintegration of Demobilised Combatants Through (Self-)employment and Training', prepared for the Expert Meeting on the Design of Guidelines for Training and Employment of Ex-Combatants, Harare, 11–14 July.

—— (1995e) 'Reintegrating Demobilised Combatants: The Role of Small Enterprise Development', prepared for the Expert Meeting on the Design of Guidelines for Training and Employment of Ex-Combatants, Harare, 11–14 July.

Independent Commission on Disarmament and Security Issues (1982) *Common Security: A Programme for Disarmament* (London: Pan Books).

Inkeles, Alex and David Smith (1974) *Becoming Modern* (Cambridge, MA: Harvard University Press).

IOM (International Organization for Migration) (1996a) 'After One Year: What is the Status of Reintegration in Mozambique?' (Maputo: Information and Referral Service/Provincial Fund for Demobilized Soldiers).

—— (1996b) 'IRS/PF InfoReport', January–April (Maputo).

—— (1997a) 'People on the Move' (Maputo).

—— (1997b) 'Executive Summary of the Information and Referral Service/Provincial Fund Final Evaluation' (Maputo).

Jamison, Dean T. and Peter R. Moock (1984) 'Farmer Education and Farm Efficiency in Nepal: the Role of Schooling, Extension Services, and Cognitive Skills', *World Development*, 12(1): 67–86.

Juhn, Tricia (1998) *Negotiating Peace in El Salvador: Civil–Military Relations and the Conspiracy to End the War* (Basingstoke: Macmillan).

Kaldor, Mary (1991) 'After the Cold War: Obstacles and Opportunities in Cutting Arms Budgets', *Proceedings of the World Bank Annual Conference on Development Economics 1991*, pp. 141–58.

Kazoora, Benjamin (1998) 'The Ugandan Reintegration Experience', in K. Gebrewold (ed.), 'Converting Defence Resources to Human Development', Proceedings of an International Conference, 9–11 November 1997, Report 12 (Bonn: BICC), pp. 31–7.

Kiggundu, Moses (1989) *Managing Organizations in Developing Countries: An Operational and Strategic Approach* (West Hartford, CT: Kumarian Press).

—— (1997) 'Retrenchment Programs in Sub-Saharan Africa: Lessons for Demobilization', BICC Paper 10 (Bonn: BICC).

Kiker, B.F. (1966) 'The Historical Roots of the Concept of Human Capital', *Journal of Political Economy*, February–December, pp. 481–99.

Kilby, P. (1988) 'Breaking the Entrepreneurial Bottle-neck in Late-developing Countries: Is there a Useful Role for Government?', *Journal of Development Planning*, no. 18, pp. 221–49.

King, Kenneth (1990) 'Research, Policy and the Informal Sector: an African Experience', in D. Turnham, B. Salomé and A. Schwarz (eds), *The Informal Sector Revisited* (Paris: OECD Development Centre), pp. 131–53.

Kingma, Kees (1996) 'The Role of Demobilization in the Peace and Development Process in Sub-Saharan Africa: Conditions for Success', *African Security Review*, 5(6): 33–42.

—— (1998) 'Demobilization and Reintegration: an Overview', in K. Gebrewold (ed.), 'Converting Defence Resources to Human Development', Proceedings of an International Conference, 9–11 November 1997, Report 12 (Bonn: BICC), pp. 12–20.

—— and Kiflemariam Gebrewold (1998) 'Demilitarisation, Reintegration and Conflict Prevention in the Horn of Africa', Discussion paper (London: Saferworld and BICC).

—— and Vanessa Sayers (1995) *Demobilization in the Horn of Africa: Proceedings of the IRG Workshop, Addis Ababa, December 1994*, Brief 4 (Bonn: BICC).

Klingebiel, Stephan, Inge Gärke, Corinna Kreidler, Sabine Lobner and Haje Schütte (1995) 'Promoting the Reintegration of Former Female and Male Combatants in Eritrea' (Berlin: German Development Institute).

Koester, Marco and Nicola Pape (1996) 'ERREC/OBS – On-the-job Training – Whereabouts of Graduates and Training Conditions', Otto-Benecke-Stiftung (unpublished).

Kumar, Krishna (ed.) (1997) *Rebuilding Societies after Civil War: Critical Roles for International Assistance* (Boulder, CO and London: Lynne Rienner).

Lauglo, Jon and Anders Närman (1988) *Diversified Secondary Education in Kenya: The Status of Practical Subjects and their Uses after School*, Pergamon Comparative & International Education Series, vol. 6 (Oxford: Pergamon Press), pp. 235–56.

Levin, Henry M. (1983) *Cost-Effectiveness: A Primer – New Perspectives in Evaluation*, vol. 4 (Beverly Hills: Sage Publications).

Longhurst, Richard (1994) 'Conceptual Frameworks for Linking Relief and Development', *IDS Bulletin*, 25(4): 17–23.

Lucas, Robert E. (1988) 'On the Mechanics of Economic Development', *Journal of Monetary Economies*, January, pp. 3–22.

Maglen, Leo R. (1990) 'Challenging the Human Capital Orthodoxy: the Education–Productivity Link Re-examined', *Economic Record*, 66(195): 281–94.

Massoud, Tanza G. (1996) 'War Termination', *Journal of Peace Research*, 33(4).

Mathews, Jessica Tuchman (1989) 'Redefining Security', *Foreign Affairs*, 68(2): 162–77.

Matthies, Volker (1994) *Äthiopien, Eritrea, Somalia, Djibouti: Das Horn von Afrika* (Munich: Beck).

—— (ed.) (1995) *Vom Krieg zum Frieden: Kriegsbeendigung und Friedenskonsolidierung* (Bremen: Temmen).

McClelland, David C. (1961) *The Achieving Society* (Princeton, NJ: Van Nostrand).

McLaughlin, Stephen D. (1989) *Skill Training for the Informal Sector: Analyzing the Success and Limitations of Support Programs*, Education and Employment Division, PHREE Background Paper no. PHREE/89/05 (Washington, DC: World Bank).

McNabb, Robert and Keith Whitfield (1994) 'The Market for Training: an Overview', in R. McNabb and K. Whitfield (eds), *The Market for Training* (Aldershot: Avebury), pp. 1–18.

Mehreteab, Amanuel (1997) 'Assessment of Demobilisation and Reintegration of Ex-Fighters in Eritrea', unpublished MA thesis, University of Leeds.

Metcalf, David H. (1984) 'The Economics of Vocational Training: Past Evidence and Future Considerations', Staff Working Paper no. 713 (Washington, DC: World Bank).

Mingat, Alan *et al.* (1989) *L'Enseignement Technique court au Niger: Une Evaluation par le Marche* (Dijon: IREDU).

Mondo, Emilio (1994) 'Demobilization and Reintegration Experiences in Uganda: December 1992–December 1994', paper presented at IRG Workshop on Demobilization in the Horn of Africa (Addis Ababa, December).

—— (1995) 'Uganda's Experience in National Management of Demobilization and Reintegration', in J. Cilliers (ed.), *Dismissed: Demobilisation and Reintegration of Former Combatants in Africa* (Halfway House, South Africa: Institute for Defence Policy), pp. 90–103.

Motumi, Tsepe and Penny McKenzie (1998) 'After the War: Demobilisation in South Africa', in J. Cock and P. McKenzie (eds), *Defence to Development: Redirecting Military Resources in South Africa* (Cape Town: David Philip), pp. 181–207.

NGO Networking Service (1995) 'Demobilisation and Reintegration Issues in the Horn of Africa', in J. Cilliers (ed.), *Dismissed: Demobilisation and Reintegration of Former Combatants in Africa* (Halfway House, South Africa: Institute for Defence Policy), pp. 72–89.

Nölker, Helmut and Eberhard Schoenfeldt (1985) *Glossar: Internationale Berufspädagogik* (GTZ: Expert Verlag).

Nübler, Irmgard (1993) 'Training Microentrepreneurs – Does it Pay?', *Small Enterprise Development*, 3(4): 34–44.

—— (1995) 'Management Training for Women Microentrepreneurs: an Evaluation Methodology and Case Studies from Africa', PhD thesis, Free University of Berlin.

—— (1996) *Management Training for Women Microentrepreneurs: An Evaluation Methodology and Case-Studies from Africa* (Berlin: Gesellschaft für Technische Zusammenarbeit, Overall Verlag).

OECD/DAC (Organisation for Economic Co-operation and Development/ Development Assistance Committee) (1998a) 'Military Expenditures in Developing Countries: Security and Development', Final Report and Follow-up to the Ottawa Symposium, co-sponsored by the Government of Canada and the OECD/DAC (Paris: OECD).

—— (1998b) 'Conflict, Peace and Development Co-operation on the Threshold of the 21st Century', Development Co-operation Guidelines Series (Paris: OECD).

Pearce, David W. and R. Kerry Turner (1990) *Economics of Natural Resources and the Environment* (Baltimore, MD: Johns Hopkins University Press).

Pole, David (1982) 'Ethiopia and Eritrea: the Pre-colonial Period' (Rome: Research and Information Centre on Eritrea).

Poulton, Robin-Edward and Ibrahim ag Youssouf (1998) *A Peace of Timbuktu: Democratic Governance, Development and African Peacemaking* (Geneva: United Nations Institute for Disarmament Research).

Presidência da República (1996) 'Proposta do Plano Económico e Social e Política Orçamental para 1997' [Proposal of the social and economic plan and the budgetary policy for 1997] (Maputo).

Preston, Rosemary (1994) 'Demobilising and Reintegrating Fighters after War: the Namibian Experience' (Warwick: International Centre for Education in Development, University of Warwick).

Prokopenko, Joseph (1989) *Productivity Management* (Geneva: ILO).

Pronk, Jan and Mahbub ul Haq (1992) *Sustainable Development: From Concept to Action*, Report of the Hague Symposium, convened by UNCED, with co-sponsorship of UNDP and the Government of the Netherlands (New York: UNDP).

Psacharopolous, George (1988) 'Education and Development: a Review', *World Bank Research Observer*, 3(1): 99–116.

Ratilal, Prakash (1990) 'Mozambique: Using Aid to End Emergency' (New York: UNDP), April.

Renner, Michael (1996) *Cost of Disarmament: An Overview of the Economic Costs of the Dismantlement of Weapons and the Disposal of Military Surplus*, Brief 6 (Bonn: BICC).

Roemer, Michael and Joseph Stern (1974) *The Appraisal of Development Projects: A Practical Guide to Project Analysis with Case Studies and Solutions* (New York: Praeger).

Rosen, Sherwin (1987) 'Human Capital', *New Palgrave* (London), pp. 681–9.

Sandler, Todd and Keith Hartley (1995) *The Economics of Defense*, Cambridge Surveys of Economic Literature (Cambridge: Cambridge University Press).

Schultz, Theodore W. (1961) 'Investment in Human Capital', *American Economic Review*, II: 1–17.

—— (1975) 'The Value of the Ability to Deal with Disequilibria', *Journal of Economic Literature*, 13(3): 827–46.

Sen, Amartya K. (1988) 'The Concept of Development', in H. Chenery and T.N. Srinivasan (eds), *Handbook of Development Economics*, vol. 1 (Amsterdam: Elsevier Science), pp. 9–26.

Shaw, Timothy, Sandra MacLean and Katie Orr (1998) 'Peace-Building and African Organizations: towards Subcontracting or a New and Sustainable Division of Labour', in K. van Walraven (ed.), *Early Warning and Conflict Prevention: Limitations and Possibilities* (The Hague: Kluwer Law International), pp. 149–61.

SIPRI (Stockholm International Peace Research Institute) (1997) *SIPRI Yearbook: Armament, Disarmament and International Security* (Oxford: Oxford University Press).

Solomon, Hussein and Jakkie Cilliers (eds) (1996) *People, Poverty and Peace: Human Security in Southern Africa*, IDP Monograph Series no. 4 (Halfway House, South Africa: Institute for Defence Policy).

Srivastava, Ramesh (1994) 'Reintegrating Demobilised Combatants: a Report Exploring Options and Strategies for Training Related Interventions' (Geneva: ILO).

Stewart, Frances (1993) 'War and Underdevelopment: Can Economic Analysis Help Reduce the Costs?', Centro Studi Luca d'Agliano/Queen Elisabeth House Development Studies Working Paper no. 56 (Oxford: University of Oxford).

—— (1995) *Adjustment and Poverty: Options and Choices* (London and New York: Routledge).

Stone, E.F. (1982) 'Research Design: Issues in Studies Assessing the Effects of Management Education', in R.D. Freedman *et al.* (eds), *Management Education: Issues in Theory, Research, and Practice* (Chichester: John Wiley & Sons).

Tendler, Judith (1989) 'Whatever Happened to Poverty Alleviation', in J. Levitsky (ed.), *Microenterprises in Developing Countries* (London: Intermediate Technology).

UNDP (United Nations Development Programme) (1990) *Human Development Report 1990* (New York: Oxford University Press).

—— (1994) *Human Development Report 1994* (New York: Oxford University Press).

—— (1997a) *Human Development Report 1997* (New York: Oxford University Press).

—— (1997b) 'Reintegration Programmes for Demobilized Soldiers in Mozambique', report prepared by Sam Barnes for UNDP/RSS (Maputo).

UNDP/RSS (1996) 'Preliminary Results of the Quantitative Data Obtained during Interviews with 1000 Demobilized Soldiers' (Maputo), 28 May.

United Nations (1995) *The United Nations and Mozambique, 1992–1995*, Blue Books Series, vol. V (New York: UN Department of Public Information).

—— (1998) 'The Causes of Conflict and the Promotion of Peace and Sustainable Development in Africa', report of the UN Secretary-General. A/52/871–S/1998/3/318 (New York: UN).

USAID (1995) 'Mid-Term Evaluation: Demobilization and Reintegration Support Project' (656–0235), Mozambique (submitted to USAID by Nicole Ball, Overseas Development Council, Washington, DC) (Maputo).

Vroom, Victor H. (1964) *Work and Motivation* (New York: John Wiley & Sons).

Waal, Alex de (1996) 'Contemporary Warfare in Africa: Changing Context, Changing Strategies', *IDS Bulletin*, 27(3): 6–16.

—— (1997) *Famine Crimes: Politics and the Disaster Relief Industry in Africa* (London: Africa Rights and the International African Institute, in association with James Currey and Indiana University Press).

War-Torn Society Project (WSP) (1996) 'Eritrea Country Note', January (Asmara).

WCED (World Commission on Environment and Development) (1987) *Our Common Future* (Oxford: Oxford University Press).

Welch, Finis (1970) 'Education in Production', *Journal of Political Economy*, 78(1): 35–59.

Welsh-Honwana, Gita (1994) 'Mozambique: Feasibility Study', report of a Fact-finding Mission (London: International Alert).

Wilde, Kerstin and Anteneh Belete (1996) 'Lessons Learned in Ethiopia', paper presented at the Workshop on the Experiences with the Demobilisation and Reintegration of Ex-combatants (Addis Ababa: GTZ).

Williamson, Oliver E. (1975) 'Franchise Bidding for Natural Monopolies', *Bell Journal of Economics*, 7: 73–104.

Woldegiorgis, Techlemicael (Rosso) (1996) 'The Challenges of Reintegrating Returnees and Ex-Combatants' (Asmara: War-Torn Societies Project, Eritrea, November).

World Bank (1989) *Sub-Saharan Africa: From Crisis to Sustainable Growth* (Washington, DC: World Bank).

—— (1990) *World Development Report 1990: Poverty*, published for the World Bank (Oxford, New York: Oxford University Press).

—— (1993) 'Demobilization and Reintegration of Military Personnel in Africa: the Evidence from Seven Country Case Studies', Africa Regional Series Discussion Paper IDP-130, October (Washington, DC).

—— (1994) 'Eritrea – Options and Strategies for Growth', Country Operations Division, East Africa Department, Africa Region Report no. 12930-Er.

Wulf, Herbert (1992) 'The Demobilization of Military Personnel as a Problem and a Potential for Human Development', paper prepared for the UNDP Human Development Report 1993 (Hamburg).

Zacarias, Agostinho (1993) 'Prospect for Demobilization and Integration of the Mozambique Armed Force', in Joseph N. Garba (ed.), *Towards Sustainable Peace and Stability in Southern Africa*, vol. 1: papers from a conference organized by the Southern Africa Peacekeeping and Peacemaking Project in Harare, Zimbabwe, 30 June–2 July 1993 (New York: Institute of International Education), pp. 70–4.

Zartman, I. William (ed.) (1995) *Collapsed States: The Disintegration and Restoration of Legitimate Authority* (Boulder, CO: Lynne Rienner).

# Index